Praise for *The Learning Challenge*

by James Nottingham

I have witnessed first-hand in my own district, and in that of others, the power of the Learning Challenge in developing student ownership over their own learning. This book provides the blueprint for empowering students to plunge deep into the learning pit and have the mindset and tools necessary to make them climb out and back in again. This book gives students the understanding and permission to challenge prior knowledge, biases and misconceptions to substantially enhance learning. I'm thrilled to see a book that guides students toward the "voice" and "choice" they need to advocate for their own learning and to choose the path less traveled by to benefit their learning and that of their peers.

—Michael McDowell, *EdD, Author,* Rigorous PBL by Design
Superintendent, Ross School District
Ross, CA

James Nottingham provides educators with a practical way to get students to challenge their thinking, through questioning and dialogue. *The Learning Challenge* is jam-packed with ideas on how to take a simple concept and turn it into a full-blown learning experience.

—Kelly Fitzgerald, *Instructional Coach*
Rouse High School
Leander, TX

We all recognize that schooling is no longer about imparting information in the hope that it will be put to good use. We know good schooling is about providing students with continuous opportunities to develop the ability and practices to think deeply. Deep learning is hard work. It is complex, complicated and not particularly comfortable at times (see "The Pit"). In *The Learning Challenge*, Nottingham takes us through the four stages of the Learning Challenge, a framework for thinking and learning, in which students learn to step out of their comfort zone so that they can make meaning and connections in order to engage in deep thinking.

John Hattie states that 90% of what is taught in schools is at the surface level. That is not a comforting statistic. In *The Learning Challenge*, James Nottingham has provided us a clear path for engaging students in deep and meaningful learning complete with student-friendly language, stages and steps, examples, tools and tactics to guide us in engaging students in rigorous learning.

—Barb Pitchford
Co-Author, Leading Impact Teams: Building a Culture of Efficacy
Aspen, CO

Research into how we learn has continued to highlight the value of desirable difficulties. Wrestling with big ideas, although uncomfortable at times, leads to stronger, deeper learning. However, in the age of accountability, classroom teachers are finding it difficult to set aside time for such wrestling in exchange for more test preparation. James Nottingham has provided a clear, concise and research-based approach to creating cognitively challenging classrooms that captivate, activate and invigorate learners. This book takes every reader through the learning pit, challenging their prior beliefs, and leads them to construct and consider a new and innovative way to promote stronger and deeper learning for their students.

—John Almarode, *Professor of Education*
Co-Director of the Center for STEM Education and Outreach
James Madison University, College of Education
Harrisonburg, VA

In this era of rapid change, cognitive conflict is a constant challenge to be faced. James Nottingham's *The Learning Challenge* offers learners of all ages a place to be and a process to recognize and engage with. Offering young learners the opportunity to contend with the tension that goes with being "in the Pit" and think and talk about their own learning is immensely valuable. My experience, working with this concept, is that it works!

—Simon Feasey, *School Principal*
Bader Primary School
Thornaby, Stockton-on-Tees, England

James Nottingham's work on Challenging Learning is a critical element of creating Visible Learners. This new series will help teachers hone the necessary pedagogical skills of dialogue, feedback, questioning and mindset. There's no better resource to encourage all learners to know and maximize their impact!

—John Hattie, *Professor and Director, Melbourne Education Research Institute*
University of Melbourne
Melbourne, Australia

In *The Learning Challenge*, James Nottingham shows us how to use generative concepts as focal points for engaging deep student thinking and discourse. His visual model of "pits and peaks" helps us realize that cooperatively grappling with cognitive conflicts in the pit is necessary to eventually reach new peaks of understanding. Nottingham provides a wealth of strategies, tools and examples to aid the teacher. The vast array of questions to stimulate student thinking is second to none.

—H. Lynn Erickson, *Educational Consultant*
Author, Concept-Based Curriculum and Instruction for the Thinking Classroom
Everett, WA

The Learning Challenge is an incredibly valuable book for anyone seeking to motivate students, deepen their learning and improve the quality of their thinking. It contains outstanding explanations and examples on every page. I highly recommend this book!

—Julie Stern, *Author,* Tools for Teaching Conceptual Understanding
Educational Consultant
Bogotá, Colombia

The Learning Pit has become one of the most powerful and popular heuristics of learning over the past 10–20 years, and Nottingham's new book will become the go-to resource for its fullest explication and application over the next two decades. Though weighted heavily toward classroom practice, it is happily respectful of the many theoretical connections, and both theory and practice support each other beautifully.

—Barry J. Hymer, *Professor of Psychology in Education*
University of Cumbria in Lancaster
Lancaster, England

Nottingham's *The Learning Challenge* is a seminal piece and should be considered mandatory reading for every educator. The examples included throughout help to paint a clear picture of how teachers can create the conditions to encourage and support students' deep understanding of complex concepts.

—Jenni Donohoo, *Author,* Collective Efficacy
Curriculum and Assessment Policy Branch
Ontario, Canada

Nottingham has used trending research to develop a step-by-step process for educators to engage students in their learning journey. In understanding the student perspective, educators will be empowered in their professional practice to understand their own learning journey.

—**Karen L. Beattie,** *Principal*
Chisholm Elementary School
New Smyrna Beach, FL

The Learning Challenge provides a valuable balance between practical tools, applications and underpinning theoretical constructs. The format of each section makes concepts clear and develops understanding of the principles explored in practice. It is ideal for teachers who are planning for the effective use of the Learning Challenge and the Learning Pit to deepen pupils' understanding and support their progression.

—**Pippa Leslie,** *QKS School Direct University Program Lead*
University of Cumbria
Lancaster, United Kingdom

Profound, practical and precise: James Nottingham tells you how to make your classroom a place where young people would love to be.

—**Guy Claxton,** *Author,* Intelligence in the Flesh
King's College
London, England

Nottingham provides real-life instructional lessons that deepen students' thinking by taking them in and out of the learning pit. Schools will create deep thinkers by making the Learning Challenge part of their instruction. Nottingham's message in *The Learning Challenge* gives new traction to the old term *metacognition*.

—**Genie Baca,** *Principal*
Eastridge Elementary
Amarillo, TX

James Nottingham compels the reader to feel the urgency in recognizing that learning is a journey and not an end, and can only be achieved when we transform learning from "knowing *what* to think" to "knowing *how* to think." *The Learning Challenge* offers a framework and practical strategies educators of all levels and disciplines can use to educate the mind to think critically and the heart to act independently.

—**Mariko Yorimoto,** *Vice Principal*
Kaimiloa Elementary
St. Ewa Beach, HI

The name *James Nottingham* is virtually synonymous with the Learning Challenge—the study of thinking as a process of inquiry, or better known to many as "The Learning Pit," in which students are challenged to think more skillfully. His coverage is comprehensive, ranging from the processes educators can use to get students deeply engaged and collaboratively involved in their learning to practical suggestions for lesson design . . . moving the educational culture from one of input and teaching to one of learning and impact.

—**Julie Smith,** *PhD, Consultant*
Co-Author, Evaluating Instructional Leadership
Vancouver, WA

James Nottingham has searched the world and understands what learning looks like. This is a must-read not only for teachers but also for students to understand and be deliberate about the way they approach the challenges, thrills and processes of learning.

—Summer Howarth, *Director of Learning Design and Events*
Education Changemakers
Melbourne, Australia

In beautifully simple and clear language, *The Learning Challenge* presents a comprehensive methodology to bring philosophical inquiry to everyday learning. Nottingham makes a strong case for the didactic value of cognitive conflict, and offers K–12 teachers the tools and theory they need to make the learning pit a core part of their work in the classroom.

—Daniel Fisherman, *Educational Foundations*
Montclair State University
Montclair, NJ

THE
LEARNING
CHALLENGE

Challenging Learning Series

The Learning Challenge: How to Guide Your Students Through the Learning Pit to Achieve Deeper Understanding

by James Nottingham

Challenging Learning Through Dialogue

by James Nottingham, Jill Nottingham and Martin Renton

Challenging Learning Through Feedback

by James Nottingham and Jill Nottingham

Creating a Challenging Learning Mindset

by James Nottingham and Bosse Larsson

Challenging Learning Through Questioning

by James Nottingham and Martin Renton

Learning Challenge Lessons, Elementary

by James Nottingham, Jill Nottingham, Lucy Bennison and Mark Bollom

Learning Challenge Lessons, Secondary ELA

by James Nottingham, Jill Nottingham, Lucy Bennison and Mark Bollom

Learning Challenge Lessons, Secondary Mathematics

by James Nottingham, Jill Nottingham, Lucy Bennison and Mark Bollom

Learning Challenge Lessons, Secondary Science/STEM

by James Nottingham, Jill Nottingham, Lucy Bennison and Mark Bollom

THE
LEARNING
CHALLENGE

*How to Guide Your Students Through the
Learning Pit to Achieve Deeper Understanding*

JAMES NOTTINGHAM

Foreword by John Hattie

CORWIN

A SAGE Publishing Company

FOR INFORMATION

Corwin
A SAGE Company
2455 Teller Road
Thousand Oaks, California 91320
(800) 233-9936
www.corwin.com

SAGE Publications Ltd.
1 Oliver's Yard
55 City Road
London, EC1Y 1SP
United Kingdom

SAGE Publications India Pvt. Ltd.
B 1/I 1 Mohan Cooperative Industrial Area
Mathura Road, New Delhi 110 044
India

SAGE Publications Asia-Pacific Pte. Ltd.
3 Church Street
#10-04 Samsung Hub
Singapore 049483

Note on this book's title: The "Pit" metaphor used to describe the cognitive conflict that is common to the learning process was first used in the Transformational Learning Model of Dr. Jim Butler and Dr. John Edwards, as further described in the Acknowledgments of this book.

Printed in the United States of America.

ISBN: 978-1-5063-7642-4

US Edition

Acquisitions Editor: Ariel Bartlett
Senior Associate Editor: Desirée A. Bartlett
Editorial Assistant: Kaitlyn Irwin
Production Editor: Melanie Birdsall
Copy Editor: Sarah J. Duffy
Typesetter: Hurix Systems Pvt. Ltd.
Proofreader: Caryne Brown
Indexer: Jean Casalegno
Cover Designer: Janet Kiesel
Marketing Manager: Anna Mesick

This book is printed on acid-free paper.

SUSTAINABLE FORESTRY INITIATIVE
Certified Chain of Custody
Promoting Sustainable Forestry
www.sfiprogram.org
SFI-01268
SFI label applies to text stock

17 18 19 20 21 10 9 8 7 6 5 4 3 2 1

CONTENTS

Chapter 3: The Learning Challenge Culture 33

Chapter 4: Concepts 45

Chapter 5: Cognitive Conflict 75

Chapter 10: The Learning Challenge in Action   191

Appendix   223

LIST OF FIGURES

THE CHALLENGING LEARNING STORY

Challenging Learning was the title I used for my first book back in 2010. I chose the title because it brought together two key themes of my work and it gave a relevant double meaning—challenging the way in which learning takes place *and* showing how to make learning more challenging.

More recently, Challenging Learning is the name I've given to a group of organizations set up in seven countries across Europe and Australasia. These educational companies bring together some of the very best teachers and leaders I know. Together we transform the most up-to-date and impressive research into best pedagogical practices for schools, preschools and colleges.

This book continues in the same tradition: challenging learning and making learning more challenging. The main difference between this book and the original *Challenging Learning* title is that this one focuses on practical resources for use by teachers, support staff and leaders. There is still some theory, but now the emphasis is on pedagogical tools and strategies. Across this new series you will find books about questions and the zone of proximal development, dialogue and language, mindset and self-efficacy, coaching for professional development and leadership and organization.

This particular volume focuses on the Learning Challenge and its role in helping students to think about and articulate their thinking. At the heart of the Learning Challenge is "the pit," a metaphor that can be used to describe the feeling of stepping out of the comfort zone to explore ideas or contradictions that are complex and perplexing.

The Learning Challenge promotes meaningful communication. It offers participants the opportunity to think and talk about their learning, and to push for a depth of understanding that is oftentimes difficult to achieve within a busy curriculum. At its very best, the Learning Challenge can be one of the best ways to learn good habits of thinking and communication.

As you read this book, you will notice that I have referred mainly to *teachers* and *teaching*. Please do not take this to mean this book is only for teachers. In fact, the book is aimed at support staff and leaders as much as at teachers. I simply use the terms *teacher* and *teaching* as shorthand for the position and pedagogy of all the professions working in schools.

Most chapters begin with a preview. This is to give you a chance to think about your current practice before diving in to see what our recommendations are. Chatting with a colleague about what you think works well (and how you know it does); what you would like to change; and, in an ideal world, what you would like your pedagogy to be like will definitely help you use this book as the reflective journal it is intended to be.

At the end of most chapters is a review. This is focused on repertoire and judgment. A broad repertoire—or tool kit of teaching strategies, as some authors call it—is crucial to improving pedagogy. Yet repertoire alone is not sufficient; good judgment is also needed. So, whereas the strategies in this book should be sufficient to broaden your repertoire, your good judgment will come from reflections on your own experiences, from trying out the new strategies with your students and from dialogue with your colleagues. My suggestions for review are there to help you with your reflections.

As a teacher, teaching assistant or leader you are among the most powerful influences on student learning. Back when you were a secondary student and went from teacher to teacher, you knew exactly which member of staff had high expectations and which had low; which had a good sense of humor and which you suspected had not laughed since childhood. It is the same today. Your students know what your expectations and ethos are. So it is not the government, students' parents or the curriculum that sets the culture (though they all have influence). It is *you* who sets the culture, and so it is *your* actions that count most.

With this book I hope I can inspire you to ever more expert actions.

With best wishes,

James Nottingham

FOREWORD

The Learning Challenge is written by my friend and colleague, James Nottingham. James and I oversee work in many schools throughout the world, are interested in the same problems and conundrums in learning and share many interests in beer, kids, dogs and the trials and tribulations of our favorite sports teams (where of course we differ as to which teams). James has deep knowledge of schooling and a great sense of humor. Most important, there is seemingly no challenge he is unprepared to take on to make a difference to the learning lives of children. This book illustrates many years of practice, research, insight and thinking. It is not for nothing that it is titled *The Learning Challenge*.

So often teachers and students believe learning should be easy. Just ask colleagues and children who are the best learners and why. Too many of them will point to those who "just seem to get it," who know stuff without seeming to have to try or who are considered "naturally" talented. Yet these are the very attributes that do *not* relate to learning. Learning is more a challenge.

Learning involves being on the edge of knowing and not knowing. It involves acknowledging what we do not yet know but could with effort and strategy. It sometimes involves reorganizing what we already think we know into something different and giving up some previous and sometimes precious knowledge to reach a deeper and more flexible understanding. As Piaget famously said, it involves *disequilibrium*. That is, learning occurs when there is an imbalance between what is understood and what is encountered. When our equilibrium is imbalanced, we have the possibility to grow and develop.

Thus, an aim of teaching is to create situations where there is disequilibrium, to create disharmony, to challenge current ways of thinking with different and more correct or integrated notions.

Sadly, this is not what it feels like in many classes where there is a quietness of "tell and practice," a sense that "work" is about getting things right, and where teachers talk and talk. Students in these classes come to learn that there is a bank of things they need to know and know how to do, and it is their teachers' role to share this bank with them. No wonder so many students claim that the most knowledgeable person is the one who knows most; no wonder so many tests and tasks involve showing how much you know; no wonder so many classroom dialogues focus on getting the answers right; no wonder so many students become turned off by this "banking" model of learning!

One of my favorite books remains Paulo Freire's (1970) *Pedagogy of the Oppressed*, as the theory underlying Visible Learning owes much to this work. My fellow graduate friend Colin Lankshear introduced me to this work, and it has remained with me ever since. A fundamental notion is that learners must come to understand how the myths of dominant discourses are, precisely, myths that oppress and marginalize them—but that can be transcended through transformative action (Lankshear & McLaren, 1993, p. 43).

The other favorite book of that time was Neil Postman's (1969) *Teaching as a Subversive Activity*. Freire (1970) critiqued the then (and still) dominant mode of schooling: a "careful analysis of the teacher-student relationship at any level, inside or outside the school, reveals its fundamentally narrative character" (p. 72). That is, the teacher narrates and the student is expected to listen. "The teacher talks about reality as if it were motionless, static, compartmentalized and predictable. . . . [The teacher's] task is to 'fill' the students with the contents of his narration" (Freire, 1970, p. 72). Education, claimed Freire, is suffering from narration sickness, and there is a sonority of words and a loss of their transforming power. Not surprisingly, students come to believe that learning is listening to these deposits from the bank of knowledge and ideas of others, which then needs to be received, filed and stored—for the day someone checks the status of the bank account in each child's mind.

Some students love this form of teaching and build large banks of knowledge to be trotted out when needed. Some parents welcome teachers who bestow these gifts of deposits, and many societies welcome this safe, nonchallenging and manageable model. Freire argued that such a model gives low priority to developing critical consciousness and is the preferred model of the oppressors to preserve the status quo. Most important, this banking model minimizes disequilibrium, rarely engages students in seeing or making relations between ideas and reduces the challenge of learning to short-term memory, knowing lots and regurgitating the deposits of teaching.

The alternative is the Learning Challenge. To entice, educate and invigorate students and teachers into the thrill of the challenge of building their realities and understandings about themselves and the worlds around them.

It should be obvious: we go to school to learn that which we do not know or understand, and we are more likely to learn when we are at the edge—the edge between what we know or think we know and what we do not know. To form new relations between what we know and what we are learning. Yes, this does require knowing things, building a bank, but it involves then using this bank of knowing to make relationships between ideas, between what we know and do not know. It involves taking risks, being in circumstances where we may not know what to do next and having others help us make the optimal connections between ideas. This book highlights this balance between knowing lots (surface-level learning) and relating ideas (deep learning). There is a place for both, and the art of teaching is knowing when to highlight the surface, when to highlight the deep, when to move from surface to deep, and then how to transfer the new deep thinking to near or far transfer situations. This is the strength of Nottingham's analysis. It is not surface *or* deep; it is *when* to be surface and deep.

For example, moving students through the Learning Challenge needs to occur at the right time in the learning equation—when the students have too much information, when they are ready to make links in their ideas. As noted in this book,

> A person could be said to be "in the pit" when they are in a state of cognitive conflict. When a person has two or more ideas that make sense to them but when compared side by side, appear to conflict with each other. . . . [T]he pit represents moving beyond a single, basic idea into the situation of having multiple ideas that are yet unsorted.

In terms of the SOLO taxonomy, moving from multistructural (having many ideas) to relational (making relations between ideas). Or to use Nottingham's notions, moving from concepts to identifying contradictions, examining all options, striving to form meaning, connecting and explaining.

The Learning Challenge is not a panacea. It is to be used deliberately at certain phases of learning, it needs considerable preparation and safety nets, and progress needs to be continually evaluated by students and teachers (at the right times) to see if it has made the difference moving from surface to deep learning.

I particularly point out the conflict stage—akin to what Piaget called disequilibrium. For Piaget, this uncomfortableness, this realization that things I know may not fit anymore, is the moment for learning to occur. It is when we make a mistake, question a misconception, encounter something that does not fit with what we think we know, err and meet desirable difficulties.

Of course, some students are so compliant that they will do most of what we ask of them. Yet when they are by themselves and face difficulties, they often fail (and often then withdraw). These students need to learn the power and skills of the Learning Challenge. Going through a learning pit tests our abilities, asks us to prove or justify our thinking,

This book includes so many worthwhile processes to invoke the various stages of learning, to show the connections between these stages and to identify evidence of impact from techniques that have been tried and tested in many contexts around the world by James Nottingham and his team. It is a pleasure reading a book that puts the challenge back into learning.

Challenging LEARNING

questions the truth or validity of ideas, seeks falsifiable hypotheses and tackles challenges with skill, energy and determination.

Nottingham argues that it is part of the teacher's role to create cognitive conflicts by creating "wobblers"—the shaking, unsteady feeling we experience when we are out of our comfort zone. This shows the importance of challenge in learning: It is not all sunshine and roses. Such challenge demonstrates the importance of effort, building trust and having confidence to take risks, knowing how to ask for and listening to feedback, learning to question oneself and others, putting in effort and learning how to become assessment-capable to evaluate progress. It is a way of thinking. It is a series of mind frames.

This book includes so many worthwhile processes to invoke the various stages of learning, to show the connections between these stages and to identify evidence of impact from techniques that have been tried and tested in many contexts around the world by James Nottingham and his team. It is a pleasure reading a book that puts the challenge back into learning.

I will leave the second last word to Freire (1970):

> We must abandon the banking concept of teaching and learning, and adopt instead a concept of students as conscious beings. We must pose problems of human beings in relation to their world, the development of the critical intervention into reality, developing dialogue with one's ideas and with others to break any circles of certainty that imprison reality and the growth of understanding.

And I will leave the last words to James Nottingham. Please read on.

—John Hattie
Director, Melbourne Education Research Institute

PREFACE

This book describes the theory and practice of guiding your students through the Learning Challenge. It is a practical book filled with ideas for making lessons engaging, thought provoking and collaborative.

In many ways, it has taken far too many years to write this book. After all, the model was born in the early part of my teaching career more than two decades ago. Yet this is the first book about it. In other ways, I am glad to have waited this long because the book is all the better for it. If I had written something when the model first came to people's attention, then it would have included only ideas that I had tried in my own schools. Now, though, I can share the full Learning Challenge after it has been tried and tested in hundreds of classrooms in dozens of countries around the world.

> The Learning Challenge is for all teachers, leaders and support staff who wish to help students develop a language for learning.

The Learning Challenge (LC) is for all educators. It is for the teachers, leaders and support staff who wish to guide their students in the development of critical, creative, caring and collaborative thinking. It is a model that provides learners with a language to think and talk about learning. It helps build participants' resilience, wisdom and self-efficacy. And when it is used as a structure for learning, it can improve teacher clarity and raise expectations of success.

The book covers everything from background to rationale, from establishing a learning culture to techniques for challenging, motivating and guiding students through a pit of learning. The chapters cover the following topics:

Chapter 1: the story of the Learning Pit and the Learning Challenge

Chapter 2: what the Learning Challenge looks like in practice

Chapter 3: how a culture of challenge, respect and reasoning can be created

Chapter 4: how to use concepts to enrich learning

Chapter 5: the best ways to challenge your students

Chapter 6: the best ways to help your students make sense of the world around them

Chapter 7: proven techniques for developing metacognition and reflection in education

Chapter 8: how to build students' self-efficacy

Chapter 9: links to the SOLO taxonomy and Philosophy for Children

Chapter 10: seven full lesson plans to help you make the most of the Learning Challenge

> The LC is part of a series of books that aim to support and improve pedagogy. Other titles include Challenging Learning Through Dialogue and Challenging Learning Through Feedback.

The Learning Challenge forms part of the Challenging Learning series of books that I am delighted to have written with some of the most talented and thoughtful people I know. Other books in the series focus on feedback, questioning, dialogue and a growth mindset. This book provides a perfect introduction to all of those topics and more.

Thank you for reading it.

ACKNOWLEDGMENTS

The Learning Challenge (LC) has been strongly influenced by the work of John Dewey (1859–1952) and Matthew Lipman (1922–2010). Both Dewey and Lipman placed thinking and dialogue at the core of educational aims and practices. They understood thinking as a process of inquiry. Dewey's and Lipman's ideas featured prominently in the Philosophy for Children (P4C) training I received as a trainee teacher as well as in the broader pedagogical training I undertook. These experiences greatly influenced my thinking.

The theoretical basis of the Learning Challenge also owes much to the work of the educational psychologist Lev Vygotsky (1896–1934). Among the many ideas he shared with the world, Vygotsky wrote that the communication processes used between people become internalized into verbal thought. That is to say that the ideas and processes a person experiences in dialogue with others influence the way in which he or she thinks in the future. Thus external dialogue becomes internal dialogue. In other words: thinking. That means the dialogues that form the basis for Learning Challenge experiences are vital not only to learning in the moment but also to the very nature of participants' thinking henceforth.

> The LC is strongly influenced by the principles and practices of Philosophy for Children.

During the 1990s, I developed Four Steps to Learning: Concept, Conflict, Construct and Consider. It was working well and my students were engaging purposefully with the steps. Then I saw John Edwards present the notion of a pit at the International Conference on Thinking in 2003. As I wrote in my first book, *Challenging Learning* (2010, p. 185):

> The Learning Challenge has grown from the Transformational Learning Model of Dr. Jim Butler and Dr. John Edwards. They developed the model in the 1990s to explain how deep, or transformational, learning often involves initial dips in performance. Faced with a worthwhile challenge, people are likely to fall into what Butler and Edwards described as a "learning pit" before emerging with enhanced attitudes, skills or knowledge. The model has undergone a number of developments as Butler and Edwards have applied it in a range of settings. The Learning Challenge describes my version of their concept of the pit.

There are many other people who have had an influence on the Learning Challenge. The most significant of whom is Jill Potter (now Nottingham!). Jill was the first person outside of the schools I taught in to fully engage with the Learning Challenge and to adapt it to work with children as young as three. She has since written a wide variety of resources to support the Learning Challenge, including many of the ideas in this book. And she is the one who has edited, challenged and reworked my early thoughts into what you find in this book today: a model that will actually work not just in theory but also in practice in every classroom.

> The LC works with students from the age of three onward.

Then there is Will Ord, a longtime confidante who has done more than anyone else I know outside of Challenging Learning to promote an accurate interpretation and uptake of the model. Will's sense of humor and ability to spot the essence of an idea are a joy to behold.

There is Roger Sutcliffe, who sat next to me the day I heard John Edwards talk about the notion of a pit and who was a wonderful guide and encourager during my early years as a teacher and trainer. There is Steve Williams, who has been brilliant ever since I started book-writing at ensuring that what I claim makes sense and stands up to rigorous inspection. If I can get it past Steve, I can get it past anyone. There is Martin Renton, who with a comment, question or out-of-hours text always reminds me we're in this together. There are my colleagues of old, Paul Dearlove, David Kinninment, Louise Brown, Mike Henry and Joanne Nugent, all of whom used and adapted the pit in so many brilliant ways. And there is Helen Richards, who has also been through thick and thin with me at work and is still there with an encouraging word, a healthy dose of sarcasm to keep my feet on the floor and a whole lot of recommendations for improvement.

There are also Åse Ranfelt, Bengt Lennartsson, Bitte Sundin, Bosse Larsson, Kari Eliassen, Marianne Skogvoll, Øivin Monsen and Ragnhild Isachsen, with whom I have had some wonderful chats through the years about how best to translate the Learning Challenge into Danish, Norwegian and Swedish. The nuances and problems of translation, as well as their questions, cultural insights and, most important, friendship, have helped me better understand and adapt my work accordingly.

There are some schools that have gone above and beyond in their application and sharing of the Learning Challenge. These include Brudenell Primary School and Bournville Juniors plus many, many schools in Midlothian, Northumberland, Newcastle and County Durham in the United Kingdom; Yinnar and Cambewarra schools and Rose Rainbow Kindergarten in Australia; Douglas Park School and Stonefields School in New Zealand; *all* the schools in Flora and Ås in Norway and in Norrköping in Sweden; some of the schools connected with SURN in Virginia, in the United States; plus many more—too many to mention, in fact—that have taken on the Learning Challenge with aplomb. To them all, I say thank you for making all the effort worthwhile.

Finally, the biggest thanks goes to my wonderful team at Challenging Learning, particularly Helen, Jill, Lucy, Mark and Sarah, and to Ariel Bartlett at Corwin. They have all been brilliant in so many ways.

> Search online for the "learning pit" and you will find hundreds of ways in which the LC is being used to support and engage learners around the world.

PUBLISHER'S ACKNOWLEDGMENTS

Corwin would like to thank the following reviewers for their editorial insight and guidance:

John Almarode, Professor of Education
Co-Director of the Center for STEM Education and Outreach
James Madison University, College of Education
Harrisonburg, VA

Simon Feasey, School Principal
Bader Primary School
Thornaby, Stockton-on-Tees, England

Kelly Fitzgerald, Instructional Coach
Rouse High School
Georgetown, TX

Barb Pitchford, Author/Consultant
Corwin
Aspen, CO

Michele Thomas, Headteacher
Pembroke Dock Community School
Pembrokeshire, Wales, UK

ABOUT THE AUTHOR

James Nottingham is the founder of Challenging Learning, a company based in the United Kingdom, Australia and Scandinavia. His passion is in transforming the most up-to-date research into strategies that really work in the classroom. He has been described by the Swedish Teaching Union as "one of the most talked about names in the world of school development."

Before training to be a teacher, James worked on a pig farm, in the chemical industry, for the American Red Cross and as a sports coach in a school for deaf children. At university, he gained a first-class honors degree in education. He then worked as a teacher and leader in primary and secondary schools in the United Kingdom before co-founding an award-winning, multimillion-pound social regeneration project supporting schools and businesses across the United Kingdom.

In 2009, James was listed among the Future 500—a "definitive list of the UK's most forward-thinking and brightest innovators."

THE LANGUAGE OF LEARNING

The following terms have been used in the following ways in this book:

ASK Model: a modern-day version of Bloom's Taxonomy of Educational Objectives. It brings together a focus on Attitudes, Skills and Knowledge.

Attitudes: a tendency or preference for something. In the case of learning, we would try to encourage the attitudes of curiosity, determination, open-mindedness and so on.

Coaching: an approach to instruction that questions, challenges, encourages and guides the learner.

Cognitive Conflict: broadly defined as the mental discomfort produced when one is confronted with new information that contradicts prior beliefs and ideas.

Concept: a general idea that groups things together according to accepted characteristics.

Construct: shorthand for Stage 3 of the Learning Challenge in which participants construct meaning by connecting, explaining and examining patterns and relationships.

CRAVE Questions: a framework of questioning techniques inspired by the Socratic tradition.

Culture: the behaviors and beliefs that characterize a group of people. Used in the context of developing a positive culture for feedback.

Dialogue: conversation and inquiry. Dialogue combines the sociability of conversation with the skills of framing questions and constructing answers.

Educere: the root word in Latin from which the word *education* comes. It is used in the book as an acronym for seven categories of thinking: engage, desire, understand, create, explore, reason, evaluate.

Eureka: taken from the Greek word for "I found it," the eureka moment is reached as students climb out of the pit with a new sense of clarity and understanding.

Fixed Mindset: from the work of Carol Dweck (2006, 2012, 2014). A mindset is a self-perception or self-theory that people hold about themselves. A fixed mindset refers to a belief that talents are abilities more or less fixed by genetics.

Generalization: a statement based on an identified group of common characteristics.

Growth Mindset: also from the work of Carol Dweck, a growth mindset refers to a belief that talents are abilities that are grown rather than bestowed by birth.

Knowledge: acquaintance with facts, truths or principles. Generally considered to be a step removed from understanding, which refers to when someone is able to relate, explain and evaluate.

Learning Focus: a learning focus includes an emphasis on questioning, challenging, striving to get better and beating personal bests. This is in contrast to a performance focus that hinges on grades, attainment and beating other people. In other words, a learning focus is intrinsic, whereas a performance focus is extrinsic.

Learning Intention: what students should know, understand or be able to do by the end of the lesson or series of lessons.

Learning Zone: the Teaching Target Model's equivalent of Vygotsky's zone of proximal development.

Metacognition: literally meaning "thinking about thinking," metacognition is an important part of feedback. It encourages students to think about *how* they are giving and receiving feedback as well as *what* the feedback messages are.

Performance Focus: a performance focus hinges on grades, attainment and beating other people. This is in contrast to a learning focus that emphasizes questioning, challenging and beating personal bests.

Pit: a metaphor to identify the state of confusion a person feels when holding two or more conflicting thoughts or opinions in their mind at the same time.

Potential Ability: what a student could potentially do next. It represents the limit of the zone of proximal development.

Preview: gives students an idea about what they will be learning in advance of the lesson. This allows them to prepare beforehand. The effect can be significantly positive.

Process: the actions that lead to the learning goal. Focusing on process is particularly important when teaching students *how* to learn as much as *what* to learn.

Reflection: giving serious thought or consideration to a thought, idea or response.

Self-Regulation: an ability to control impulses, plan strategically and act thoughtfully.

Self-Review: when a student gives himself or herself feedback.

SEN: special educational needs, a collective term for students with conditions such as autism, Down syndrome, attention deficit hyperactivity disorder.

Skills: the abilities to carry out processes necessary for gaining understanding, completing tasks or performing in any given context.

SOLO Taxonomy: the Structure of Observed Learning Outcomes model describes levels of increasing complexity in the understanding of subjects, originally proposed by John Biggs and Kevin Collis.

Success Criteria: the key steps or ingredients students need to accomplish the learning intention. They include the main things to do, include or focus on.

Taxonomy: a classification representing the intended outcomes of the educational process.

Understanding: mental process of a person who comprehends. It includes an ability to explain cause, effect and significance, and to understand patterns and how they relate to each other.

Wobblers and Wobbling: user-friendly terms to describe a state of cognitive conflict.

Zone of Proximal Development: used by Lev Vygotsky to describe the zone between actual and potential development.

This book would not have been completed on time without the ideas and encouragement of Jill Nottingham, Lucy Bennison, Mark Bollom, Sarah Unwin and Ariel Bartlett.

Thank you all. I owe you much more than a pint!

> "All which the school can or need do for pupils, so far as their minds are concerned . . . is to develop their ability to think."
>
> (Dewey, 1916)

INTRODUCTION TO THE LEARNING CHALLENGE

1.0 • PREVIEW

The most important points in this chapter include:

1. The Learning Challenge encourages learners to investigate contradictions and uncertainties so that they might more deeply understand what it is they are thinking about.

2. The Learning Challenge is a frame of reference for students to talk and think more accurately and extensively about their own learning.

3. At the heart of the Learning Challenge is the pit. Someone is said to be in the pit when they have a set of unresolved, contradictory ideas about something they are trying to understand.

4. Learners are *not* in the pit when they have *no* idea. To be in the pit is to have *many* ideas that are as yet unsorted.

5. The Learning Challenge is designed to help learners step out of their comfort zone so that they might discover insights that are more meaningful and long-lasting.

1.1 • INTRODUCTION

The Learning Challenge (LC) is designed to help students think and talk about their learning. In some ways, it is a child-friendly representation of Vygotsky's (1978) zone of proximal development in that it describes the move from actual to potential understanding. It can help develop a growth mindset (Dweck, 2006), prompt people to explore alternatives and contradictions, and encourage learners to willingly step outside their comfort zone.

The Learning Challenge can work with all school-age students as well as with adults. Originally, I developed the model to help nine- to thirteen-year-olds understand the role of uncertainty in learning but then broadened its application to be useful for anyone from the age of three onward. Although it wasn't published until I wrote my first book, *Challenging Learning,* in 2010, it has been shared far and wide at education conferences and workshops since the late 1990s. Since then, it has captured the imagination of educators, students *and* their parents. It has featured in many periodicals, articles and books. It appears on many classroom walls around the world. It has even made it into the UK's *Financial Times* newspaper (Green, 2016).

I'd like to think its popularity is due to its contribution in making learning more engaging and long-lasting. And from what many people tell me, that is indeed a key reason. But of course it doesn't explain the whole story. Other reasons include how well it sits alongside John Hattie's *Visible Learning for Teachers* (Hattie, 2011) and Carol Dweck's (2006) *Mindset.* The model also helps to explain and build on the SOLO taxonomy (Biggs & Collis, 1982) and is an effective way to structure Philosophy for Children (P4C) and other approaches to dialogue. It can guide metacognitive questions such as these: How does my final answer compare to my earlier thoughts? Which strategies worked best for me this time? What could I do better next time? It also offers a rich language and framework for talking about—and thinking about—learning in general.

Perhaps the main reason for the popularity of the Learning Challenge is its simplicity. It is easy enough to be understood by the youngest learners in schools and yet complex enough to keep the most advanced learners interested. Although that can also be a bit of a double-edged sword leading to some "interesting" misinterpretations, the simplicity *and* complexity are also part of what makes the Learning Challenge relevant to so many people.

As with so many models, the Learning Challenge did not start life as the one you see described and illustrated in this book. In fact, it began life as the Teaching Target Model (Figure 1).

I created the Teaching Target Model early in my teaching career as a way to explain to my students what progress looks like. This is how I explained it to them:

> The CA line represents current ability. This is the upper limit of what you are able to do independently.

> The SA line represents subconscious ability. This is what you are able to do automatically. It is something you can do without having to think at all about it, like hold a pen, walk normally, say your name and so on.

> The PA line represents potential ability. This is how far you can reach *beyond* what you can do comfortably right now. Typically, you will need to be challenged and/or supported to get to this next stage of development.

A good example to think about is learning to ride a bicycle. Presumably the first bike you rode had stabilizers (or trainer wheels) on the back. Though you might have found it

---

The LC sits comfortably alongside John Hattie's Visible Learning, Carol Dweck's Growth Mindset, Matthew Lipman's P4C and Biggs and Collis's SOLO taxonomy.

The LC began life as the Teaching Target Model that in itself is a description of Vygotsky's zone of proximal development.

▶ Figure 1: The Teaching Target Model

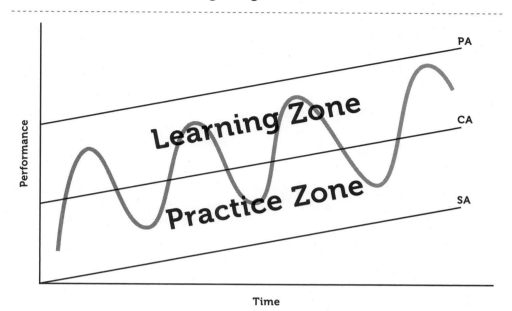

Note: PA: potential ability; CA: current ability; SA: subconscious ability

strange to begin with, no doubt you will have got the hang of pedaling and before long will have been riding a bike with stabilizers with ease. This is what we could call an action within your Practice Zone. You didn't need to deliberately think about it; you just got on, and away you went.

Later, one of your parents will have suggested taking your stabilizers off the bike. Then what happened? You wobbled. You fell off and got back on again. You probably complained that it was easier before and asked why you had to do it. Nonetheless you persevered with encouragement and kept going until eventually you got the hang of it. Throughout that time of wobbling, feeling unsure, wondering if you would ever succeed, you were in the learning zone. One of the best-known educational psychologists, Lev Vygotsky, called this the zone of proximal development, but we will call it the learning zone (or the Wobble Zone if you prefer).

That is what learning is all about: wobbling. If you are doing something that you can already do, then you are practicing, whereas learning requires you to step out of your comfort zone, to go beyond your current ability (CA) and try things that will make you wobble. Playing it safe by staying in your comfort zone and doing what you can already do will probably result in correct answers and completed work. I used to remind my students that we are here to *learn* together, not just *do* together. So I encourage you to take every opportunity you can to go beyond your CA and be prepared to wobble. If you are wobbling, then you are learning. And if you are learning, then you will flourish.

When a learner steps outside their comfort zone, then they begin to wobble.

My students generally responded very well to this model. They felt as if they were being given permission to take risks, try new things and get things wrong. This contrasted with a common belief they had developed earlier in their school life that the most important thing was to get things right, even if that meant playing safe and going for the easier option. Of course I wanted them to get things right, but I also wanted them to learn. So *if* it was a choice between getting things right or learning through mistakes, then I was very much in favor of the latter.

A drawback to the Teaching Target Model, however, was that I would represent the movement between practice and learning as a series of peaks and troughs, as you can see in Figure 1. My students would often interpret this as a series of mountains and valleys, with the top of the mountain representing the most wobbly part of learning. Though in many ways this was nice, it just didn't quite feel right to me. On the one hand, I was trying to use the model to reassure my students that learning often makes people feel uncertain and vague, but on the other hand, they were recalling the feelings of achievement and satisfaction people often feel when they reach the top of an actual mountain.

So I knew it had to change, but I wasn't sure how. Then when I heard John Edwards talking about a pit (see Acknowledgments), I had my *aha* moment. I just needed to invert the Teaching Target Model and make the wobbly bit a pit rather than a mountain! That way, the uncertainty and risk of learning could be represented by a pit rather than a mountaintop. And so the Learning Challenge evolved into the model you see today, one that has a pit at the core (see Figure 2).

▶ **Figure 2: The Learning Challenge**

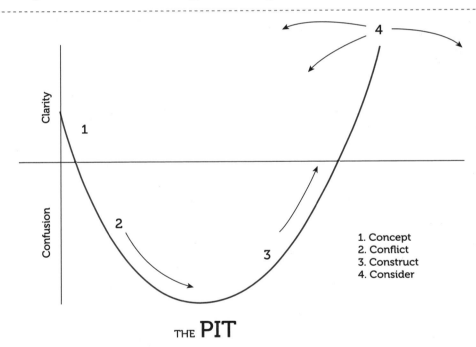

THE **PIT**

1. Concept
2. Conflict
3. Construct
4. Consider

1.2 • THE LEARNING CHALLENGE: A QUICK GUIDE

The Learning Challenge promotes challenge, dialogue and a growth mindset. It offers participants the opportunity to think and talk about their own learning. It encourages a depth of inquiry that moves learners from surface-level knowledge to deep understanding. It encourages an exploration of causation and impact, an interpretation and comparison of meaning, a classification and sequencing of detail and a recognition and analysis of

> The Learning Challenge is designed to encourage (literally: give courage to) your students so that they might better understand themselves and each other, so that they develop a sense of clarity and discernment in their thinking; and ultimately so that they become more aware of who they are and what they stand for. As one of my students once said, "How do you know what you think until you've thought it?"

pattern. It builds learners' resilience, determination and curiosity. And it nurtures a love of learning.

At the heart of the Learning Challenge is the pit. A person could be said to be in the pit when they are in a state of cognitive conflict. That is to say, when a person has two or more ideas that make sense to them but that, when compared side by side, appear to be in conflict with each other.

Deliberately and strategically creating a state of cognitive conflict in the minds of learners is at the heart of the Learning Challenge.

Here are some examples of cognitive conflicts that commonly arise during Learning Challenge episodes:

- I believe that stealing is wrong, but I also believe that Robin Hood did the right thing.

- Children are taught that an odd number cannot be divided into two, but three cakes can be shared equally between two friends.

- I think it is wrong to kill animals, but I also eat meat.

- Young children should not talk to strangers but are advised to approach a police officer or shop worker if they are lost.

- A liquid is thought of as a substance that flows freely, but so does sand, and that is not a liquid.

- Students know that studying will help them improve but often can't see the point in studying more.

- Telling a lie is viewed as a negative, but writing fictional stories is viewed as positive. So what is the difference?

- Food is a substance that gives energy, yet many things give energy (e.g., sunshine, encouragement) but are not normally regarded as food.

- A hero is someone who takes risks on behalf of others, but then so do terrorists.

- Justice is seen as a good thing, whereas revenge is thought of as a negative, yet they both seem to be about settling a score. So what is the difference?

- When we hold discussions with our students, we expect them to show respect for other people's ideas, yet there are many extreme views that perhaps we would not want them to respect.

When people think through these or other examples of cognitive conflicts, then they are said to be in the pit. There are more examples of cognitive conflict throughout Chapters 5 and 10.

Being in the pit represents being in a state of cognitive conflict.

Cognitive conflict occurs when a person has two or more contradictory ideas in their mind at the same time.

Here are some common examples of cognitive conflict.

It is important to note that learners are *not* in the pit when they have *no* idea. The pit represents moving beyond a single, basic idea into the situation of having multiple ideas that are as yet unsorted. This happens when a learner purposefully explores inconsistencies, exceptions and contradictions in their own or others' thinking so as to discover a richer, more complex understanding.

The SOLO taxonomy can help you understand the LC (and vice versa).

In SOLO taxonomy terms, being in the pit represents the multistructural stage of learning and, as learners come out of the pit, the relational stage of learning (see Sections 1.3.7 and 9.1).

And that is the point of the Learning Challenge: to make learning more challenging and thought-provoking. In other words, to get people into the pit! Though this might seem perverse—particularly given the ever-increasing pressures of the curriculum—the justification is that through challenge, your learners will develop more resilience, gain greater self-efficacy and build many of the strategies they will need for learning in—and beyond—school. Being in the pit is also where your students will think more deeply, more critically and more strategically.

The Learning Challenge typically has four stages:

Stage 1: Concept

The Learning Challenge begins with a concept. The concept can come from the media, conversation, observations or the curriculum. As long as *some* of your students have at least *some* understanding of the concept(s) you wish them to explore, then the Learning Challenge can work. This first stage equates to the unistructural stage of learning in the SOLO taxonomy (Biggs & Collis, 1982).

Stages 1 through 4 of the LC correspond directly with Stages 1 through 4 of the SOLO taxonomy.

Stage 2: Conflict

The key to the Learning Challenge is to get your students into the pit by creating cognitive conflict in their minds. This deliberate creation of a dilemma is what makes the Learning Challenge such a good model for challenge and inquiry, reasoning and reasonableness. Stage 2 of the Learning Challenge is equivalent to the multistructural and relational stages of the SOLO taxonomy (Biggs & Collis, 1982).

Stage 3: Construct

After a while of being in the pit (and I'm being purposefully ambiguous by saying "after a while" because it depends on context), your students will begin to make links and construct meaning. They will do this by examining options, connecting ideas together and explaining cause and effect. Often (though not always) this leads them to a sense of eureka in which they find new clarity. This sense of revelation is one of the reasons that the effort of going through the pit is so worthwhile.

Stage 4: Consider

After achieving a sense of eureka, your students should reflect on their learning journey. They can do this by considering *how* they progressed from simplistic ideas (Stage 1), to the identification of more complex and conflicting ideas (Stage 2), through to a deeper understanding of how all these ideas interrelate to each other (Stage 3). Now at Stage 4, they can think about the best ways to relate and apply their new understanding to different contexts. This final stage of the Learning Challenge is equivalent to the extended abstract stage of the SOLO taxonomy (Biggs & Collis, 1982).

1.3 • UNDERPINNING VALUES

There are many values and beliefs upon which the Learning Challenge is based. Here are the most important ones.

1.3.1 • Challenge Makes Learning More Interesting

At the heart of the Learning Challenge is the belief that challenge makes learning more stimulating and worthwhile. This is in contrast to making learning simpler and more elementary, which has its place but is not ideal much of the time.

To illustrate the point, please compare the two paths shown in Figure 3. As you see, the path on the left is straightforward and is likely to get you to your destination quickly, whereas the path to the right is filled with obstacles and will require greater effort to reach your goal. Of course, if you were in a rush, then the obvious path to take is the one on the left.

▶ Figure 3: The Path to Challenge

> Linking challenge to making things more difficult can be off-putting, whereas describing challenge as making things more interesting can make it much more attractive to students.

> The LC encourages participants to take the challenging route.

But if I were to ask you to choose the path most *interesting,* then which one would you go for? Which one looks to be the more engaging and thought-provoking? Which one is most likely to lead you into discussion with other people about the best strategies going forward? Which one are you most likely to look back on and review with enthusiasm?

Which is going to give you the most satisfaction when you eventually reach your goal? And which route are you most likely to remember months, maybe even years from now because of the effort you had to put in to get through it?

Hopefully you've answered "the right path" to each of those questions. If not, then I've got a persuasion job on my hands as well as an instructional one!

This imagery is one way to describe the Learning Challenge journey. Taking on the Learning Challenge and going through the pit is the equivalent of taking the path to the right.

The Learning Challenge promotes a more rigorous and exploratory path to learning as a way to reach a deeper understanding of concepts.

That is not something that I would advocate in every situation or in every lesson. Of course, there are many situations in which an easy answer is needed. But I do think every student should frequently engage in the Learning Challenge so they will, as Guy Claxton (2002) would put it, "build their learning muscles."

1.3.2 • Dialogue Enhances Learning

The Learning Challenge relies on high-quality dialogue. At its best, dialogue is one of the most effective vehicles for learning how to think, how to be reasonable, how to make moral decisions and how to understand another person's point of view. It is supremely flexible, instructional, collaborative and rigorous. Done well, dialogue is one of the best ways for participants to learn good habits of thinking.

As my co-authors and I explored in more depth in our book *Challenging Learning Through Dialogue* (2017), Professor Robin Alexander (2010) found the following to be true:

1. Dialogue is undervalued in many schools when compared with writing, reading and mathematics.

2. Dialogue does not get in the way of real teaching. In fact, by comparing PISA and other international tests, he shows it is possible to teach more through dialogue and yet still be at or near the top of the tables.

3. Dialogue is the foundation of learning because it allows interaction and engagement with knowledge and with the ideas of others. Through dialogue, teachers can most effectively intervene in the learning process by giving instant feedback, guidance and stimulation to learners.

4. Dialogue in education is a special kind of talk in that it uses structured questioning to guide and prompt students' conceptual understanding.

The Learning Challenge involves the type of reflective, respectful dialogue described. The focus for participants is in challenging each other, asking appropriate questions, articulating problems and issues, imagining life's possibilities, seeing where things lead, evaluating alternatives, engaging with others and thinking collaboratively.

A different way to describe this is to talk of the co-construction of understanding. Written about by many theorists, most notably Lev Vygotsky (1978) and Jerome Bruner (1957), the idea of co-construction can be described using these main features:

- Learning and development is a social, collaborative activity. We don't learn inside a vacuum; we learn by mimicking and engaging with others.

- Social construction is connected to real life in that it focuses on matters that are important and relevant to participants.

- Learning has a social context; participants learn from each other and influence each other's learning.

And so it is with the Learning Challenge. Lessons that are based upon or involve the Learning Challenge can be distinguished by these characteristics of co-construction.

1.3.3 • We Are All Fallible

The Learning Challenge encourages *all* participants, including the teacher or facilitator, to be open about their own fallibility and to willingly explore flaws in their own thinking so that everyone may learn more together. This means that phrases such as "I'm not sure," "perhaps," "maybe," and "I was wondering" are to be encouraged throughout the dialogue. To some people, these sorts of phrases reveal ignorance or weak-mindedness. Yet in the context of the Learning Challenge, they are intended to reveal the ideals of open-mindedness and hypothesis-testing.

It is as Bertrand Russell wrote in an essay lamenting the rise of Nazism in 1933, "The fundamental cause of the trouble is that in the modern world the stupid are cock-sure whilst the intelligent are full of doubt." Or as the celebrated Irish poet W.B. Yeats (1919) wrote in *The Second Coming*, "The best lack all conviction, while the worst are full of passionate intensity."

So when you engage your students in the Learning Challenge, please encourage—and model—the values of open-mindedness and exploration since these are vital for the success of this approach.

Linked to these ideals is the notion that there might not be one, agreed "right" answer at the end of it all. Although most of the time some form of agreement is reachable, there are occasions, particularly with the more open-ended, philosophical questions, when no satisfactory conclusion is achievable in the time frame you have. But that is not to say the experience will be any less worthwhile, as is explored in the next section. However, it would be worth mentioning that:

> **Sometimes participants in the Learning Challenge will enter the pit and stay there! They should not feel disheartened by this. Nor should they feel abandoned as they are likely to be in the pit with others. Instead, they should feel invigorated by finding one of life's great, unanswered questions.**

1.3.4 • Process Is as Important as Outcome

The process of learning is often more important than getting the right answer, particularly with Learning Challenge sessions. A learning focus includes an emphasis on questioning, challenging, striving to get better and beating personal bests. This contrasts

The dialogue generated by the LC leads to social construction of ideas.

The LC relies on the values of open-mindedness and a willingness to learn from others.

with a performance focus that hinges on grades, attainment, showing what you can do and beating each other.

As numerous teachers and their students will testify, far too many schools focus primarily on performance ("it's the grades that count"). And yet, improved performance comes from a learning focus, whereas learning does *not* always come from a performance focus.

> **If you and your students focus on *learning,* then their performance grades will also increase. However, if you and your students focus on grades alone, then rich learning opportunities might be missed along the way.**

That is why *process* is more important than getting the answer right in the Learning Challenge. Of course, if you can get your students to deeply engage in learning *and* help them reach a satisfactory answer, then that is ideal. But if your students go into the pit and don't come out (yet), then don't worry; it doesn't mean they haven't benefited from the experience. So long as you keep encouraging them to go beyond their first answers to seek alternative explanations; ask questions such as why, if, and what about; see problems as part of the learning process rather than things to be avoided; make connections, find the significance of parts in relation to the whole and look for ways to transfer ideas to other contexts, then they will *improve* their competence rather than simply *prove* they have got the right answer.

1.3.5 • Hattie's Mindframes for Learning

John Hattie is currently Laureate Professor and director of the Melbourne Education Research Institute. He is known throughout the world for his groundbreaking comparison of thousands of studies relating to learning. In his seminal book, *Visible Learning* (Hattie, 2009), he ranked 138 effects taken from 800 meta-analyses that included more than 50,000 studies in education. He updated this list to 150 effects in his follow-up book, *Visible Learning for Teachers* (Hattie, 2011) and more recently to a list of 195 effects in *The Applicability of Visible Learning to Higher Education* (Hattie, 2015), in which he compared more than 1,200 meta-analyses relating to influences on learning and achievement.

From all of this work, one of the many powerful messages is related to beliefs about learning: what Hattie calls Mindframes. Hattie has proposed ten Mindframes so far. Of these, the ones that the Learning Challenge contributes toward include the following:

> *I enjoy challenge.* **Hattie asserts that we should teach students to recognize the benefit of challenge. He has found that too many of us rush to the aid of our students, whereas it would be better to encourage our students to persevere and to learn from their errors. This idea is at the very heart of the Learning Challenge.**

I engage in positive relationships. Hattie has shown that teacher-student relationships influence learning almost twice as much as the average effect. These relationships, whether student-teacher relationships or the relationships students have with peers, tend to be improved by going through the pit together. Indeed, it is the social effect of uniting to get through the pit that is very often the first benefit noticed by teachers and leaders after their students have engaged with the Learning Challenge.

I use the language of learning. Hattie has found a strong link between a focus on learning (rather than a focus on teaching) and improved educational outcomes. The Learning Challenge offers an opportunity for students to talk about very abstract notions of learning in a more user-friendly and practical way. For example, being in the pit is shorthand for cognitive conflict or cognitive dissonance, coming out of the pit is a way to talk about social construction and reviewing the learning journey is one way to make metacognitive strategies a part of daily conversation in the classroom.

I engage in dialogue, not monologue. The Learning Challenge is founded on challenge through dialogue. Sometimes this dialogue is internal. More often it is interpersonal, exploratory talk among students, and between students and their teachers. And what they talk about are concepts, strategies and attitudes for learning—all of which are building blocks for educational success.

I see learning as hard work. The Learning Challenge makes learning more engaging and long-lasting by making it harder work. The Learning Challenge takes a seemingly simple concept and reveals its complexities in such a way as to intrigue and beguile students. By working through these nuances, students ultimately reach a eureka moment that convinces them that effort is worthwhile and that actually the harder learning is, the more satisfying it can be.

> *I talk about learning rather than about teaching.* **The Learning Challenge brings the focus back to learning—learning about, learning with and learning because. It provides a rich and accessible language for all participants (teachers and their students) to be better able to talk about learning.**

1.3.6 • Dweck's Growth Mindset

Carol S. Dweck is the Lewis and Virginia Eaton Professor of Psychology at Stanford University. Her best-selling book *Mindset* (Dweck, 2006) has sold more than a million copies. In 2009, she received the E.L. Thorndike Award for Career Achievement in Educational Psychology. Previous winners include B.F. Skinner, Benjamin Bloom and Jean Piaget, so she is in good company!

Her research focuses on the beliefs people have about intelligence and talents and how these mindsets affect behavior. She examines the reasons that people get into different mindsets and the impact these differing beliefs have on motivation, resilience and success.

From her decades of research, Professor Dweck has described two contrasting mindsets: fixed and growth. People in a fixed mindset think of talents and intelligence as relatively stable and innate. They say things such as "I've always been good at this but I couldn't possibly do that" or "I'm naturally good with languages but I don't have a musical bone in my body." In other words, people in a fixed mindset believe that either you can or you can't and that's that.

On the other hand, people in a growth mindset think of talents and intelligence as highly responsive to nurture. They don't deny the role that genetics plays, but they see nature as the starting point rather than as the defining quality. So someone in a growth mindset would be likely to say, "I have developed a talent for writing, but I have never really

> The more students go through the LC, the more likely they are to get into a growth mindset.

> People in a growth mindset are more likely to enjoy challenge, engage with learning and step out of their comfort zone.

▶ Figure 4: A Comparison of Fixed and Growth Mindsets

	Fixed Mindset	Growth Mindset
Beliefs	Intelligence and ability are fixed. Nature determines intelligence and ability.	Intelligence and ability can grow. Nurture significantly affects intelligence and ability.
Priorities	Prove myself Avoid failure	Improve myself Learn from failure
Response to challenge	Feel inferior or incapable Seek ego-boosting distractions	Feel inspired to have a go Seek advice, support or new strategies
Mottos	If you're really good at something, you shouldn't need to try. Don't try too hard; that way you've got an excuse if things go wrong.	No matter how good you are at something, you can always improve. Always try hard; that way you've more chance of success and making progress.

committed to learning a musical instrument (yet)." Notice the word *yet*, a very powerful word in the context of learning. Indeed, the title for Dweck's (2014) TED talk that has been viewed five million times already and that I was honored to introduce to the live audience, was originally titled "The Power of Yet."

Compare some of the differences between fixed and growth mindsets, as shown in Figure 4. As you read through them, note that the Learning Challenge encourages and teaches the attitudes and behaviors of the growth mindset.

> *The Learning Challenge* particularly focuses on effort, having a go, taking risks, trying new strategies, seeking advice, looking for challenges, questioning yourself and others, persevering and making progress. All of which are essential attitudes and behaviors of a growth mindset.

1.3.7 • The SOLO Taxonomy

The SOLO taxonomy stands for the Structure of Observed Learning Outcomes. It is a model first proposed by John Biggs and Kevin Collis (1982) in *Evaluating the Quality of Learning: The SOLO Taxonomy*.

SOLO is a means of classifying learning in terms of complexity, which in turn helps to identify the quality and depth of students' understanding.

> The SOLO taxonomy and the LC fit together very well.

> Many people use the SOLO taxonomy to describe a learner's progress from surface-level knowledge through to a deep, contextual understanding. This is also an aim of the Learning Challenge and so, together, the two models sit perfectly alongside each other.

No Idea
SOLO Term: Prestructural
Learning Challenge Stage 0

This is when your students have no idea about the concept or topic you have chosen. At this stage, the Learning Challenge will *not* work. Before you can get your students into the pit, they will need at least *some* idea about the concept in question. For example, you are unlikely to get six-year-olds into the pit about a concept as complex as global development, but you could probably get them into the pit about friendship or fairness.

One Idea
SOLO Term: Unistructural
Learning Challenge Stage 1

This is when your students have one idea or at least a basic set of notions about the concept or topic you have chosen. At this stage, the Learning Challenge is ready to begin. Generally you can start by asking what the concept means. For example, "What is a friend?" or "What is global development?" And as long as *some* of your students (and not just the outliers) are able to give a reasonably accurate answer involving one or two facts about the concept, then the Learning Challenge can begin.

Many Ideas
SOLO Term: Multistructural
Learning Challenge Stage 2

This is when your students have many ideas about the concept or topic in question. At this stage, your students will be heading down into the pit, if they are not there already. Generally, you will have encouraged your students into this stage by helping them spot contradictions or problems with what they have said. For example, "You say that friends are people you know, but you know lots of people who aren't your friends, don't you?" or "If global development is the equivalent of wealth, then what about the wealthy countries with high levels of child poverty: are they developed?"

Connecting Ideas
SOLO Term: Relational
Learning Challenge Stage 3

This is when your students begin to connect their ideas together and understand the relationships between them. In Learning Challenge terms, this is where your students construct understanding to the point of reaching a eureka moment. With this newfound sense of clarity and meaning, your students will feel a sense of accomplishment, and their answers will be noticeably more exact and developed.

Reviewing and Linking Ideas
SOLO Term: Extended Abstract
Learning Challenge Stage 4

This is when your students extend and apply their understanding to new contexts. In Learning Challenge terms, this is the point at which students look to blend their new discoveries with past knowledge so that they might better understand the bigger picture. They also innovate and create new applications for their understanding.

Further links between the Learning Challenge and the SOLO taxonomy will be explored in depth in Chapter 9. For now, though, see the brief overview on the previous page.

1.3.8 • A Language for Learning

A key strength of the Learning Challenge is its role in providing student-friendly language to describe abstract notions such as metacognition, quantitative versus qualitative aspects of learning and cognitive conflict.

> The LC provides child-friendly language to help students talk about their learning spontaneously and sincerely.

For example, most teachers will have studied Vygotsky's (1978) zone of proximal development, but how many students regularly use Vygotskian terminology? However, with the Learning Challenge even the youngest school-age child is able to indicate when they are in their zone of proximal development by saying, "I'm in the pit!"

Here are examples of other language regularly used by participants in the Learning Challenge to help them describe abstract notions of learning:

Wobbling, wobblers and *being in the pit*: user-friendly terms to describe a state of cognitive conflict (see Section 5.4.1)

Concept stretching: a way to describe the actions involved in challenging the meanings and applications of concepts (see Section 5.6)

Scaffolders: a collective term for a variety of strategies and tools used by participants to make sense of their learning (see Section 6.3)

Eureka: the revelatory state a person achieves after working hard to achieve a moment of clarity (see Section 6.5)

Stage 1: a nonprejudicial way to describe having only basic, surface-level knowledge about a concept (see Section 9.1)

Stage 2: an alternative to saying "I'm in the pit" (see Section 9.1)

Stage 3: a way to indicate progress from quantitative to qualitative stages of learning (see Section 9.1)

Stage 4: indicating a participant is engaging in a metacognitive review of their learning journey (see Section 9.1)

Unpacking: a nice term to describe investigation into the underlying or hidden aspects of a concept or idea

1.3.9 • A Structure for Learning

> The LC gives a structure to dialogue so that teachers can plan their lessons carefully if they wish to.

One of the most common reasons given for the popularity of the Learning Challenge is its usefulness as a tool for planning and delivering a challenging, dialogue-based lesson.

As a novice teacher, I was told again and again that classroom dialogue would help my students learn. Looking at Hattie's research more than two decades later, it turns out that advice was spot-on: classroom discussion is ranked tenth in the *Visible Learning* list of factors influencing achievement with an effect size of 0.82, equivalent to double the average effect of 0.4 (Hattie, 2015).

However, back then I was apprehensive about starting anything remotely open-ended because of the fear of not being able to predict the topics that might come up or anticipate the questions my students might ask. I worried that I might not know the answers to the questions that came up. I also felt pressure from the school leaders to have written plans for each stage of every lesson. Funnily enough, it seemed the leaders weren't happy to accept the plan "have a chat with the kids and see what happens."

That was one of the drivers behind the Learning Challenge—to create a framework that would allow me to know where the lesson would go while also allowing enough flexibility for my students to follow lines of inquiry that were interesting and relevant to them.

Thus the Learning Challenge allowed me to predict the following stages of an open-ended, dialogue-driven lesson:

Here are the seven main steps of the LC.

1. Identify a key concept.

2. Ask students for their initial ideas about the concept (these will usually be simple, undeveloped notions).

3. Create cognitive conflict by identifying contradictions and exceptions to students' early answers.

4. Ask students to compare their differing ideas by searching for similarities and differences.

5. Help pairs or groups select a thinking tool that will help them explain, sort and relate the ideas together.

6. Challenge students to develop a robust definition of the concept that will stand up against "what if" and "how about" questions.

7. Consider how students' final definitions apply to new contexts and reflect back over the learning journey.

This sort of plan seemed to satisfy my leaders much better. More important, it gave me the confidence to introduce dialogue into lessons safe in the knowledge that I had a good idea of where the lesson might go!

This step-by-step plan is explored in much more depth in Chapter 2.

1.3.10 • Learning for All

As you might have noticed in a couple of places in this chapter, I mentioned that the Learning Challenge works as long as *some* of your students have *some* understanding of the key concepts. This is because the Learning Challenge is collaborative in nature, bringing with it an expectation that participants will explain to and question each other. Those students who are initially unsure about the meanings of concepts tend to pick up interpretations from their more informed peers. That is assuming of course that those peers are not so far ahead that they use terminology or language that is incomprehensible. Thankfully this tends to be unlikely other than in the cases of the outliers. If those instances do occur, then you can get students in the middle to help those outliers make links and to explain or question in more accessible ways. This is covered in more depth in Sections 9.3 and 9.4.

The LC can work for all students who have a basic understanding of the chosen concept.

In fact, it is very often those students who are *not* normally confident in lessons who excel more in earlier Learning Challenge lessons. That is not to say the higher-achieving students do not benefit; it is just that they tend to sit back in earlier episodes to weigh it all up. Perhaps they are so used to "getting things right" in class that they are perplexed by the lack of an obvious answer or solution. Or maybe they are worried about appearing to be less "perfect" in front of their peers? Either way, those who are used to getting top grades tend to hang back at the beginning while those who normally struggle in lessons generally take to the Learning Challenge like ducks to water.

That is not say that the Learning Challenge is suitable for everybody right out of the box, as it were. Adaptation is sometimes needed. For example, participants with some forms of autism can find the standard Learning Challenge approaches a bit too open and free-flowing. But, of course, as with any other pedagogical strategy, we should use our professional judgment and experience to adapt these approaches so that they provide positive and beneficial experiences for all of our students. Having worked in special education settings as well as in mainstream education, I know this is sometimes not easy, but it *is* possible, and it *is* very rewarding for teacher and student alike when we get it right. This is explored in Section 9.3.

1.4 • A PIT IS CENTRAL TO THE LEARNING CHALLENGE

The idea of a pit fits perfectly with the notion that challenge is often unsettling and irregular.

A small portion of the people I meet say they like the Learning Challenge but would prefer it not to include a pit. They argue that the connotations are too negative. There are also issues with translation because some languages have no word for *pit*. This has led to interesting variants such as gold mine, a black hole or even the iron pot that hangs over old cooking stoves. And these are all in addition to the problem of *pit* being a rude word in Swedish!

In this brief section, I would like to justify the use of the term and idea of a pit and in so doing, explain a bit more about why I think a pit works best.

> The *aim* of the Learning Challenge is to get participants out of their comfort zone. This is a deliberate and strategic objective. It is neither incidental nor casual. It is not something that happens parenthetically. The very purpose of the Learning Challenge is to step outside the familiar to explore ideas and experiences that are neither effortless nor soothing. And that is why the idea of a pit works so well.

When your students get into the pit, you should expect them to feel uncomfortable. I don't mean anxious. I don't mean overwrought or afraid. I mean the opposite of contented. I mean needled: spurred on to think, try more and question more. That is why the idea of a "learning mountain" or a "cooking pot" does not work as well: neither of these evoke the feelings or the situation that the Learning Challenge is trying to create. A pit works because it is uncomfortable without being frightening. It is provocative without being aggressive. It is consuming, but you can always see out of it—unlike a mine that takes you right underground.

Of course, a pit doesn't suit every purpose. There are times when it is better to allow your students to get through a task without being challenged. It can mean fewer behavior problems, more time to support particular individuals, and it can give some students a sense of satisfaction at reaching their goals without having to ask for help or think too hard. Yet there are problems with this approach too. If your students stay in their comfort zone too much, then they will not get as much opportunity to develop life skills such as resilience, persistence and determination. There will not be as much need to think collaboratively or to search for alternative solutions. And they will rarely feel compelled to look beyond the obvious or take intellectual risks.

So it is all about balance: balance between practice tasks and challenging tasks, between feeling the satisfaction of arriving at the answer easily and taking time to engage in lots of trial and error before reaching the eureka point, balance between watching the world go by and getting into the pit to see what you can learn!

> The pit represents being out of your comfort zone. This should not happen all of the time but should certainly be a common feature of learning.

1.5 • REVIEW

In addition to the main points identified in the preview, this chapter has covered the following:

1. Although many people refer to the Learning Challenge as the Learning Pit, it is more accurate to say that the Learning Challenge *includes* a learning pit.

2. Being in the pit represents a state of cognitive conflict in which a person has two or more ideas that they agree with but, when compared side by side, appear to be in conflict with each other.

3. There are four stages of the Learning Challenge: concept, conflict, construct, consider.

4. The Learning Challenge contributes significantly toward the *Visible Learning* Mindframes (Hattie, 2015).

5. There are also strong parallels between the SOLO taxonomy (Biggs & Collis, 1982) and the Learning Challenge.

Figure 5:
The Main Steps in the Learning Challenge

Easy Learning

Deep Learning

Concept
Find a concept worth exploring that you know a little bit about.

Question
Find the problems, the nuances and the exceptions to your concept. You can do this by comparing your concept with another, considering if it always applies or trying to find a definition that works in all cases.

The Pit

Cognitive Conflict
If you've uncovered lots of examples and exceptions to your concept, and realized how complex your chosen concept is, then you are in the pit! This is where deep learning really gets going.

Construct
Identify patterns, relationships and meanings between all the ideas you've uncovered. Distinguish between them by sorting, classifying, grouping or ranking. Use your findings to create a more precise understanding of your concept.

Eureka!
Eureka: you found it! The feeling of enlightenment and discovery you feel at this stage is the ecstasy of learning. This is what makes the learning journey so worthwhile. Congratulations for persevering!

Consider
Look back at your learning journey. Which strategies worked best? What would you change next time? How can you apply your new understanding to different contexts?

Review

Transfer

Apply

Adapt

Challenging LEARNING
© The Learning Pit

THE LEARNING CHALLENGE IN PRACTICE

2.0 • PREVIEW

In this chapter, I run through a full Learning Challenge (LC) from Stage 1 to Stage 4. This is to encourage you to jump in with both feet and have a go at a Learning Challenge before returning to this book to find ways to make things work even better.

In Section 9.4.3, I recommend the Ready-Fire-Aim approach. That is when we get ready to have a go at something free from the anxiety of needing to be an expert before we begin, then we fire by taking a few early attempts at the new action and *then* we aim more accurately by interrogating the guide in a more focused way. I think this is a very practical way for three reasons:

> The Ready-
> Fire-Aim
> approach
> encourages
> a "try now,
> refine later"
> approach.

1. It reduces the worry that so many of us in education have, that we need to be the expert in the room. Instead, this approach encourages us to learn alongside our students.

2. People are in a much better position to pick up on nuances and implied messages when they have experience under their belts to reflect upon.

3. It fits perfectly with the classic educational mantra of "Plan-Do-Review."

It is worth bearing in mind that the different steps of the Learning Challenge are not set in stone. They are recommendations for what could be used to support your students' thinking. As with all pedagogical processes, they should be adapted to suit your students, your context and your purpose.

The most common steps are shown below, with the ones in bold being those that would be attended to in every single Learning Challenge experience. The others are either optional or assumed.

The text in bold shows the steps that would ordinarily be taken in every LC experience.

1. Create the Learning Challenge culture (see Chapter 3).
2. Remind your students of the ground rules for dialogue (see Section 3.4).
3. Share the Learning Intentions of the lesson (see Section 9.4.4.2).
4. **Sit in a circle with your students** (see Section 3.4.2).
5. Share a stimulus such as an image, a book or an object (see Section 4.3).
6. **Identify the most interesting concepts** (see Section 4.3).
7. Create thought-provoking questions about the concepts (see Section 4.4).
8. Select the best question (see Section 4.5).
9. **Invite your students to share their first thoughts** (see Section 4.6).
10. **Encourage your students to listen and respond to each other appropriately** (see Sections 3.1 and 3.5).
11. **Identify contradictions in the thoughts of participants** (see Sections 5.3 and 5.4).
12. **Explore alternatives and strive for meaning** (see Section 6.1).
13. **Connect ideas and explain reasons** (see Section 6.3).
14. **Construct a more sophisticated understanding of the central concept** (see Section 6.3.3).
15. Reach a eureka moment (see Section 6.5).
16. Review the learning journey and look for other applications for the new learning (see Section 7.2).

2.1 • STAGE 1: CONCEPT

The LC always begins with a concept. Section 4.2.1 lists concepts that are commonly used in LC sessions.

The Learning Challenge needs a concept to begin with. For the reasons discussed in Section 4.1, facts are not enough; the Learning Challenge needs a concept that your students have some knowledge about.

Good examples include art and design, democracy, evidence and proof, fairness and fair test, food, good and bad, growth and development, happiness, love, money, names and identity, number, theory, truth. Many more concepts are explored throughout this book.

For the purposes of showing you the classic way to run a Learning Challenge, I have chosen the concept of *real*. It is an idea that often comes up with very young children as well as with the most mature students. There are many ways to draw out or identify key concepts with which to begin a Learning Challenge, and they will be explored later in the book. For now, I am simply going to say what the concept is.

Concept: Real

The concept of real is an interesting one. Some philosophers have said that all our experience (including dreaming) is a different real from the reality of the physical world that exists independently of human experience. Though this is far from a globally accepted view, it is an interesting one nonetheless. It might lead your students to draw a distinction between real and imaginary or between real things that are tangible compared to things that are abstract.

> Here is an example of how a concept such as real can be explored.

Other interesting questions around this topic include the following:

1. If I pretend to be a police officer, then what part of that role-play is real?

2. If I blow a dog whistle that makes a sound humans can't hear, then is the sound real?

3. In history, there are very often at least two different versions of events: one from the victors and one from the losers. How can we know which is the real version of events?

4. How do you know when what you see is really how *it is* rather than just how you *see it*?

5. What is the difference between real and opinion?

6. What do people mean when they say that is a "fake watch" rather than a real one?

7. Is reality TV real?

8. Is there any way to be absolutely sure that aliens are not real?

9. In what ways are the Harry Potter stories by J.K. Rowling real?

10. Can a lie be real?

Another way to explore the concept is to look at its opposite; in this case, *un*real. For example, in what ways is a plastic toy, a dream, pretend money, magic or a folk tale unreal? Though they might all be thought of as unreal, they seem to be unreal in different ways. And that is without bringing in such things as optical illusions such as the famous duck-rabbit illusion.

To begin a Learning Challenge session about real with your students, you could pick any of the questions above. Or you could do something like this:

Get hold of a real version and a toy version of the same thing: for example, a real apple and a toy apple. Then place these items in front of your students and ask them to talk about the *three* apples in front of them. By saying "three apples," I am including an invisible apple in this scenario.

Once your students have started to share their initial thoughts about the concept, it is time to set up some cognitive conflict so as to take them into the pit.

Show students an apple, a plastic apple and an "invisible" apple, and ask them to decide which one or ones are real. This is a good way to begin exploring the concept of real.

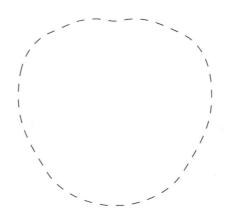

Invisible apple

2.2 • STAGE 2: CONFLICT

Stage 2 of the Learning Challenge is concerned with purposefully creating cognitive conflict in the minds of participants. This is principally because when people are in a state of cognitive conflict, they tend to be spurred to think more deeply and urgently about their ideas. Compare this to when someone has an answer that they are satisfied with: that is when they typically relax and feel no compulsion to think further; they know the answer, so why think more?

> **Cognitive conflict is about prompting people to seek solutions or alternative answers, to try to identify the cause and effects, to ask for advice, to think about the relative merits of one approach compared with another and so on. In other words, the point of cognitive conflict is to get people to think.**

Further reasons for cognitive conflict and how to set it up in the minds of your students will be explored in depth in Chapter 5. For now, though, let's look at one way to create cognitive conflict in the minds of your students: through the use of wobblers (see Section 5.4.1).

Start with the three apples shown in Figure 6.

You:	What do you think of these three apples?
Students:	Which three apples? There are only two of them.
You:	No, there are three. (Count out all three, including the invisible one.)
Students:	There are only two (point to the two that can be seen).
You:	(Hold up the invisible one and pretend to caress it and sniff it.)
Students:	That's not real. You are just pretending.
You:	What makes you say that?
Students:	Because we can only see two.
You:	Does that mean it is only the things that you can see that are real? For example, at the moment, I can't see my dog. Does that mean he is no longer real?
Students:	No, he is real because you've seen him before, so you know he's there. He's just not with you at the moment.
You:	OK, but what about things that I have never seen before, such as the Great Wall of China? Does that mean that is not real because I haven't seen it before?
Students:	But you have seen it on TV or online or in a photograph, haven't you?
You:	Yes, but I have seen all sorts of things on TV and online that are definitely not real!
Students:	(Students suggest things they have seen online that are not real. You could respond directly to the most interesting of these examples or you could continue with the following dialogue.)
You:	So let's leave out the invisible apple for now. What about the other two apples: are they both real?
Students:	No, one is real and one is pretend.
You:	What do you mean by that?
Students:	One is plastic.
You:	Does that mean the plastic one is not real?
Students:	Yes.

> This is an example of how a dialogue might proceed if you were to ask students which of the apples in Figure 6 is real.

You:	But does that mean everything that is plastic is not real, for example, this chair? This chair is plastic, so does that mean it's not real?
Students:	No!
You:	Then why is this plastic apple not real?
Students:	It is real.
You:	So they are both real, is that right?
Students:	Yes. No. Not sure.

With a dialogue similar to this, you will get your students into the pit. Once they are in the pit, you could use some of the following questions to deepen their dilemma:

Additional questions to ask three- to seven-year-olds:

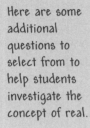

Here are some additional questions to select from to help students investigate the concept of real.

- When we dress up, are we real?
- Are your dreams real?
- Are toys real? What about toy cars or plastic animals?
- Are things that we can't see real?
- How do you know if something is real or not real?
- Is television real?

Additional questions for seven- to eleven-year-olds:

- What is the difference between being real and being alive?
- When you look in the mirror, is your reflection real?
- Do you need to be able see, touch, feel, smell or taste something to know it's real?
- When are stories real?
- Is what's real for you the same as what's real for your friends?
- Is the sky real?
- Are rainbows real?

Additional questions for eleven- to fourteen-year-olds:

- Can something be real and not real at the same time?
- What's the difference between reality and perception?
- How do you decide when to believe what you see?
- What are the connections between reality, truth and fact?
- Can something that doesn't exist be real?
- Are people who have died still real?

Further questions to ask fourteen- to eighteen-year-olds:

- What is the difference between reality and virtual reality?
- What is real about reality TV?
- Does one enter a different reality in one's dreams?
- If something has not happened yet but is inevitable, is it real?
- What did Albert Einstein mean when he said, "Reality is merely an illusion, albeit a very persistent one"? What matters most, the answer to what is real or what we believe to be real?
- Are ideas real? Are they the only thing that is real?
- How do we know that our perceptions are real?
- Is mind or matter more real?

2.3 • STAGE 3: CONSTRUCT

While struggling in the pit together, your students will begin to create meaning through social construction. To do this they will find patterns; make links; think about cause and effect; identify similarities and differences; and organize, distinguish, relate and analyze their ideas. This ultimately leads to a resolution of sorts, be it the "right" answer or, more usually, the "best" answer given the resources available.

Figure 7 shows an example thinking activity for helping students think through different types of real.

To help them with this process, you could offer one or more of the following "pit tools." There are many more to choose from in Section 6.3.

2.3.1 • Pit Tools to Help Young Students Construct Meaning

Suitable for three- to seven-year-olds

▶ **Figure 7: Concept or Not?**

	Real	Not Real	Not Sure	Reason
Toys				
Barbie				
Aliens				
Plastic money				
Teddy bear				
What you see in the mirror				
What you can see when you close your eyes				
Sounds you can't hear				
Shadows				
Optical illusions				
Emotions				

Early Venn Diagrams

Though Venn diagrams are more often used with older students, they can also help young children think through concepts. This is particularly true if you use two hoops and keep them separate to begin with. Only when the children discover that some objects can go into both hoops should you suggest that the hoops could be overlapping to take this into account.

▶ **Figure 8: Concept Venn Diagram**

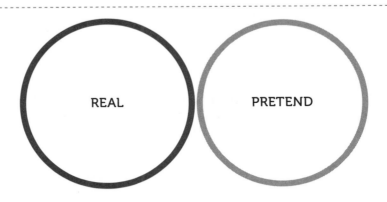

Venn diagrams can help students think through concepts. Even young children can use them if the circles are kept separate to begin with.

Objects for the children to place into the hoops:

Here are some things for young children to sort into the real category or the pretend category.

Toy money	A photograph of a house	Paper to represent an invisible object
Real money	A drawing of a house	An empty cup to represent a pretend drink
A book	A toy house	
A mirror	A banana	A toy teapot
A child's costume	A plastic banana	A teabag
A doll's shoe		

You could also ask your students these questions:

Here are some additional questions to help young children think about the differences between real and pretend.

- What is the difference between a real nurse and when we dress up as a nurse?
- What is the difference between imaginary play and physical play?
- Is all play pretend? If so, does that mean play is not real?
- What is the difference between dressing up, for example, as a superhero, and getting dressed?
- If dressing up is pretend, then are you not real when you dress up?
- If you play with a friend, does that mean you haven't really been doing anything?
- What is the difference between playing and pretending?

2.3.2 • Additional Pit Tools for Older Primary Students

Suitable for seven- to eleven-year-olds

In addition to the ideas shared in Section 2.3.1, you could also pick from the following tools for older students.

▶ Figure 9: Concept Line

REAL   **NOT REAL**

Older students could use this concept line to decide what is real.

Place these words and concepts at the appropriate place along the line shown in Figure 9. For further explanation about using Concept Lines, see Section 6.3.6.

Role-play	Pretend	Forgery	Dressing up
James Bond	Monsters	Toy soldier	Pets
Doll	The sky	Dreams	Thoughts
Rules	Words	Imaginary friend	Television
The news	Shadows	Aliens	Fake watch
Love	Happiness	Anger	Joke
Terrorism	Sports	Games	Disability
Online friends	Names	Photographs	Art

▶ Figure 10: Concept Circles

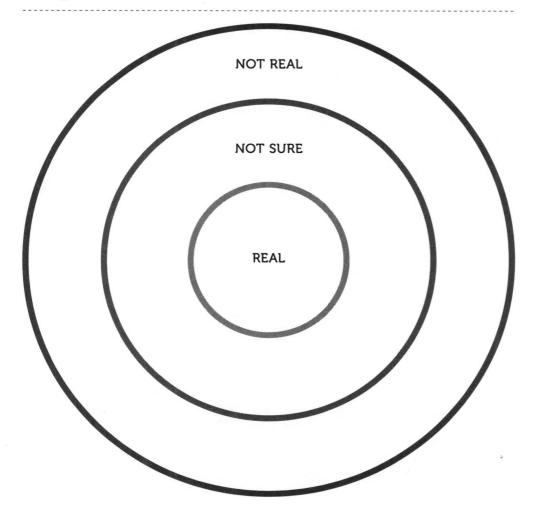

Concept circles are a useful pit tool for thinking about concepts.

Place these words and concepts in the appropriate circle shown in Figure 10. For further explanation about using Concept Circles, see Section 6.3.7.

Fake	Authentic	Pretend	Good	Bogus
Genuine	Realistic	False	Bona fide	Counterfeit
Copy	Mock-up	The sun	Mother Earth	Ancient gods
International laws	School rules	Beliefs	Television	Virtual reality
Online gaming	Wrestling	Boxing	Praying	Advertising
Glamour shots	Space travel	Space tourism	Video game violence	

2.3.3 • Additional Pit Tools for Teenagers

Suitable for eleven- to eighteen-year-olds

Describe the similarities and differences between these pairs of concepts.

- Real and not real
- Reality and truth
- Fact and fiction
- Real and imaginary
- Reality and feeling
- Reality TV and TV news
- Real and dead
- Real and supernatural
- Reality and perception
- Real and make-believe
- Real and pretend
- Real and tangible
- Reality and virtual reality
- Real and alive
- Real and copy
- Real and authentic

Creating a Resolution

Once your students have found patterns, made links, thought about cause and effect, identified similarities and differences and organized and analyzed their ideas, then they will be closing in on *an* answer. Sometimes this might be the right answer, but more usually it is the best answer that they are able to create given the resources available. An example of the sort of resolution your students might create can be seen in Figure 24 in Section 6.3.3.

2.4 • STAGE 4: CONSIDER

The fourth and final stage of the Learning Challenge is to consider the learning journey. Though you should be encouraging your students to think about their thinking throughout the Learning Challenge, Stage 4 is also a great point at which to engage in metacognition.

In his book *Unified Theories of Cognition*, Allen Newell (1991) points out that there are two layers of problem solving: using a strategy to solve a problem and thinking about *how* to select and monitor that strategy. As he puts it, good problem solving often depends as much on the selection and monitoring of a strategy as it does on its execution. This is one way to describe metacognition. I will look in depth at other ways in Chapter 7.

Metacognition Questions to Help Consider the Learning Journey

- What did you originally think *real* meant?
- How confident were you of your answer at the beginning?
- Which challenges caused you to think again?
- How can we tell if something is real or not?
- Can something be real and not real (or fake) at the same time?
- How can we be sure that our lives are real?
- Is the future real?
- What helped you make sense of the ideas you had in the pit?
- How sure are you that you have not accepted easy answers?
- How does your notion of real differ now from the beginning of the lesson?
- What questions about real are you left with?
- What strategies did you use this time that could help you next time you're in the pit?

> These questions can help students reflect on their learning journey throughout the LC experience.

2.5 • WHEN, WHERE, HOW?

This chapter has shared one example of a classic Learning Challenge lesson. In Chapter 10, there are seven more full examples. In the meantime, I think it would be good to consider when, where and how you might set up a Learning Challenge.

It is fair to say that some people like to run a full Learning Challenge from start to finish every day of the week. Others design a whole series of Learning Challenge episodes that span a full topic of work. Some spot an opportunity during a lesson to set up an impromptu Learning Challenge and go for it. Others run Stages 1, 2 and 3 in class and then set Stage 4 for homework. Or set Stage 1 as a preview activity, perhaps for homework, and then run Stages 2, 3 and 4 in class. The thing is, even with the plainest of varieties, there are still many ways to run the Learning Challenge. It is entirely up to you how to organize it.

As a school leader, I used to encourage the following approach:

> Term 1: Each member of staff runs a stand-alone Learning Challenge lesson at least once a week without feeling the need to integrate it into existing programs of study.

> Here are some ways to get the LC going in a school.

Learning Intentions come from broader educational aims such as learning attitudes and skills rather than from the more subject-specific knowledge-based goals.

Term 2: Each member of staff runs a full Learning Challenge once a week within the normal programs of study. For example, a history teacher investigates a concept such as truth with an older class one week and a concept such as nation with a younger class the next, or a primary school teacher picks a literacy concept such as friendship one week and a science concept such as proof the next.

Term 3: Each member of staff runs an impromptu Learning Challenge episode when they spot the opportunity to do so. They don't plan any full sessions but instead look for ways to integrate the approach into "normal" curriculum lessons. Ideally they find at least one or two opportunities per week.

Term 4: The schools I worked in had only three terms, but many of the schools I've supported since have had either four terms or two semesters. So a fourth stage to the development can be for staff to identify Learning Challenge episodes for small groups within a whole class. For example, a different Learning Challenge concept can be used for each collaborative group or, more likely, the same concept for just a few groups, with the rest of the students in the class working on a different set of tasks altogether. Typical sizes of the collaborative groups ranged from three to six, with three or four being the optimum.

If you were to run a sequence such as this, you would have opportunity to develop facilitation skills in the earlier stages free from the constraints of the curriculum. Then in the latter stages, you would build up your experience of spotting opportunities to run Learning Challenge experiences as part of everyday learning. That would give you the best of both worlds: time to practice and play then time to refine and normalize.

As for the length of each Learning Challenge episode, this depends on the experience and maturity of the students. Typical sessions last between forty and seventy-five minutes or sometimes more if time and concentration levels permit.

As to the question of where, the Learning Challenge can pretty much be run by anyone with anyone. Normally it is school, kindergarten or college staff—teachers, leaders and support staff—who run Learning Challenge sessions. And yet, sometimes youth leaders, parents and businesspeople try the approach with the people they spend time with. Though the example I have shared in this chapter is very reliant on language and focuses on what we might say is a philosophical concept, that is not to say the Learning Challenge is restricted to such conditions. As I will share throughout this book, the Learning Challenge can work with different types of concepts and for different purposes. So long as you would like to engage people in deep thought, then this approach is relevant for you.

The typical length of an LC is between forty and seventy-five minutes. That said, some sessions are split into two shorter sections for the youngest students.

2.6 • REVIEW

In addition to the main points identified in the preview, this chapter has covered the following:

1. The Learning Challenge begins with a concept. Facts are not enough to get your students into the pit with.

2. At the heart of the Learning Challenge is cognitive conflict, the purpose of which is to get people to think more.

3. Constructing meaning to climb out of the pit involves making links; thinking about cause and effect; identifying similarities and differences; and organizing, distinguishing, relating and analyzing ideas.

4. Metacognition plays an important role in the Learning Challenge. This involves getting your students to think *about* their own thinking. I discuss this in more detail in Section 7.1.

> "A major purpose of education is to cultivate open-mindedness and intelligence.
>
> Defined in terms of the aptitude for acquiring knowledge, intelligence depends upon an alert curiosity. The cultivation of intelligence depends on freedom to exercise curiosity."
>
> (Jiddu Krishnamurti, 1895–1986, described by the Dalai Lama as one of the greatest thinkers of the age)

THE LEARNING CHALLENGE CULTURE

3.0 • PREVIEW

This chapter focuses on the best ways to build a Learning Challenge culture, from creating ground rules to ensure your students engage respectfully and positively with each other through to identifying the skills and attitudes that will come out of Learning Challenge experiences.

The most important points in the chapter include:

1. As the facilitator, you set the culture of the Learning Challenge. Your responsibilities include encouraging and guiding your students by asking questions, showing interest, challenging ideas and asking for opinions, reasons, examples and comparisons.

2. You will notice positive effects if you ask your students to increase the amount of wait time between a person saying something and someone else responding to three or more seconds.

3. Ways to develop trust and respect among participants in the Learning Challenge include humor, humility, playfulness and an emphasis on challenge rather than point scoring.

4. One of the most important aims of the Learning Challenge is to teach your students how to learn the skills and principles for and of learning.

5. The Learning Challenge will benefit from—and can play a significant role in developing—a broad range of intellectual values such as being articulate, empathetic, rational and reasonable.

3.1 • THE FACILITATOR'S ROLE

I will begin by looking at the role of the facilitator in creating a suitable culture for Learning Challenge experiences. For now, I will assume that that role will be taken by you, but over time I would expect your students to grow more and more into the role.

Once we've looked at the role of facilitator, we will examine the behaviors and attitudes you should expect of all participants.

Please note that I am using the term *facilitator* cautiously. Many people understand the term to mean someone who makes things easier. In many ways, though, that is contrary to the role in a Learning Challenge lesson. As I explain in Sections 1.3.1 and 5.2, the aim of Learning Challenge sessions is to make things more challenging and demanding. The focus is definitely *not* on making things easier, as the term *facilitator* would suggest. However, perhaps we could say that the facilitator is there to facilitate the orchestration of the process rather than to make the process itself easier. The facilitator should aim to make the running of the lesson more straightforward while also making the cognitive demands on participants anything but easy.

With that said, one of the most important functions of the facilitator is to show participants that you regard them as thinkers who have interesting and valuable ideas and actions to contribute.

> The role of the LC facilitator is to orchestrate the process so that participants listen, challenge, question and engage with each other.

As a facilitator, you should take an encouraging stance to make clear to your students the following attitudes:

- **I am interested in and respect your ideas.**

- **I will show my interest by listening to you, questioning you and encouraging you to elaborate.**

- **I am confident you are the sort of person who can come up with relevant questions, opinions, reasons, examples and comparisons.**

- **I will work as much as I can with your questions, understandings, interests and values.**

- **I am creating a classroom community in which we are a group of thinkers who can tackle questions together and work toward the best answers and understandings.**

- **We should all feel secure enough to take intellectual risks.**

> Mary Budd Rowe found that the average amount of time a teacher waits after asking a question before asking another is less than one second.

Showing patience is also an important function of the facilitator's role in creating the right atmosphere for the Learning Challenge. According to Mary Budd Rowe (1973), the average amount of time a teacher waits after asking a question is one second or less. That is not a lot of time for your students to think, and it does not show a lot of patience!

All participants in the Learning Challenge should be encouraged to wonder, elaborate and pause for thought. Rowe suggested a very simple way to make this more likely is by introducing wait time. She observed that when teachers wait for a minimum of three seconds *before* taking an answer from their students and then wait another three seconds *after* taking an answer, the effects can be staggering:

- The length of explanations increases fivefold among advantaged groups and sevenfold among disadvantaged groups.

- The number of volunteered, appropriate answers by larger numbers of students greatly increases.

- Failure to respond and "I don't know" responses decrease from 30 percent to less than 5 percent.

- The number of questions asked by children rises.

- Students' scores on academic achievement tests tend to increase.

Rowe's research is as relevant today as it was back then. And it is doubly pertinent to Learning Challenge lessons seeing as they so often rely on high-quality dialogue. It is also worth bearing in mind that Rowe's research has been repeated many times in many different countries since her work in the 1970s, and the results are consistent: in the typical classroom students get very little time to process information, language and ideas and are therefore restricted in how well they can contribute to a dialogue.

There are also benefits for facilitators in increasing wait time for participants. Robert Stahl (1990) noticed the following improvements when the wait time was increased to three seconds:

- Teachers' questioning strategies tend to be more varied and flexible.

- Teachers decrease the quantity and increase the quality (and variety) of their questions.

- Teachers ask additional questions that require more complex information processing and higher-level thinking on the part of their students.

Incidentally, you can find out more about this research and some corresponding recommendations in a book my colleagues and I have written called *Challenging Learning Through Dialogue* (Nottingham, Nottingham & Renton, 2017).

A classic way to increase thinking time is through the use of the strategy Think-Pair-Share. This is a simple and effective way to give your students time to process their ideas and select the language needed to contribute to the dialogue. The convention typically follows these steps:

- Someone asks a question.

- Participants *think* to themselves for a minimum of three seconds.

- In *pairs*, participants discuss possible responses.

- Volunteers are invited to *share* their ideas with the larger group.

The advantage to this approach is that your students will get more opportunity to prepare and practice the language they need before responding. By preparing independently first, then verbalizing their ideas, then comparing with other students' ideas, they will have time to rehearse and formulate their views. This in turn causes your students to be more willing to contribute their ideas, make better use of accurate subject language and more willing to take intellectual risk. All of which should be encouraged in Learning Challenge lessons.

Increasing wait time to three or more seconds can have a dramatic effect on learning.

Do not be frightened of silences during an LC experience! Silence can give participants more opportunity to think.

Think-Pair-Share is a useful strategy for increasing wait time.

3.2 • TRUST AND RESPECT

Research by Bryk and Schneider (2002), among others, has shown that nurturing trusting relationships is one of the key features of improving student learning. By trust, they mean the firm belief in a person's reliability, benevolence and honesty.

When trust is a part of Learning Challenge experiences, then your students will feel able to take risks, make mistakes, express opinions and collaborate with each other.

The following are some of the ways that you can build trust and respect as facilitator:

3.2.1 • Challenging, Not Point Scoring

The Learning Challenge owes much to the Socratic tradition of education. Socrates (469–399 BCE) often posed a series of questions to help a person reflect on their underlying beliefs and the extent of their knowledge. Such questioning was not about point scoring or proving someone wrong. Indeed, it is said of Socrates that he questioned his fellow Athenians not through an arrogant sense of his being right and their being wrong but through a desire to unearth contradictions and misconceptions that were blocking the way to true wisdom.

And so it is with the Learning Challenge. It is not designed to make your students feel bad about what they don't know or to worry them by being in the pit—quite the reverse actually.

> **The Learning Challenge is designed to cause participants to think more deeply and more compellingly about their learning. It promotes a spirit of exploration to identify complexity and subtlety. It is not about point scoring but about awareness, understanding and the synthesis of new ideas.**

3.2.2 • Humor and Humility

Humor and humility are difficult to convey in a book, but they are absolutely key aspects of the Learning Challenge.

If you were to give the impression of attempting to interrogate your students during a Learning Challenge episode in an effort to discredit or disprove their hypotheses, then that would be both arrogant and discouraging. Instead, you should take a lighthearted and self-effacing attitude. This means using phrases such as "Sorry, I don't understand" or "I don't think I am very clear about this." It means laughing with rather than at your students, admitting you don't have all the answers, asking unpretentious questions and using a tone of voice and body language that suggest you are in the pit with your students.

3.2.3 • Playful Trickery

As you read through the example dialogue in Section 2.2, you might have thought it looked as if I were suggesting that you trick your students. This is perhaps partly true. I do advocate a type of trickery in Learning Challenge lessons but *only* in the playful way that we might engage with young children. I definitely do not mean in the way that a con artist might try to trick someone. Think the "coin behind the ear" trick rather than the "watch off your wrist before you know it" trick!

The LC follows in the Socratic tradition of questioning to understand, rather than questioning to defeat.

Humor and humility will help LC participants engage with each other in a more respectful and thoughtful manner.

You might also be interested to know that the root word for *challenge* comes from the Latin *calumnia*, and it originally meant "trickery"!

3.3 • LEARNING HOW TO LEARN

When people are hesitant about the Learning Challenge, it is often because they are not sure of its purpose. Generally these people are keen to have a go but can't quite see how to justify its inclusion in an already overfilled curriculum.

One way to respond to this question is to say the Learning Challenge is process-based learning; it teaches people *how* to learn as well as *what* to learn. If we focus deliberately on ways *of* learning and teach each other the skills and principles *for* learning, then we can increase the rate and depth at which we learn how to learn.

> The LC focuses on teaching participants *how* to think rather than *what* to think.

For me, the realization that we need a more deliberate focus on learning how to learn came during a Philosophy for Children (P4C) conference in Bulgaria in 2003. During the event, I was asked to facilitate a P4C session with a group of local teenagers for the other delegates to observe.

I began the session with a fictional story about two hunters, Hank and Frank, who are chased by a talking bear. The teenagers then created a number of philosophical questions from which they chose their favorite: "Why sacrifice yourself for others?" After a short pause for quiet reflection, I invited an eager young man to start us off by giving his first thoughts. This is what he said:

> It seems to me that "sacrifice" is the most important concept in this question. I think someone might sacrifice themselves based on instinct, impulse or intuition. Of course, two of these are in the cognitive domain and one is in the affective domain, so I suppose we need to determine which of these is more likely in any given situation before we can answer the question effectively.

All the other delegates were nodding approvingly at the boy's apparent confidence in thinking about and analyzing the concept of sacrifice. As for me, I was like a rabbit caught in the headlights; I certainly had not been expecting that response!

To grab some thinking time for myself, I asked the teenagers to decide what these terms—*instinct, impulse* and *intuition*—had in common. While they did that, I asked a friendly philosopher to suggest what I might do next.

Reconvening, I asked one girl to give her group's answer. She will forevermore be a favorite of mine after replying, "Instinct, impulse and intuition have one thing in common: they are all names of perfumes." (At last: someone on my wavelength!)

Once the hour-long discussion had finished, I made a beeline for the organizers and moaned that they had staged all this: "You could've told me you'd invited only the most talented philosophers from across Bulgaria to join us!" They laughingly explained they had simply invited volunteers from the local area to take part; there had been no selection process.

"So how come they're so adept at thinking?" I inquired. "Because they've been taught how to think from an early age," they said. "But so have children in the United Kingdom and yet I haven't come across young teenagers as skilled in thinking as your students," I countered. Their response was something that initially vexed, then intrigued and ultimately emboldened me: "From what we've seen in Western countries, you don't seem to teach children how to think; instead you only teach them what to think."

The more I work in schools around the world, the more I think these Bulgarian teachers may have been right.

For example, if I ask children at the end of primary school (nine- to eleven-year-olds) if they think stealing is wrong, they all answer yes. But if I then ask why Robin Hood is thought of as a good man if stealing is wrong, they always retort, "Because he robbed from the rich and gave to the poor." Perhaps there's nothing too controversial there yet, but if I press them to decide whether it would be OK for me to steal, let's say from a bank, and give the proceeds to poor people, they almost always say yes. Rarely do the children seem troubled by the fact that stealing from anybody, no matter what the funds are used for, is against the law.

I wonder if this suggests the Bulgarian teachers might be right—that too many children are being taught what, rather than how, to think?

Yet teaching students how to think feels like something of an abstract concept. Perhaps the simplest way to picture it is to consider one strategy for thinking that we all use when faced with a difficult choice: to list advantages and disadvantages. Creating this structure in our head is common to all of us. But it is not a structure we were born with; we were taught it, and it has become one of our "thinking tools." The Learning Challenge allows us to model structures for thinking, for example, by asking questions, giving counterexamples, asking for reasons, justifying answers, adding to the last idea you heard. All of these are new thinking structures, and the Learning Challenge encourages you to purposefully and strategically model and teach these skills to your students.

Another example: I often notice teachers and parents praising children for saying the "right" thing: "it is wrong to kill," "we must always be nice," "you should never lie" and so on. And on the face of it, this might seem reasonable. After all, we want young people to be moral and to do the right thing. However, what happens if they are faced with a dilemma but, up to that point, have only ever followed instructions? Such dilemmas might include eating meat while maintaining that killing is wrong, always telling the truth even if it is likely to hurt someone, always being nice even to someone who is being racist or bullying a friend. What then?

Many parents will reply that they trust their children to do the right thing. But how do children know what the right thing is unless they have learned how to make moral decisions for themselves? In other words, how can they be moral if they haven't learned how to think for themselves?

The Learning Challenge is a great way to teach your students *how* to think, how to be reasonable, how to make moral decisions and how to understand another person's point of view. It is supremely flexible, instructional, collaborative and rigorous. At its very best, the Learning Challenge is one of the best ways for your students to learn good habits of thinking.

This is also backed up by research. Learning-to-learn strategies—also known as metacognition and self-regulation approaches—have a very high impact on learning. Indeed, a number of systematic reviews and meta-analyses have consistently found high levels of impact for strategies related to metacognition and self-regulation. And although most of these studies have looked at impact on language or mathematics, there is evidence from other subject areas such as science that suggest the approach is widely applicable.

Creating cognitive conflict is one way to create the conditions in which students want to learn how to think.

The LC uses structures for thinking that help participants make more considered decisions.

Metacognition is a key feature of the LC.

Analysis of results from the PISA 2009 and 2012 showed that the difference in reading performance between those students who generally know how to learn and those who don't was 107 points—the equivalent of more than two years of schooling.

3.4 • GROUND RULES

The Learning Challenge relies heavily on dialogue. Indeed, the model is inextricably linked with high-quality, exploratory talk.

Unfortunately, though, Rupert Wegerif (2002) found that much of the talk that goes on in classrooms is not educationally productive or helpful for extending students' skills and understandings. It seems that many students do not use talk to work well together—and perhaps do not know how to do so.

To help improve the situation, Wegerif (2002) proposed the following ground rules as a basis for improving the quality of dialogue:

3.4.1 • Our Talking Rules

- We share our ideas and listen to each other.

- We talk one at a time.

- We respect each other's opinions.

- We give reasons to explain our ideas.

- If we disagree we ask "why."

- We try to agree in the end if we can.

Remember: these are rules for talk. They are not the same as class rules for behavior. If you also have class rules, then they should be kept separate from the dialogue rules so that your students know the dialogue rules are there to help them learn how to talk with each other rather than learn how to behave. There might be some crossover, but it is important to keep each set of rules separate and distinct.

Of course, these rules are not set in stone. You do not have to use these rules. Indeed, it might be better to ask your students to agree on their own set of rules. Either way, you should ensure there is an opportunity for your students to talk about the meanings of the rules and to agree on the precise wording of the rules.

Make sure the ground rules you settled upon are displayed prominently for easy reference and reminding. This might seem unnecessary, yet researchers have found that a simple set of agreed-upon ground rules that are constantly referred to have far greater influence on improving the quality and focus of dialogues that are established and not frequently referred to. This is particularly true when students are working in the sort of smaller collaborative groups that Learning Challenge episodes often break into.

3.4.2 • The Learning Challenge Circle

The Learning Challenge works best when your students arrange themselves in a circle. If your students are going to learn to respond to one another, they need to be able to see each other face to face. It is not a good idea to have your students in rows at their desks or in a big huddle in front of the teacher, as is common is so many primary schools. You do not want to have something as elementary as the physical setting working against what you are trying to do.

> Ground rules can help to improve the quality of dialogue in a LC experience.

> The LC works much better when participants sit in a circle with each other. This improves nonverbal as well as verbal communication.

If you have a large group of students, then you might consider splitting them up into two circles—an inner circle and an outer one, as mentioned in Section 4.6. The inner circle can take part in the Learning Challenge dialogue, and the outer circle can take notes, reflect on skills and pit tools used or gather their thoughts for when it is their turn in the inner circle. Every five to ten minutes or so, you can invite your students to swap places with each other so that the inner circle move to the outer circle and the outer to the inner. As they switch places, you could also give them time to compare notes with the person they are trading places with. My colleagues Jill and Martin and I have covered the variations on this idea and the resources you might use to support your students in *Challenging Learning Through Dialogue* (Nottingham, Nottingham & Renton, 2017).

Whether your students are set in one big circle or split into two, make sure that you are also set alongside them. The Learning Challenge is about thinking *together*. It is not about your students thinking and you watching. It makes a powerful statement about the collaborative aspects of learning if you are part of the Learning Challenge circle.

Unfortunately, it makes an equally powerful but opposing message if you are stood up and your students are set down. Though that is a common stance in classrooms, it implies a power relationship of "I am in charge. I talk. You listen." This is *not* something that sits very well alongside the Learning Challenge. Do all you can to arrange the space so that all of you—your students and you—can sit together and think together.

3.5 • LEARNING CHALLENGE VIRTUES

> This is a long list of virtues. It is best to focus on just one or two during each LC experience.

The Learning Challenge will benefit from—and can play a significant role in developing—a broad range of intellectual virtues. Below is a comprehensive list of virtues. I recommend that you select one or two of them to have as a focus for each Learning Challenge episode.

Being Socially Sensitive

Including how to respond to others in socially appropriate ways (with respect and confidence, using tentative language, listening attentively, being supportive, taking turns and encouraging others)

Being Intellectually Sensitive

Including how to use critical, creative, logical, sequential, structural and semantic routines to develop the quality of thinking

Being Collaborative

Including how to oppose as well as support others in such a way as to improve the quality of everyone's thinking

Being Coherent

Including how to structure your own thinking and how to identify coherence and incoherence in others' thinking

Being Articulate

Including how to express ideas clearly so that others may understand them and respond appropriately

Being Empathetic

Including how to understand ideas in the way in which others do and sometimes to think on behalf of others

Being Discerning and Selective

Including how to recognize and distinguish between different kinds of response—whether it is in relation to a question, a problem or another participant—and then how to respond most appropriately in return

Being Abstract

Including how to move from thinking concretely to thinking abstractly and to be able to apply abstract insights to concrete notions

Being Rational

Including how to respond appropriately to the demands of reason and logic, and how to recognize good and bad reasons

Being Sequential

Including how to approach problems in the right order according to rational, logical demands

Being Reasonable

Including how to support your own thinking with good reasons and to expect that of others irrespective of agreement or disagreement

Being Judicious

Including how to make balanced judgments with the aim of making decisions that are wise and fair

Being Resilient

Including how to resolutely defend your own position in the face of others' opposition if it helps in terms of seeking the truth

Being Open-Minded

Including how to show a willingness to change your mind and how to be open to the ideas of others

Being Self-Critical

Including how to reflect analytically on the quality of your own reasoning and how to find ways to improve it

Being Comfortable With Discomfort

Including how to challenge others and be challenged by them even if it causes discomfort and to be comfortable with that discomfort

Being Quizzical

Including how to respond with curiosity to cognitive conflict and how to approach the problem positively and strategically

Being Holistic

Including how to think about the dialogue as a whole and to consider the roles played by yourself and others

Being Autonomous

Including how to think for yourself, making judgments based on the quality of reasons rather than on what others think would be the right thing to do

Being Habitual

Including how to take all of these intellectual and social virtues into all areas of your life rather than reserve them solely for Learning Challenge lessons

3.6 • REVIEW

In addition to the main points identified in the preview, this chapter has covered the following:

1. Talking rules such as sharing ideas and listening to each other, giving reasons and explanations, talking one at a time and respecting each other's opinions can improve the quality of Learning Challenge experiences.

2. The Learning Challenge is a great way for participants to learn good habits of thinking.

3. A number of seemingly contrary habits of thinking are actually complementary and interdependent. These include being resilient while also being open-minded, being collaborative as well as autonomous and being self-critical at the same time as being comfortable with discomfort.

Figure 11:
Using Concepts to Move Through the Learning Challenge

Concept
How many concepts are you thinking about right now? Which one is the most interesting, relevant or puzzling? Let's call your concept "x." Why did you choose that one?

Question
What is x? How do we know what x means? How do we difference between x and concept y? What's the When would x be good/bad/ different/relevant/irrelevant? Is it possible to always/never use x? What if x meant y?

Cognitive Conflict
What problems can you find with concept x? If you are saying that concept x means y, then does y always mean x? In what ways does your definition of x come unstuck?

Construct
When you compare all the ways you found to describe concept x, which one works best? If you were to rank all your ideas about concept x, which one(s) would you prioritize?

Eureka!
How clear is your understanding of x now? What makes x more complex than you first thought? What advice could you give someone who hasn't reached the eureka point yet?

Consider
How could you apply concept x to another situation? What strategies did you use to go through the pit that could also work next time?

The Pit

Easy Learning

Deep Learning

Review

Transfer

Apply

Adapt

CONCEPTS

4.0 • PREVIEW

This chapter focuses on the importance of concepts and why they are the best starting point for thinking activities such as the Learning Challenge.

The most important points in the chapter include:

1. If lessons focus on concepts then there is more opportunity for your students to wonder, question, challenge and think. Facts are useful, of course, but concepts more readily allow thinkers to go on a journey of exploration.

2. Concepts underpin our thinking by allowing us to recognize a thing and to distinguish it from another thing.

3. Every discipline and subject matter includes a vast array of concepts. In Sections 4.2 and 4.2.1 you will find some of the concepts most commonly used in Learning Challenge episodes.

4. It is particularly effective to draw out concepts from everyday language or from books that your students are reading. There are examples of how to do this in Section 4.3 plus recommended books from which to draw out concepts in Figure 14 and the Appendix.

5. You should help your students form questions that are based on key concepts. Techniques for beginning this are shown in Section 4.4.

6. Figure 11 gives an overview of the questions you might use to help your students think about the meanings of concepts.

4.1 • THE ROLE OF CONCEPTS

> **The Learning Challenge begins with a concept. Facts are not enough. The aim of the Learning Challenge is to create cognitive conflict in the minds of your students. And to do *that*, you need to begin with a concept.**

Having identified a concept to begin with, the focus of the LC is to identify contradictions and nuances so that the general principles and theories that evolve are more exact and complete.

Having a concept of something means being able to recognize that something and being able to distinguish it from other things. The question "How old am I?" is a factual question, whereas the question "Am I old?" is a conceptual question because it invites the exploration of meanings, uses and interpretations. That is what makes concepts so interesting and why I say you need a concept with which to begin a Learning Challenge (LC) journey.

Lynn Erickson and Lois Lanning's (2013) Structure of Knowledge makes the difference between concepts and facts clear, as shown in Figure 12.

▶ **Figure 12: The Structure of Knowledge**

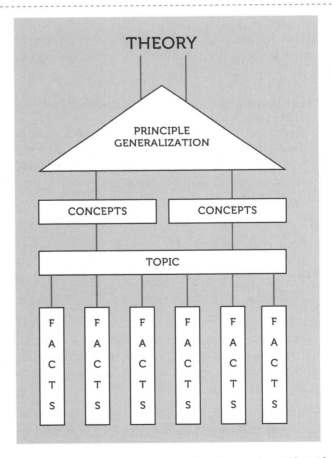

Source: The Structures of Knowledge and Process. Reprinted from *Transitioning to Concept-Based Curriculum and Instruction: How to Bring Content and Process Together* (p. 25), by H. Lynn Erickson and Lois A. Lanning, 2013, Thousand Oaks, CA: Corwin. Copyright 2014 by Lynn Erickson. Reprinted with permission.

I am not saying that facts are irrelevant, of course. It is just that when focusing on facts, any resulting dilemmas tend to be short-lived because correct answers can be established with relative ease. That is unless the so-called facts are based on nebulous statistics that politicians have a reputation for playing with—but that is another story for another, more politically focused book!

The facts I'm talking about here are the generally accepted ones. Examples might include vegetables are food, Washington, DC, is a capital city, J.K. Rowling wrote the Harry Potter series. Your students might not know all these facts yet, but nonetheless they are statements that can be verified pretty quickly. That makes the chances of creating an engaging dilemma for your students to think about deeply really quite slim.

Compare this to statements such as "art is in the eye of the beholder," "revenge is not the same as justice," or "there is no such thing as original thought." Even as you read them here, you are probably beginning to question their validity and accuracy. And so it will be with your students: generally speaking, they will approach facts as things to be learned, whereas they will view concepts as things to question and wonder about.

With all that said, there are often concepts to be found within statements of fact. Take the examples I gave before: vegetables are food, Washington, DC, is a capital city, J.K. Rowling wrote the Harry Potter series. Within these statements of fact are concepts that could be worth exploring as part of the Learning Challenge experience.

In the first example, "vegetables are food," there are two concepts: vegetables and food (though arguably there is a third concept: the verb *to be*). With my students, I would be likely to ask them, "What is food?" Of course, this might seem to be a silly question or at least a question with an obvious answer, but actually there is quite a lot of room to create some cognitive conflict.

Ask your students, "What is food?" Your students might answer, "Something we eat." To which you can reply, "Does that mean everything we eat is food? For example, if I accidentally swallow a pen lid, would that make it food?" They are of course likely to say no, meaning you can then ask for an alternative definition. As they give more answers (e.g., something that gives us energy, something we grow, something that farmers produce, something that keeps us alive), you can help them find counterexamples and so take them into the pit.

The same principles would apply to the fact that "Washington DC is a capital city." The concept I would choose within this is capital city. If you were to ask your students what a capital city is, they might suggest these are the most important cities, the most historical, the largest, where the president lives and so on. In response, you can use some of the techniques described in the next chapter to find counterexamples and so create cognitive conflict in your students' minds.

Similarly with "J.K. Rowling is the author of the Harry Potter series." The concept is author. Your students will probably explain an author as someone who came up with the ideas (but what about writers of nonfiction?), the person who wrote the words (what about journalists who are reporting other people's words?), the person who published the book (surely that's the publishers' role, not the author's role?) and so on.

There are an almost limitless number of concepts worth exploring. Some of the more popular ones for Learning Challenge experiences are presented in the next section.

4.2 • IDENTIFYING CONCEPTS

Concepts are all around us. Indeed, not a day goes by without a multitude of concepts being used to underpin our everyday interactions. These might include deliberately curriculum-focused concepts such as the ones mentioned above. They will also be apparent in day-to-day conversation once you start listening for them. The sorts of examples I'm thinking about here include the list shown below.

Common phrases heard in schools containing concepts worth exploring (main concepts shown in bold)

Here are the sorts of concepts used in everyday interactions. Each one of these could form the basis for an LC experience.

It's not **fair**.

Are we still **friends**?

Please will you **help** me?

Stop calling me **names**!

That is **bullying**.

What are you **thinking** right now?

Stop **daydreaming** and pay attention!

Act your age!

That was a **foolish** thing to do.

That was the **best** one yet.

Why the **sad** face?

It's lovely to see you looking so **happy**.

What great **listening**.

Who **knows** the answer?

Come on, play the **game**!

I was only **joking**.

That was a **kind** thing to do.

What a great **team** you make.

Make sure you **share** properly.

You can all go **home** now.

Are you telling me the **truth**?

That was a stroke of **luck**.

Tell me what is **wrong**.

Play nicely together.

Can you **explain** what you did?

Work together on this.

I don't **understand**.

Stop **telling tales**.

We need to show **respect** for each other.

Each of these concepts could be used to begin a Learning Challenge session. I say this because each one could be used to create open, searching questions that invite your students to examine meanings more closely. Take, for example, the first claim, "It's not fair," something that as parents and teachers we hear more than enough! This assertion could be turned into the question "What makes something fair?" which could then begin a dialogue that leads your students into the pit.

Here is an example from a Learning Challenge session I led recently:

Here is the transcript from part of a dialogue typically encountered during an LC session.

Me: What makes something fair?

Students: When everyone gets what they want.

Me: What about the Olympics that are taking place at the moment? Will everyone get what they want there?

Students: No!

Me: Go on.

Students: Well, everyone wants to win a gold medal but not everyone can, so that means not everyone gets what they want.

Students: Yes, but only the best deserve the medal, so it is fair.

Me: So are we saying that fair means getting what you deserve?

Students: Yes.

Me: But what about the athletes who want it more? They train harder than anyone else. They have to overcome more difficulties to get to the Olympics. Maybe they have had to scrape by with no funding for years. Don't they deserve it more than the athletes in the opposite circumstances with all the advantages you could ever wish for?

Students: Yes and no. They do deserve it more but that's not sports. Sports are decided by whoever is the best. Not who deserves it most.

You: So are sports fair?

Students: Yes, sports are fair. Unless the athletes cheat.

Students: How can it be fair if the winners aren't always the most deserving ones? What about the team that wins because of an error by the referee?

Students: Or the athlete that wins despite being a drug cheat? (This student named a high-profile athlete known for being a "drug cheat.")

Students: Well, that's life! Life is not fair.

Me: Wow, that's a pretty strong statement to make. What do you mean by that?

Students: There's never ever a situation in which everything is fair to everyone. There's always someone with the upper hand. Or someone who deserves it more. Or someone not getting what they want.

Me: So what does someone mean when they say "It's not fair"? Are they basically stating the obvious? Such as the world is round or the sun is hot?

Students: Maybe they mean it's even more unfair than normal?

Students: But if it's never fair, then how can it be even more unfair?

Me: But surely there are some situations that could be described as fair, aren't there?

Students: We don't know. Looks like we're in the pit!

At this point in the dialogue, I split my students into groups of three and asked them to come up with examples of the way in which we understand the term *fair*. Here are the suggestions they came up with:

1. Something is fair if people get what they deserve.
2. Something is fair if everything is equal.
3. Something is fair if it doesn't hurt anyone or anything.
4. Something is fair if people are happy with the outcome.
5. Something is fair if it follows all the rules.
6. Something is fair if everyone the thing affects thinks it is fair.
7. Nothing is absolutely, totally fair.

Coming together as a whole class once again, we then looked at each of these suggestions in turn and tried to find counterexamples for each one. In Chapters 5 and 6, I will show you what followed in terms of deepening the inquiry and then climbing out of the pit.

Remember: all of this came from the seemingly routine assertion that "it's not fair." That shows the potential that concepts have for thinking. Indeed, as Matthew Lipman (2003, p. 181) wrote in his wonderful book *Thinking in Education*, "Concepts are the vehicles of thought, entities by which thought is carried on."

4.2.1 • Useful Concepts for the Learning Challenge

Traditional philosophy generally splits concepts into seven main categories.

In philosophy, concepts and ideas are generally divided into seven main categories:

Metaphysics: What is real? What exists?

Including realism, idealism, phenomenalism and universalism

Epistemology: What can be known? In what ways can it be done?

Including belief, truth and opinion; skepticism; rationalism; and empiricism

Ethics: What is good/bad? What is right/wrong?

Including virtues, utilitarianism, ego and relativism

Philosophy of Mind: If there is a mind, what is it?

Including idealism, dualism, materialism, monism and epiphenomenalism

Aesthetics: What is art?

Including form theory, idealism, institutional theory and intentional theory

Philosophy of Politics: How should people live together?

Including theories from Plato, Hobbes, Locke, Rousseau and Mill

Philosophy of Science: What is and what is not science?

Including induction, deduction, falsification, paradigms and externalism

These are, of course, very broad categories and have been written about in depth in many books. For the purposes of the Learning Challenge, you might find the following school subject–related categories more familiar and therefore more useful:

This list shows the concepts most commonly explored in LC sessions with school-age students.

Arts	
Art	Meaning
Beauty	Music
Color	Perspective
Copy	Primary colors
Expressionism	Real
Imagination	Reproduction
Impressionism	Surrealism
Light and dark	
Citizenship	
Bravery/courage	Hatred
Bullying	Is
Community	Justice/just desert
Conscience	Life choices
Consequence	Love
Courage	Nation
Culture	Reconciliation
Democracy	Responsibility
Duties	Revenge

Enterprise	Rights
Equal treatment	Risk
Fairness	Talent
Famous	Truth
Freedom	Value
Friends	Welfare
Friendship	Willpower

Design Technology

Audience	Originality
Economy	Purpose
Effectiveness	Simplicity
Elegance	Value
Market	

Early Years

Being nice	Hygiene
Choice	Language
Dreaming	Me
Emotions	Pets
Fairness	Real
Fairy tales	Same
Friends	Shape and space
Growth/change	Superheroes
Health	Telling lies
Home	Thinking

> The term *Early Years* is used here to mean ideas suitable for three- to seven-year-olds.

English (Language/Literature/Drama)

Anger	Justice
Anti-hero	Language
Chivalry	Love
Democracy	Madness
Dilemma	Poem
Drama	Politics
Fairness	Power
Goodness	Romance
Hero	Story
Honor	Verb

(Continued)

(Continued)

Humanities (History/Geography/Social Sciences)	
Biodegradable	Interpretation
Border	Justice
Cause	Migration/immigration
Cultural globalization	Mountain
Culture	Nation
Democracy	Poverty
Empire	Race
Equality	Rivers
Evidence	Social diversity
Globalization	Tourist
History	Truth
Home/place	Urbanization

Math	
Argument	Prime numbers
Continuous	Probability
Equal	Proportion/ratio
Infinite	Shape
Logical	Significance
Measurement	Size
Nil/zero	Unit
Number	Value
Odd numbers	

Media	
Entertainment	Morality
Game	Reality
Knowledge	Social media
Legality	

Modern Foreign Languages	
Communication	Identify
Culture	Language
Foreign	Nationality
Globalization	Understanding

Physical Education	
Competition	Performance
Condition	Race
Confidence	Sports
Drugs	Success/failure
Fair	Talent
Games	Team

Religious Education	
Belief	Tolerance
Culture	Tradition
Faith	Truth
Fate	Value
Morality	

Science	
Biodegradable	Human
Cause	Invention
Discovery	Knowledge
Drugs	Proof
Elements	Same (cloning)
Evidence	Science
Evolution	Significant
Experiment	Species
Exploration	Theory
Fair test	Universe
Forces	Waste
Genetic	

Throughout the book, there are many other concepts that have been used to exemplify how the recommended techniques should be applied. You can find an Index of Concepts at the back of the book.

One of the best ways to choose the concept needed to begin the Learning Challenge is through the *educere* approach to learning. *Educere* is the root word in Latin from which the word *education* comes. Original meaning: "to draw out." So rather than giving your students a concept to begin with, instead you could support them to draw out concepts from a suitable stimulus such as a story, image, object or experience.

> **Remember: the Learning Challenge should begin with a concept that your students comprehend enough for them to engage in some cognitive conflict about. If they have no idea about a concept, then there will be nothing to conflict with and therefore you will not be able to take them into the pit. This means the educere approach of getting your students to draw out concepts from a stimulus is doubly effective: not only will their involvement generate a sense of ownership, but also it will show you which concepts your students are ready to engage with.**

That said, there are a number of concepts that your students might understand better than it seems at first glance. For example, I have seen a lot of younger students attempting to use a ruler to measure something without seeming to realize they need to start from zero (or if not starting from zero then taking into account the starting point when calculating the final measurement).

Getting students to identify the concepts they can notice in a story, image or piece of music is one of the best ways to start an LC.

However, if we were to strip this back to basics, then we could say that the concept is about always starting at the same point rather than about idea of zero. Apply this to a running race or a throwing competition and even the youngest school-age children will understand that everything or everyone has to start from the same place. After that, we can say that zero is the equivalent of starting at the same place, but the point is that even if students don't know the language or the concept's application yet, they just might understand the concept more than we realize. So don't be too quick to dismiss the suitability of a concept even if your students don't respond accurately the first time round.

The cartoon image in Figure 13 could provide a good starting point for your students to draw out concepts.

You could show your students this image and then ask them the following questions:

These questions can help to tease out the main concepts from an image.

- What are the main ideas in this picture?
- What does this picture make you think of?
- What story do you think the cartoonist is trying to portray?
- What do you think the character sat down is thinking?
- How would you describe the characters stood around the table?

As your students volunteer their ideas, record each of the concepts they mention. Writing these on a board for everyone to refer back to is ideal. Try to strike the balance between collecting the concepts and showing that you value every contribution. By

▶ Figure 13: Example Picture to Draw Out Concepts

Ask students to identify the main concepts in this cartoon image.

that I mean your students might call out things that are not necessarily concepts. For example, one of your students might say in response to Figure 13, "The food doesn't look very nice." From this you could write down the concepts "food" and "nice." Or if another student says, "Yuck," you could ask them to explain a little more; perhaps they might say, "I don't like peas." To which you could write down "taste" as the concept that they are implying.

One way to determine whether a word is a concept or not is to put "What is . . . " in front of it. If that generates a question that seems likely to lead to a thought-provoking and exploratory discussion, then it is probably a concept. Though this is not a fail-safe approach, it tends to be good enough to make a start in the absence of more nuanced techniques.

Here are some examples taken from the ideas offered recently by a group of students responding to the cartoon image in Figure 13, with the "what is" questions in brackets and the concepts I wrote on the board in bold:

These are the sorts of concepts that students identify from the cartoon image in Figure 13.

> The boy in the middle is greedy. (What is greed?) **Greed**
>
> Maybe they're all friends. (What is a friend?) **Friendship**
>
> He looks very happy. (What does happy mean?) **Happiness**
>
> They're at school 'cause they're wearing school uniforms. (What is school? What are uniforms?) **School, uniform**
>
> Why is the fattest kid getting all the food? He doesn't need it! (What is food? What is fair? What is need?) **Food, fair, need**

For older students particularly, a quote can sometimes be a good stimulus from which to draw out concepts. For example:

"Everything we hear is an opinion, not a fact. Everything we see is a perspective, not the truth." Marcus Aurelius (180 CE)

Quotes, videos, song lyrics and picture books can all lead to the identification of concepts suitable for LC experiences.

Music can be a great source for inspiration. Be wary, though, of songs that are packed full of concepts. "Imagine" by John Lennon (1971) is a wonderful piece of music, but the lyrics contain so many ideas that your students might find it difficult to pick out the most significant ones.

The Literacy Shed (www.literacyshed.com) is very popular among teachers as a go-to collection for video clips to stimulate writing. Many of them work equally well for identifying concepts too.

Perhaps the most popular type of stimulus is picture books. Though these tend to be regarded as suitable only for younger children, I actually find many of them can be used with older students too. Figure 14 gives examples of some of my team's favorite picture books for using in Learning Challenge sessions and shows the concepts that are at the heart of the stories and the age range we have used them with.

Remember, even just the front cover of some of these books can be enough to draw out as many as ten to fifteen concepts. If your students struggle at first, then you can ask them to imagine the thoughts and emotions of the main characters or to think about the supposed intentions of the author. In that way, you will help them look beyond the obvious and find some of the more subtle inferences and assumptions.

There are ten books listed here and fifty more in the Appendix.

▶ **Figure 14: Drawing Out Concepts From Books**

Book Details	Concepts	Ages	Overview and Potential Questions
Boys Are Best Manuela Olten	Gender Stereotypes Nature/nurture Difference Understanding Misconceptions Power Equality Best	4–11	A case of two self-assured boys with the opinion that all girls are silly. When the subject of ghosts comes up, they soon realize they are not so perfect themselves! • Do boys and girls think differently? • Are boys and girls equal? • If things are equal, does that mean it is fair?
Cheese Belongs to You Alexis Deacon	Power/position Possession Dominance Hierarchy Sharing Survival of the fittest Law/law of nature Finders keepers Good manners Envy Greed	5–12	A story of a rat that found some cheese and ultimately decided to share politely with everyone. • If you have possession of something, does that make it yours? • Do you have power only if others allow you to? • If we don't share something, are we being greedy? • Does there always need to be someone who is "the boss"?

Book Details	Concepts	Ages	Overview and Potential Questions
The Most Magnificent Thing Ashley Spires	Trial and error Perseverance Frustration Perfectionism Creativity Perspective Feedback Invention Right and wrong Success and failure Fallibility Plans and goals	7–13	A young girl learning a lesson in mindset. She discovers that she hasn't got everything right yet and what she has might not be exactly like it was up in her brain, but it'll be a truly magnificent thing just the same. • What does *regular* mean? • What does it mean to make something? • What sort of things could you unmake? • What aspects of a growth mindset did the young girl show? • What aspects of a fixed mindset did the young girl show? • Is it better to have a go and make a mistake than to not try in the first place? • What does *finest moment* mean? • What personal goals do you have, and what potential obstacles might get in your way?
Not a Box Antionette Portis	Perception Creativity Imagination Pretend play Reality Lies Experience Questioning	4–12	A story about a bunny that has lots of fun with a cardboard box. Using his imagination, Bunny makes it clear that the box can become whatever he wants it to be. • How can you imagine something if you haven't experienced it in real life? • Do we imagine consciously or subconsciously?
The Owl Who Was Afraid of the Dark Jill Tomlinson	Fear Imagination Experience Perspective Nature	4–9	Plop, the baby barn owl, is afraid of the dark. Through lots of different inspiring encounters, he realizes that through these encounters the dark is super after all. • Why did the little boy think the dark was exciting? • Do you like some things that might scare other people? • What is an excuse? • Why would someone make an excuse? • Plop is enticed to investigate the noises he hears. Is this a good idea—to go somewhere without your parents' knowledge?

(Continued)

Book Details	Concepts	Ages	Overview and Potential Questions
Lost and Found Oliver Jeffers	Loneliness Friendship Assumption	4–11	Is the penguin lost, lonely or looking for a friend? A young boy goes on an exciting adventure to discover which one. • What is the meaning of *lost*? • Why does the boy think the penguin is lost? Is it just because he is sad? • What does it mean by "some birds are like that"? • What does being disappointed feel like? • How did the boy discover about the South Pole?
The Stamp Collector Jennifer Lanthier	Power Imagination Empathy Friendship Freedom of expression Censorship Art Imprisonment Hope Perception Perspective Passion	6–16	This book offers a wonderful story about political oppression, freedom of expression and the power of stories to change lives. • What is meant by *oppression*? • How does oppression manifest itself? • What are human rights? • What is the right of freedom of expression? • What are the key aspects of the right to freedom of expression?
The Heart and the Bottle Oliver Jeffers	Emotions Grief Death Curiosity Wonder Exploration Love Youth Loss Self-preservation Attachment	5–13	A young girl sets out to liberate her heart from its glassy prison, but the bottle has been fortified by years of self-protection and it takes the innocence and limitless wonder of youth to unlock it. • What does *similar* mean? • What does it mean to be curious? • Is curiosity different from wonder? • How does someone feel delight? • What does it mean to "wear your heart on your sleeve"? • Can you ever really protect your heart? • Why was the chair no longer empty?
The Giving Tree Shel Silverstein	Nature Natural order Giving and taking Altruism Gifts Love Happiness	5–14	A story about the relationship of a boy and a tree. The boy continues to return when he needs something else, until the tree is sad because it feels like it has nothing left to give. • Can doing things to make others happy make you happy?

Book Details	Concepts	Ages	Overview and Potential Questions
The Giving Tree Shel Silverstein *(continued)*	Parents Sacrifice Loneliness Manners Love Self-sacrificing Selflessness Being reasonable Responsibility	5–14	• Do we need others in order to be happy ourselves? • Is it possible to be happy and sad at the same time? • Can an action ever be truly altruistic? • Do you think the boy is selfish? Why or why not? • Is there a word for someone who keeps on giving without thinking about himself or herself? • Do you know a person that never expects anything in return? • Why do you think the tree is not happy after giving the boy her trunk? • Have you ever given something away that you wished you hadn't? • When you are given something, should you feel like you owe something in return? • Can you be angry with someone and love them at the same time? • Do you need others in order to be happy? • Do you need a reason to be happy, or can you be happy for no reason at all? • Can you be happy and sad at the same time?
Beegu Alexis Deacon	Being alone Isolation Abandonment Feeling lonely Welcoming others	3–12	Beegu's spacecraft is stuck on Earth. Now she is lost and wandering. This book allows you to see our world through the three eyes of an unknowing outsider. • What makes a person feel lonely? • Are being alone and lonely the same thing? • What kind of people do you think of when you think of lonely people? • What is the difference between feeling lonely and enjoying being alone?

4.4 • CREATING QUESTIONS

Having identified some concepts worth exploring, the next step in a *full* Learning Challenge session is to help your students create questions about the concepts. This will help your students engage with the ideas surrounding the concepts. It will also provide a useful opportunity for first thoughts about the concepts to be aired before you lead your students into the pit.

Please note that this stage tends to be used only when you have time for a full Learning Challenge lesson. If time is tight or your objective is to get your students into the pit as soon as possible, then you might not use this stage. In fact, if you teach very young children, then you might not be able to do this stage yet. However, if you can find time for it, then the positive effects can be powerful and long-lasting. Imagine having students who are curious, reflective *and* able to verbalize their thinking in the form of great questions! That's the impact you can have by going through this stage again and again with your students.

The diagram of the Learning Challenge in Figure 11 includes some nice examples of the sorts of questions that could be used to begin exploring concepts. These include the following:

These questions can help students reflect on their choice of concepts.

- How many concepts are you thinking about right now?
- Which one is the most interesting, relevant or puzzling?
- Why did you choose that concept rather than another one?
- What does your concept mean?
- How do you know what your concept means?
- What is the difference between your concept and another concept?
- When would your concept be good/bad/different/relevant/irrelevant?
- Is it possible to always/never use your concept?
- What if your concept meant something else?

If you find these examples useful, then I suggest you share the diagram in Figure 11 with your students as a quick reference guide. Either that or you could offer them some of the question stems shown in Figure 15. By mixing and matching some of these suggestions, your students should be able to generate thought-provoking, conceptual questions worth exploring.

I suggest that you offer your students just three or four of these question stems during their first Learning Challenge experience. Then add one or two more each time until they are familiar with all of the prompts. After that, you could give them the whole set on a card or display them on the wall for reference during lessons.

Challenge your students to create thought-provoking questions by pairing one of the question stems with one or more of the concepts students identified earlier. They can then play around with the way in which the question is formed until they are satisfied that they have created a question that is worth exploring.

For example, if after looking at the cartoon image in Figure 13 your students chose the concept of greed, then they might play around with some of the question stems in Figure 15 to create the options shown below. I have put the key phrase from the question stem in bold.

These are the sorts of questions that come from pairing one of the concepts drawn out of Figure 13 with one or more of the question stems shown in Figure 15.

What is greed?

Is greed **always** a bad thing?

What is the difference between greed and hunger?

When does wanting something become greedy?

How do you decide what is need and what is greed?

What if everyone was greedy?

Is everyone greedy?

How do you know if someone is being greedy or not?

Is it possible to be greedy and kind at the same time?

What is the **opposite** of greed?

Is greed **against** the law?

Is greed **anti-**social?

Is greed **normal**?

▶ **Figure 15: Question Stems**

Question Stem	Example
What is . . .	What is belief?
What makes . . .	What makes something real?
Would you be . . .	Would you be the same person if someone stole your identity?
How do we know what . . .	How do we know what fear is?
Always or never . . .	Should we always tell the truth?
What if . . .	What if there was no such thing as curiosity?
Is it possible . . .	Is it possible to be happy and sad at the same time?
When . . .	When is a person an adult?
Who . . .	Who decides what beauty is?
Can we . . .	Can we think without language?
Why do we say . . .	Why do we say "actions speak louder than words"?
What is the difference between . . .	What is the difference between what's right and what's wrong?

These question stems are among the most productive for creating interesting conceptual questions to begin an LC session with.

Each of these questions could start off a Learning Challenge very well. They all seem likely to provoke a variety of opinions. They could lead to the generation of ideas, hypotheses, conjectures and assumptions. And each of them turns a seemingly routine concept into a provocation for explanations, possibilities and meanings.

When you record your students' questions, it is a good idea to write their names next to their questions for future reference and to give them a sense of ownership. It might also be that a particular question needs clarifying or expanding upon with additional detail about, for example, the thinking behind it. This is more easily achieved when you know at a glance whose question it is.

When your students have become familiar with this practice, you should vary the procedure. For example, you might divide your class into pairs or threes and get each pair or threesome to negotiate a question among themselves before recording it on a piece of paper or individual whiteboard. This will actively involve more of your students in the process of question formation and should eventually improve the quality of the questions asked.

You might also like to adopt the practice of encouraging your students to keep a reflection book in which they record questions that are of interest to them. This can serve a dual purpose: it can help students remember earlier questions and it can also help you identify the progress they are making in terms of the quality of questions they are creating.

Incidentally, if one of the groups creates more than one question, then ask them to select the one they think is their best one. You should be aiming for no more than about seven or eight questions from the whole class, so taking more than one question from a small group is likely to reduce the opportunities for other groups.

4.4.1 • Example Questions

Here are some example questions my students and I created by selecting two concepts from each of the categories in Section 4.2.1 and combining them with some of the question stems shown in Figure 15.

Arts

Art

> What is art?
>
> What would life be like without art?
>
> What's the difference between art and music?
>
> What's the difference between art and creativity?
>
> When does something start being art?
>
> When does something stop being art?
>
> What if art were banned in schools?

Beauty

> Who says what beauty is?
>
> What is beauty?
>
> When is beauty a bad thing?
>
> Should people focus on beauty?
>
> Can everything be beautiful?

This section shows the sort of questions that can be used to begin LC sessions in different curriculum areas.

Should we even talk about beauty?

Is it possible not to be beautiful?

It is possible to be beautiful and ugly at the same time?

Can beauty be something other than visual?

Citizenship

Truth

What is truth?

Should we always tell the truth?

What if nobody knew what the truth was?

Is it possible to always tell the truth?

What's the difference between truth and fact?

What's the difference between truth and honesty?

How do we know what truth is?

Revenge

Why do people take revenge?

Is revenge always a bad thing?

Is revenge justifiable?

What is the difference between revenge and justice?

When would it be OK to take revenge?

Can you take revenge without it being a bad thing?

Should revenge be made illegal?

Is revenge an instinctive reaction?

Design Technology

Audience

What is a good audience?

What is the difference between an audience and feedback?

Is there always an audience, even if it's just you?

Is it possible to have the perfect audience?

How many people do you need for them to be called an audience?

Can you have an audience without people?

Could animals be an audience?

Effectiveness

What is the difference between effective and efficient?

Who says when something is effective?

Does everything have an effect?

Should everything have an effect?

Is it possible for something not to have an effect?

Is effectiveness important?

Is effectiveness the same as strength?

Is it possible to be effective at something that is ineffective?

Early Years

The term *Early Years* is used here to mean ideas suitable for three- to seven-year-olds.

Pets

What is a pet?

Can anything be a pet?

Can a person be a pet?

What if everybody had to have a pet?

Should everybody have a pet?

When would having a pet be a bad thing?

Do pets have to be living things?

Can you have an imaginary pet?

Do you always have to get your pet from a pet shop?

What makes a good pet?

Being Nice

Should you always be nice?

Should you always let people play with you?

What does being nice look like?

What does being nice mean to other people?

What is the difference between being kind and being nice?

How do we know when somebody is being nice?

Should we always be nice to everybody?

Is it possible to always be nice?

Can you be nice and nasty at the same time?

Telling Lies

How do we know what lies are?

What is a lie?

Should we lie?

If somebody thinks they are telling a lie but is actually telling the truth, is it a lie?

When is a lie not a lie?

What is the difference between a lie and an opinion?

Why do people lie?

What's the difference between lying and not telling the truth?

Can you tell lies without saying anything?

English Language, Literature and Drama

- -

Romance

What's the difference between romance and love?

Is romance always a good thing?

Should romance be taught in school?

Is it possible to be in a romance without knowing you're in a romance?

Why did Shakespeare write about romance?

What is it that makes romance interesting to people?

What makes romance poetry appealing?

Story

What's the difference between a story and an event?

What if there were no such things as stories?

Is it possible to teach children without the use of stories?

Do stories always have a beginning, middle and end?

How do we know what makes the best stories?

What if stories had to be factual?

Does language development depend on stories?

Humanities

- -

Home

What is the difference between place and home?

Is a home where someone belongs?

Does a home have to be a physical thing?

Does everything have a home?

Do people always need a home?

Should we make it illegal for people to be homeless?

When would having a home be a bad thing?

Is it possible to be homeless and have a home at the same time?

To call somewhere home, do you have to live in it?

Is it possible to have more than one home?

Equality

Is equality fair?

What's the difference between equality and fairness?

Is equality for everybody possible?

Is inequality good?

How would we know if equality had been achieved?

Is equality just a state of mind?

Does equality mean giving everybody the same thing?

Is the desire for equality the same as or the opposite of being aspirational?

If I achieve something, is that a barrier to equality?

Can equality and individualism exist together?

Information and Communications Technology

Social Media

Should children be allowed to use social media?

Is social media killing the art of conversation?

Is cyberbullying worse than physical bullying?

Can social media really be regarded as a social activity?

To use social media, should you have to share your real identity?

Does social media have to use the web?

What is the difference between social media and news?

Should contacts on Facebook really be called friends?

How would the world be different if people stopped using social media?

Entertainment

What's the difference between entertainment and information?

Is entertainment always subjective?

Is entertainment in the eye of the beholder?

Is it possible to have no entertainment?

Can you have entertainment without pleasure?

Is entertainment considered entertainment only if you enjoy it?

If somebody finds something entertaining but you don't, is it still entertainment?

Math

Number

What if numbers didn't exist?

Do numbers exist without people?

Is there ever a circumstance where numbers can't be found?

Can you do mathematics without numbers?

If you're using numbers, are you always doing mathematics?

What's the difference between numbers and math?

Does the world exist only because of numbers?

Do numbers ever stop?

Value

Does everything have a value?

What's the difference between value and number?

Is value a relational concept?

What's the difference between value and valuable?

Is it possible for value to be a constant?

Do nonhumans understand value?

What if nothing had a value?

Does everything have a value?

Modern Foreign Languages

Foreign

What's the difference between being foreign and being different?

What does *foreign* mean?

Do you have to be from another country to be foreign?

What do we mean when we talk about a foreign object?

Is it possible to be foreign in your own country?

Should it be made compulsory to study a foreign language?

Would it be a good thing for the world to agree on one common language?

Is social diversity a good thing?

What if there was no such thing as foreign?

Language

Can you think without language?

What's the difference between language and communication?

Does every living creature have a language?

Is it possible to exist without language?

If there were no humans on the planet, would that mean that there would be no language?

If we didn't have language, would anything have a name?

If we didn't have language, would we be incapable of communicating accurately?

Without language would we have emotions?

Does speaking a foreign language help you experience different emotions?

If it does, does that mean the more languages you speak the more emotions you have?

Physical Education

Success

What does it mean to be successful?

Do you have to win to be successful?

Is success about being the best?

When would success be a bad thing?

Do success and competition go hand in hand?

Is it possible to succeed and fail at the same time?

If there were no such thing as success, would there be no such thing as failure?

Is it possible to always be successful?

Should we always aspire to be successful?

Competition

Is life better with competition?

If there were no competition, would there be no success?

Is competition a human construct?

Is competition a survival instinct?

If everybody wins does that stop it being a competition?

Without competition would we have no innovation?

Is it important to decide what is fair competition?

Can any competition be fair or are there always people who have an advantage?

Religious Education

Morality

What's the difference between morality and law?

Can religion and morality be separated?

Should morality always be adapted to the context it finds itself in or is universal morality possible?

Should everything have a moral purpose?

Is it possible to be moral all your life?

Is morality a subjective concept?

In what ways does morality differ between the major world religions?

What are the links between morality and etiquette?

Should morality be taught at school?

What's the difference between morality and values?

Belief

Is it important to believe in something?

Is it possible to have no beliefs or is that a belief in itself?

Does it make something more believable the more people who believe in it?

If something is proven does that stop it being a belief?

What's the difference between belief and faith?

Should we share our beliefs with others?

Is it good to have different beliefs from others?

Is friendship strengthened by shared beliefs?

What's the difference between beliefs and values?

To what extent do your parents decide your beliefs for you?

Science

Proof

To prove something, do you need to have physical evidence of it?

Who says what proof is?

Does science always need proof?

Is proof the difference between science and religion?

When would proof be a bad thing?

Is it possible to un-prove something that has already been proven? Or would that be proof of the opposite?

How much evidence do you need for there to be proof?

Science

What is science?

Is science just another form of math?

When does science start and math end?

Can you do science without observation?

Is science always linked with progress?

Do you have to think scientifically to do science?

Do you think science will ultimately answer every question?

Can only scientists do science?

What would a country be like if science was banned in it?

Is science the opposite of religion?

What is social science?

4.5 • SELECTING THE BEST QUESTION

If you have created the opportunity for your students to create questions, then you will also need to help them select the best question to go into the pit with. So, after collecting one question from each group, give your students time to air the questions; this could be done by getting authors to give a brief insight into their own question or by asking for volunteers to say why they think each question in turn is a particularly good one.

To begin with, students will typically choose their favorite question. However, over time, you should encourage them to identify criteria so that they can choose the best question.

Once the questions have been aired, get your students to take a vote. In the first few sessions with your students, it is probably enough to encourage them to pick their favorite question. After a while, though, you should be encouraging them to select the best one. To do this, you will need to agree on some criteria for what constitutes the best. For example, the most problematic or thought-provoking one or the one most likely to create a range of opinions and disagreements.

Here are some other examples:

- Questions that offer the widest selection of possible answers
- Questions that deal with concepts most central to students' lives
- Questions that raise the most contestable concepts
- Questions that provide the greatest chance of differing viewpoints
- Questions that can't be answered with a simple yes or no

It may not be obvious which is the best question, and in some regards it may be impossible to decide for sure. However, the very process of selecting criteria and using these to make a decision can be a worthwhile end in itself.

There are many ways to select a single question to begin an LC experience with. Of the many techniques, "omni-voting" is probably the one to begin with.

Then, when it comes to the voting, there are many ways to go. Here are some popular ones:

Single vote: Each person gets one vote. The question that attracts the most votes is chosen for further discussion.

Omni-vote: Each person can vote as many times as they like. (Although it is worth reminding younger children that if they all vote for all the questions, there won't be one that stands out!) The omni-vote is generally the best method of voting for groups new to the Learning Challenge.

Multi-vote: Each person gets a set number of votes—say, three—that can then be spread between three questions or placed onto one or two questions.

Single transferable vote: This works well if you lay out the questions on the floor and ask each student to stand next to one of the questions. You can then ask the children standing next to the questions with fewest votes to recast their vote onto one of the front-runners.

4.6 • SHARING FIRST THOUGHTS

This stage is all about encouraging your students to share their first responses to the chosen question.

Give all your students some reflection time before inviting first thoughts from a few volunteers. Resist the temptation to question or challenge too soon. Encourage all the other students to listen attentively and with respect.

Do *not* feel compelled to get every student to speak!

There is a commonly held belief that we should try to ensure all students say at least one thing in each discussion. This is nonsensical because there are some people who do their very best thinking when saying nothing (while others find it easier to think well by saying lots).

One justification for this can be found in the work of Katharine Cook Briggs and her daughter, Isabel Briggs Myers. During World War II, they created the Myers-Briggs Type Indicator (MBTI; see Conoley & Kramer, 1989) to help women identify the sort of wartime jobs in which they would be most comfortable and effective. Their work was based on the theories of Carl Jung.

Of the four pairs of preferences proposed in the MBTI assessment tool, one set of opposites focused on the difference between extraversion and introversion. It identified that some people tend to "act–reflect–act" (extraversion), whereas others "reflect–act–reflect" (introversion). Or put another way:

Introverted thinking is about *thinking to talk*.

Extraverted thinking is about *talking to think*.

Of course, the MBTI is a personality test and should therefore be taken with a very big pinch of salt. It is also context-related: how many of us are introverted when dragged to a party of complete strangers but extraverted when playing host at our own party? Context obviously matters! So it is simply not true to say that we are either one way or the other *all the time*.

The key is that some people—students included—*typically* find it easier to think if they don't have to say anything whereas others *typically* find talking lots helps to clarify their thinking. Contrast this with many school-based discussions in which the teacher begins by saying:

"I'm going to pass this fluffy owl around the circle. When you've got it then, and only then, is it your turn to talk!"

Imagine if you're in the mood for some introverted thinking and you've been given the fluffy owl first. What do you do? Everyone is looking at you expectantly, but you haven't had time to think what you might say. As the pressure builds, your teacher reminds you to say "pass" if you want to. The problem is you know if you *do* say "pass," then everyone will think you're a dimwit. Meanwhile, around the other side of the circle, there's an extraverted thinker desperate to say something, with words and ideas ready to pour out of every orifice! Eventually, the extraverted child shouts out and the teacher barks at them for breaking the rules.

Oh, the joys of teaching (and yes, so very many times, I was *that* teacher).

Here are some better ways to run dialogues that encourage thinking in both an extraverted *and* introverted manner:

Reflection time: Give everyone a moment to either collect their own thoughts or share their first ideas (very quietly) with the person next to them.

Pause: Pause the Learning Challenge halfway through to give some thinking time, either overnight or for a short period during the school day. A good time to pause is once the voting has been completed so that your students can reflect on the question that has been chosen.

Inner circle and outer circle: This works particularly well if you have a group of twenty or more. Split the group in two and get half the students to sit in a circle, with the other half sat around the outside of the circle. The outer group can record the dialogue—with a mind map, concept map or similar—as well as jot down their own thoughts. If you swap the groups around periodically, perhaps every ten minutes or so, then everyone will have a chance to reflect quietly *and* speak if they want to.

It is disingenuous to try to get all students to talk. The focus of LC sessions is on thinking, and some people do their best thinking when they don't feel the need to speak.

Setting up an inner circle and outer circle affords more thinking time for participants.

Of course, many teachers might still worry if some students don't speak. However, we don't know that students are concentrating even if they *do* speak! Many students have learned phrases and tactics designed to give the impression that they are focused when actually their mind is elsewhere.

So whether you are in discussion with one student or a whole group of students, I recommend the following:

a. Pause and reflect time.

b. Feasibility language: Phrases such as *perhaps, maybe* or *I was wondering* promote a sense of open-mindedness and exploration, which is something that's vital for inquiry.

c. Thinking: Remind your students that the most important thing is to *think* about the question. So long as everyone does that, it is up to individuals whether or not to share their views with others.

Once your students begin to share their first thoughts, guide the others to respond encouragingly and to build on what has been said. This can be done in one or more of the following ways:

Repeat-Paraphrase-Connect (RPC): When a student has expressed their first idea, get others to *repeat* word for word what they've said, *paraphrase* by saying the same thing in a different way or *connect* what was said to an idea of their own.

Meaning: A particularly effective strategy is to respond to a student's contribution by asking if anybody else knows what the student meant. Some of your students will feel certain that they understood, so ask them to explain. If only two of you are in the discussion, then you could try explaining what you think the other person meant. Either way, make sure you then ask the first person if indeed that was what they meant. Usually, the explanation is close to the intended meaning but not exactly so, which gives the first person an opportunity to clarify their thoughts even more. This strategy also teaches us there is often a marked difference between what someone says and how others understand it.

Agree: A simple (and effective) convention is to ask everyone taking part in a dialogue to begin their first few responses with "I agree with . . . because . . ." as this requires participants to listen carefully to what others say.

Help participants to build their skills of listening by using some of the techniques shown here.

In addition to the main points identified in the preview, this chapter has covered the following:

1. If your students have created a range of questions from the concepts they find most interesting, then they should be given the opportunity to choose the best question for inquiry.

2. To choose the best question, they could take a vote, do a blind ballot or identify the criteria by which to judge the best question.

3. Once the decision has been made about the best question, then you should give your students time to share their first thoughts. Do not challenge them yet and do not expect everyone to speak. The most important thing for them to do is think about the possible meanings of the question and the avenues of inquiry they might follow.

4. There is no hard and fast rule about the setup phase. So long as you have helped your students identify an interesting concept worth exploring, then you are ready for Stage 2 of the Learning Challenge.

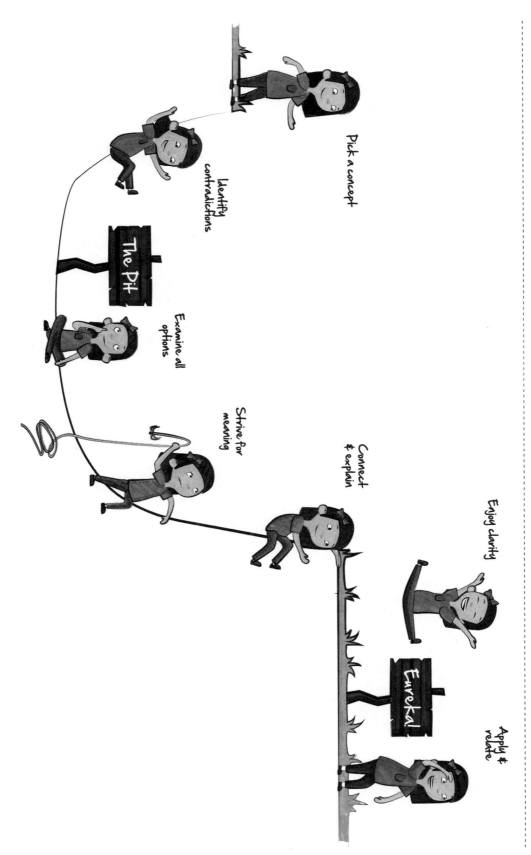

▼ Figure 16: The Seven Steps to Understanding

COGNITIVE CONFLICT

5.0 • PREVIEW

This chapter focuses on the role of cognitive conflict: what it is, why it can help your students learn and how to set it up effectively.

The most important points in the chapter include:

1. At the heart of the Learning Challenge is cognitive conflict.

2. Cognitive conflict is the disagreement between two or more of the ideas or opinions a person holds at the same time.

3. Cognitive conflict prompts people to think more urgently and purposefully.

4. There is a moral purpose to creating cognitive conflict in that it helps people become more judicious and considered.

5. There are many ways to create cognitive conflict, including through dialogue, by comparing two or more concepts together and by considering concepts in varying contexts.

6. When your students encounter cognitive conflict, then that is when they can say they are in the pit.

5.1 • WHAT IS COGNITIVE CONFLICT?

Cognitive conflict is created when contradictions are identified and options examined, as shown by Steps 2 and 3 in Figure 16. It is quite literally a conflict within a person's

At the heart of the Learning Challenge is a pit. The pit represents a state of cognitive conflict.

cognition—that is to say, a disagreement between two or more of the ideas or opinions a person holds concurrently. This conflict can be unsettling, but at the same time, it can cause more reflection and the questioning of assumptions.

For example, if school-age children are asked if Robin Hood was a "good man," they are most likely to say yes. This is idea one: "Robin Hood was a good man." However, if they are then asked whether it would be good if someone in the class stole from a supermarket and gave the proceeds to the poor, their usual answer is no. This then prompts the second idea in their minds: "It is wrong to steal."

The conflict of opinions between thinking that Robin Hood was a good man while also believing that stealing is wrong creates the tension that causes the children to reflect more on their beliefs.

Figure 17 shows another example, this time in response to the question "What is a friend?" The character's immediate reaction is to think of a friend as being someone they trust. This is idea one. Someone else in the group then proposes that there are many people who can be trusted who would not count as a friend, for example, a member of the emergency services. This is idea two.

▶ **Figure 17: An Illustration of Cognitive Conflict**

But then the teacher suggests that many of us trust, for example, people working for the emergency services but don't count them as our friends. This prompts idea two which, when compared with idea one, is what creates the cognitive conflict.

Please bear in mind that your students need to accept, however provisionally, two or more ideas that are in opposition, otherwise cognitive conflict won't exist. That is why the Learning Challenge begins with a concept that your students have at least one idea about. If they have no idea, then there will be nothing to conflict with and therefore you will not be able to take them into the pit!

> **This also explains why you should *not* voice your disagreement with students' ideas even if you think they are wrong. For example, if one of your students said, "It is OK to hit someone," then no matter how vehemently you disagree with that opinion, for the purposes of the Learning Challenge you should not show your disapproval or disagreement. Instead, you should encourage other participants to think of counterexamples. This is as true for when you agree with your students' opinions as it is for when you disagree with them. The integrity and success of the process relies on participants being able to explore ideas without censorship.**

A nice way to capture this value is to say, "Not all of our questions answered but all of our answers questioned."

As I mentioned in Section 3.3, I am *not* suggesting that you should stop teaching your students the values of the society in which they live. What I am advocating, though, is that you use the Learning Challenge to teach your students *how* to think so that, through the course of their education, your students learn what and how to think.

5.2 • WHY IS COGNITIVE CONFLICT A GOOD THING?

Stage 2 of the Learning Challenge is all about creating cognitive conflict in the minds of participants. As described in Section 2.2, the purpose of cognitive conflict is to motivate people to think more deeply and urgently about their ideas.

The image shown originally in Figure 3, shown again as Figure 18, is a useful way to describe what cognitive conflict might feel like. Whereas the left-hand path represents tasks that are easy and straightforward, in which there is no cognitive conflict, the right-hand path represents the more challenging tasks that often generate cognitive conflict.

Let's compare the two in more detail. The left-hand path could be said to represent the route that many students take during lessons. That is not to denigrate the teaching profession or to say that it is always a bad path to take. The problem is that with an over-filled curriculum and mounting pressure to do well in exams, far too many of us feel obliged (forced, even) to guide our students along this route so that they can reach the answer as smoothly and efficiently as possible. There just doesn't seem to be time to pause and think. By contrast, the path to the right is more problematic and time-consuming but at the same time more engaging and thought-provoking.

Of course, I am not suggesting that we should never take our students on the smoother path. Indeed, there are many skills we ask them to repeat again and again—for example, reciting times tables—and we do so for the very purpose of making those skills easier and more automatic for them. That said, there are very definitely many benefits to encouraging our students along the more challenging path.

▶ Figure 18: The Learning Challenge Path

These are some of the advantages to taking your students on a Learning Challenge journey (as represented by the right-hand path shown in Figure 18):

- Causing your students to think more about their learning journey

- Prompting your students to problem solve with greater purpose and priority

- Encouraging your students to collaborate with each other so that they make more progress

- Putting your students in challenging situations in which they develop resilience, determination and tenacity

- More necessity for your students to question, elaborate, connect, predict, sequence and verify

- Creating greater demand on your students to reflect on their learning strategies and to think about their next steps (metacognition)

- An increased sense of achievement for your students when they eventually reach their learning goal

The following quotes add another dimension to the benefits I have listed:

If students do not have to work hard to make sense of what they are learning, then they are less likely to remember it in six weeks' time. (Blog post by Dylan Wiliam, on deansforimpact.org, 2016)

Memories are formed as a residue of thought. (From "Ask the Cognitive Scientist: What Will Improve a Student's Memory?" Daniel Willingham, 2009, p. 22)

> **When learners do well on a learning task, they are likely to forget things more quickly than if they do badly on the learning task; good instruction creates "desirable difficulties" (Bjork, 1994, p. 193) for the learner. (Blog post by Dylan Wiliam, on deansforimpact.org, 2016, which references "Memory and Metamemory Considerations in the Training of Human Beings," Robert Bjork, 1994)**

I have included the full reference for these quotes here as well as in the list of references at the back of the book because I think the sources are almost as interesting as the ideas themselves.

The first quote is from Dylan Wiliam (2016), one of the best-known researchers in the field of feedback, on the website Deans for Impact.

The second reference is there to help you the next time you are asked to justify your use of the Learning Challenge to a grade-obsessed colleague or student. Show them this quote and remind them that far from slowing student progress down, the Learning Challenge is likely to *increase* student success in exams! By thinking more, students are likely to remember more, and by remembering more, they are likely to do better in tests (Willingham, 2009).

The final quote comes from Dylan Wiliam again, but he quotes Robert Bjork (1994), a professor of psychology. I really wish I'd thought of that phrase: "desirable difficulties." It is a great way to describe the Learning Challenge!

The quotes above share some of the research evidence for the benefits of challenge.

At the heart of all this challenge and memory forming is cognitive conflict. Generating conflicting ideas about the concepts that are important to their lives will help students engage with the material *and* remember the lessons long into the future.

5.2.1 • The Moral Purpose of Cognitive Conflict

There is also a moral purpose to cognitive conflict in that it helps people become more judicious and deliberate. It does this by prompting them to reflect more compellingly on their assumptions and inconsistencies—that is, if they recognize that cognitive conflict exists in the first place! I say this because many inconsistencies exist in people's lives that they don't do very much about, for example, a meat eater who thinks killing animals is cruel; the driver of a large, polluting vehicle who thinks global warming should be tackled; the boss who advocates work-life balance while also expecting everyone to put in many extra hours outside the normal working week.

Before I get too political, though, let's go back to thinking about the school context. Figure 19 shows some common examples of conflicting opinions that I hear among school-age students.

These ideas exist in the minds of many students, and sometimes it is easier just to leave them as they are. Yet there are a great many benefits to be gained from examining conflicts one by one. For a start, it can be interesting and often quite funny to think about the many contradictions we live with. Secondly, it can offer your students an enjoyable way to learn how to resolve conflicts and make decisions.

There are many moral reasons for helping young people deal with cognitive conflict.

It is also worth bearing in mind that the etymology of critical thinking is *kritikos*, the Greek word for "making judgments." So if you encourage your students to analyze different sides of an argument with a view toward making reasoned judgments, then you will also be familiarizing your students with one of the central procedures of critical thinking.

Opinion	Conflicting Opinion
If I am bullied, I should tell a teacher.	If I am bullied, I should fight back.
It is wrong to steal.	Robin Hood did a good thing.
You should never lie.	Giving an honest opinion can offend.
Drugs are illegal.	Cigarettes and alcohol contain drugs.
You should always help your friends.	Helping people too much can make them dependent.
I should think for myself.	I should do what my elders tell me.
Many hands make light work.	Too many cooks spoil the broth.

Figure 19 shows examples of cognitive conflict commonly held by school-age students.

Thirdly, examining and resolving dilemmas can help your students develop their conflict resolution strategies as well as their wisdom. That sounds like a rather extravagant claim, but consider this if you will: how often do we make decisions on behalf of our students and, in so doing, inadvertently deny them the opportunity to develop their own wisdom?

A classic example is when we see two students fighting. We stop the fight and ask them to explain: one says the other one was bullying him or her. So we remind them both that in the case of bullying, they should always tell a teacher who will then put a stop to it. Their response is often to say that their parents have advised them to fight back against bullies. Now how's that for conflicting opinions: if I am bullied I should tell a teacher versus if I am bullied I should fight back.

Now consider how you would respond to that circumstance. How likely are you to say what so many of us say: "That might be what your parents say, but you are in school now and in school, you should follow the school rules."

Many school lessons teach students *what* to think. The LC provides a balance to this by teaching students *how* to think.

Perhaps this seems the right thing to do. After all, as teachers we do need to get our students to follow the school rules. But consider the inadvertent message this advice also conveys: ignore one side of the argument and do as you are told! What sort of life lesson is that?

In terms of the process, what is the difference between me saying, "Ignore what your parents say and do as I tell you" and, for example, a drug dealer saying, "Ignore what they taught you in school and just take these drugs. They'll give you an amazing high and I'll give you the first sample free."

Please know that I am *not* saying that getting your students to follow school rules is as bad as dealers peddling drugs! What I am saying is that the *process* of advising someone to ignore one side of an argument and do the opposite is the equivalent in both examples. At the risk of being alarmist, isn't that part of what led to the most common claim made at the Nuremberg trials: I was doing as I was told.

This is one of the reasons why I am saying that teaching your students to examine and resolve their cognitive conflicts has a moral dimension. The process can help them learn how to make decisions, listen to counterarguments, try to understand other people's points of view and so on.

Of course, I would not advocate starting your students off with the process of examining cognitive conflict by sharing tales of the Nuremberg trials or by thinking about the right response to bullying. That sort of thing can be examined once your students have a lot of Learning Challenge experiences under their belts. Instead, I suggest you start with any of the less confronting examples of cognitive conflict shown in Sections 4.4 and 4.4.1 and in Chapter 10.

5.3 • CREATING COGNITIVE CONFLICT

Steps 1, 2 and 3 in Figure 16 show some of the ways to build toward cognitive conflict. Here are some other methods:

Dialogue: using dialogue to reveal the complexities of a concept (see Section 5.4)

Comparisons: comparing a chosen concept with other concepts, including the use of synonyms and antonyms (see Section 5.5)

Context: reflecting on different uses of the concept in varying contexts, particularly contemporary examples (see Section 5.6)

This section explores each of these approaches to cognitive conflict in depth. As you read through them, I recommend that you highlight the techniques or examples you think will work best for your students. I have found them all to be very useful, but not all at the same time and certainly not in all contexts. For example, I think the dialogues probably work best with articulate students, whereas extensions might work better with English language learners.

> Many of the examples of cognitive conflict in this book show the teacher as main protagonist. Over time, students should take on more and more of this role.

Bear in mind that the ultimate aim is for cognitive conflict to emerge spontaneously—and even to be created purposefully by your students—without your guidance. This is unlikely to happen straightaway, which is why many of the examples in this book identify the teacher as lead protagonist (particularly in the example dialogues). Over time, though, there should be a noticeable progression from you challenging your students, to your students challenging each other, to each student challenging himself or herself. This final manifestation of challenge—students challenging themselves—can be thought of as the basis for reflection and metacognition.

5.4 • CREATING COGNITIVE CONFLICT THROUGH DIALOGUE

Dialogue is a great vehicle for getting your students into the pit. Indeed, it is such a great pedagogical tool that my colleagues and I have written *Challenging Learning Through Dialogue* (Nottingham, Nottingham & Renton, 2017) to share some of the best approaches to dialogue. Furthermore, if you watch the *Learning Challenge* (Nottingham, 2015) animation on YouTube, you will notice many of the examples are dialogue based.

The following are two examples of the use of dialogue to create cognitive conflict. Both are records of actual exchanges between some students and me. The first was with seven-year-olds; the second dialogue was with fourteen-year-olds.

The Learning Challenge With Seven-Year-Olds

Me: Two, seven and eight: Which number is different from the other two and why?

Andrew: Seven, because it's an odd number.

> This is an extract from a transcript of an LC session about odd numbers.

(Continued)

Me:	What's an odd number?
Caroline:	A number that can't be divided by two.
Me:	So if I have $7, are you saying it can't be divided into two? How much would each person have if I shared $7 between two people?
Charlotte:	$3.50 each.
Me:	So seven can be divided into two. Does that mean it's even then?
Sergei:	No!
Me:	So what is an odd number?
Sergei:	It can't be divided into two without leaving a remainder.
Me:	But when I divided $7 by two, that didn't leave a remainder.
Daniel:	But 50¢ is not a whole number. You can't divide an odd number by two without splitting a whole number.
Me:	Are you telling me that fifty is not a whole number?
Sunita:	50 cents isn't.
Me:	This (holding a 50-cent piece) is not whole? Why not? It looks whole to me.
Sunita:	But it's not a whole dollar. It's a half dollar.
Me:	So what is an odd number then?
Ben:	It's a number that can't be divided by two without changing the units.
Me:	Can you give me an example?
Ben:	If I had seven one-dollar bills then I'd have to split one of them in half first.
Me:	Does that mean anything I have to split in half, so that I can share it, is odd?
Ben:	Yes.
Me:	But what if I have a $10 bill I would have to split that to share it, wouldn't I? Does that make $10 odd?
Ben:	No.
Me:	So what about five cakes? If I had five cakes, could I share them equally between two people?
Harry:	Yes, of course.
Me:	So are five cakes odd or even?
Harry:	Odd.
Me:	And yet I can divide them into two equal portions.
Daniel:	But the bits wouldn't be whole. You'd have to have halves.
Sunita:	Yeah, so maybe an odd number *can* be divided into two but only using halves?
Sergei:	Yes, but the half-dollar piece wasn't a half. That was a whole coin. Not like the cake.
Caroline:	Ah, this is too hard!

5. Cognitive Conflict

The Learning Challenge With Fourteen-Year-Olds

This is an extract from a transcript of an LC session about bravery.

Me: What do we mean by being brave?

Sarah: Facing your fears.

Me: But if I'm scared to run across a motorway, but still do it, am I being brave?

Ellie: No, that's just stupid. You have to do something good to be brave.

Me: Such as kill someone?

Kyle: That's not good.

Me: But lots of soldiers have been awarded medals for bravery, and presumably many of them killed the enemy while being brave.

Kyle: Yes, but that was their job.

Me: So if I do my job, am I being brave? I'm doing my job now—does that mean I'm being brave?

Vijay: No, sir. You're not doing your job. You're just trying to confuse us.

(It was very tempting to ask why Vijay thought trying to confuse [or challenge] him wasn't the job of a teacher, but I wanted to stick to the topic.)

Me: So if you're just doing your job, then you're not being brave, is that right?

Sunita: What about firemen? They're brave.

Molly: My dad's a fireman and all he does is sit around playing computer games.

Me: But presumably your dad also rescues people and puts out fires when he's asked to.

Molly: Of course!

Me: So is he brave then?

Molly: Yeah, I guess.

Me: Can anyone else tell me what it is about Molly's dad's job that means he has to be brave to do it?

Ben: He puts the lives of others before himself.

Me: OK, but most parents would put the lives of their children before their own, particularly in times of crisis or danger. Are they being brave?

Jenny: Sort of. But then it's kind of expected, isn't it?

Julia: What is?

Jenny: Putting your kids' lives before your own. It's just what you do.

Me: But when firefighters put their lives in danger to save others, isn't that just what is expected? That's what they are there for, isn't it?

Jenny: True, but then that feels different. I can't explain it but it does.

Me: Can anyone help Jenny out? What do you think she might mean?

Brandon: Do you mean that it's normal? Like expected?

Jenny: Maybe, yeah. It's normal for firefighters to risk their lives to save others. And it's normal for parents to put their kids before themselves.

(Continued)

(Continued)

Me:	So is being brave a normal thing then?
Sarah:	No. Being brave is not normal; otherwise why would we talk about it? It would be like pointing at someone and saying they're human. Of course they are. All people are. So if everyone were brave, then why would we even mention it? Why would we have bravery awards if everyone were brave? I think it is something *un*usual.
Kyle:	Depends what you mean by brave.
Me:	Indeed! So how about it then? Can anyone say what *brave* means?
Students:	(groans) We're in the pit again!

Reading the dialogue above, please note that by continually asking questions and pointing out the inconsistencies in the students' arguments, I was not trying to score points or belittle them in any way; that would have been socially and morally suspect as well as counterproductive. Instead, I was aiming to get the young people thinking *more* by finding exceptions to their initial answers so that they need to think again and in so doing, develop their insights and deepen their resilience.

For example, if I had asked the seven-year-olds to explain what an odd number is and then accepted their first answer ("it can't be divided by two"), then they would not have needed to think very much; they would probably have been able to answer with a memorized response. Compare this to the dialogue shown in which I led them to think that while "an odd number cannot be divided by two," there are very obviously situations in which an odd number *can* be divided by two: for example, $7 can be divided into two lots of $3.50. This is the cognitive conflict that I was trying to set up: two thoughts that make sense but are also in conflict with each other. This then leads eventually to more reasoned answers and the development of the language needed to explain things in a more nuanced manner.

It is a similar situation in the dialogue with fourteen-year-olds: on the one hand, being brave means facing your fears, but on the other hand, facing your fears can also be foolhardy (or as my students called it, being "stupid"). In this particular example, my students went on to add more cognitive conflict: since so many people put the lives of others before themselves, this would mean bravery is "normal," yet it can't be "normal"; otherwise why would we remark on it or give awards for bravery? Again, there is a contradiction in what they are saying, and therefore a state of cognitive conflict is emerging.

5.4.1 • Wobblers

One of the best ways to create cognitive conflict in dialogue is with what I call *wobblers*. I use this term to evoke the sense of wobble we experience when learning to ride a bike. I explained this more in Section 1.1, but to summarize here, I mean the shaking, unsteady feeling we experience when we are out of our comfort zone. As I've described throughout this book, the Learning Challenge is all about encouraging our students out of their comfort zone and into the pit of learning so that they might better understand the complexities and nuances of concepts that are important to their lives. Wobblers are great tools to help with this endeavor.

Before you read through these wobblers, I recommend you revisit Section 3.2 to be sure about the ways in which these strategies should be used. In that section, I wrote about how the Learning Challenge is not about point scoring but about wobbling; it is not about belittling someone but about humor and humility, and it is not about proving anybody wrong but about finding new ways to look at familiar concepts.

Wobblers are techniques to create "wobble" in the minds of LC participants.

Wobbler 1: If A = B

This involves asking what something is, taking whatever your students say and then testing it by turning it around and adding a conflicting example. For instance:

Question: What is bravery? (This is A.)

Answer: Facing your fears. (This is B.)

Question: So if I face my fears (B), does that mean that I am being brave (A)? For example, running across a busy road?

The process looks something like this:

If A = B then does B = A?

A is the concept that you are considering, in this case bravery.

B is a student's response, in this case "Facing your fears."

Now add an example that will conflict with the definition. For example, "running across a busy road" would be facing your fears but would not normally be thought of as brave.

Note that you are not proving them wrong by finding this counterexample. Instead, you are trying to find an example that will cause your students to think again.

Examples of Wobbler 1

If bullying (A) means hurting someone (B), then does that mean that if I hurt someone (B) that therefore I am bullying them (A)? For example, if I hurt someone by committing a foul during a sports match?

If being fair (A) means giving everyone the same (B), then does that mean if I give everyone the same (B) that I am being fair (A)? For example, what if I give a baby the same amount of food as an adult? Or I give all students the same punishment even though only half of them have been misbehaving?

If justice (A) is about balancing the scales (B), then if we balance the scales (B), is that justice? For example, taking revenge? Or killing a murderer, stealing from a thief and so on.

If home (A) is where your parents live (B), then does that mean where your parents live (B) is your home (A)? For example, what if your parents decide to move to another country and you don't go with them?

If a poem (A) is something that rhymes (B), then does that mean something that rhymes (B) is a poem (A)? For example, what about *cat* and *mat*? They rhyme. Are they a poem when put together?

If food (A) is something you eat (B), does that mean something you eat (B) is food (A)? For example, what if you eat the lid from your pen? Or you swallow a fly?

Wobbler 2: Not A

Another way to create wobble in the minds of your students is to add a negative to "If A = B." Thus the formula becomes:

If A = B, then if it's *not* B, is it also *not* A?

> These examples of Wobbler 1 show the concept as (A) and the answer that students give as (B).

> Wobbler 2 adds a negative to students' responses to see if the idea also works in reverse.

A is the thing you are considering, for example, friend.

B is one of your students' responses, for example, "someone I play with."

So this time, to create cognitive conflict, we ask:

Does that mean if you do *not* play (not B) with your friend today that you are *not* friends (not A)?

Examples of Wobbler 2

If children say that fairness (A) is about being the same (B), then if we are not the same (not B) does that mean it is not fair (not A)? For example, you and I are different because we have different eye color, haircuts, arm length and so on.

If a dream (A) is the thinking we do when we are asleep (B), then if I'm not asleep (not B), does that mean I can't dream (not A)? For example, the dreams we have when we're half awake or daydreaming? Or the dreams we set our sights on achieving?

If democracy (A) is about going with the majority (B), then if the majority do not agree (not B) is it not democracy (not A)? For example, what about the presidents and prime ministers who have won an election with approximately 30 percent of the vote because so many people in the country have declined to vote?

If a lie (A) is when someone does not tell the truth (B), then if I do tell the truth (not B) does that mean I am not lying (not A)? For example, what if someone says there is no such thing as aliens but then years from now, it is proved that there are aliens on other planets? Would they be lying or telling the truth?

If a friend (A) is someone I trust (B), then does that mean someone I do not trust (not B) cannot be my friend (not A)? For example, what about the friends you have that you can't trust to be on time? Or those you would never trust with a secret or to look after your pet? Does that mean they are not your friends?

Wobbler 3: General to Specific

You may need to move between generalizations and specific examples to make the first two wobblers work, particularly with the "not A" version. For example, if you were to ask what a friend is and your students replied "someone who is nice," it would seem strange then to ask, "Does that mean someone who is not nice is not your friend?" The answer must almost certainly be yes!

However, if you were to move from the general (G) to the specific (S), this wobbler will still work and give your students more cause for thought.

Here are two more examples, with the main concept shown as (A), the students' first answer as (B), the generalization as (G) and the specific example as (S).

Question:	What is a friend? (A)
Answer:	Someone who is nice. (B)
Question:	Do friends always (G) have to be nice to each other?
For example:	What if your friend wasn't nice to you today (S)—would that mean you were no longer friends (G)?
Question:	What are living things? (A)

Answer:	Living things grow (B) and breathe and excrete.
Question:	What if a living thing did not grow for a few months (S)—would that mean it was no longer living? (G)
For example:	A plant does not grow throughout the winter months (S) but starts to grow again in springtime. Does that mean it was not living during winter?

Wobbler 4: Quantifiable

If your students make a claim about something that is quantifiable, then you can ask them to specify the exact amount. This is not such a common wobbler, but when it is used it can really help create cognitive conflict.

In the examples below, the quantifiable wobbler is marked with (Q).

> Wobbler 4 tests the extent to which something is true (its quantity).

Question:	What is a friend? (A)
Answer:	Someone you've known for a long time. (B)
Question:	How long? (Q)
Answer:	About two years.
Question:	So if I have known someone for two years (A), does that mean I will definitely be friends with them? (B)
Answer:	No.
Question:	And what about if I have not known someone for very long (not B)—let's say three weeks (Q)—does that mean I can't be friends with them? (not A)
Answer:	No. But the longer you know someone, the more chance you have of being friends with them?
Question:	Really?

5.4.2 • Dialogue Examples

Here are some more examples of the use of wobblers to create cognitive conflict through dialogue. You can also find examples in Section 2.2 and in *Challenging Learning* (Nottingham, 2016).

In the first two examples below, the following annotations are used:

(A) represents the main concept

(B) represents the students' main answer

(not A) is when the opposite to concept (A) is being tested

(not B) is when the opposite to answer (B) is being tested

(G) is a generalization

All the examples share records of actual exchanges between students and their teachers.

Concept: Knowledge

Nine- to ten-year-olds

Teacher: What does knowledge (A) mean?

Adam: It's about knowing things (B).

Teacher: If I know your name (B), does that mean I have knowledge about you (A)?

Adam: Yes.

Teacher: But do I know you in the same way that your mom knows you?

Rachel: No, that's different.

Teacher: How is it different?

Rachel: Adam's mom knows him really well. You only know him a bit.

Teacher: Which bit?

Adam: You know what she means. My mom knows me really well. She's known me a lot longer than you have.

Teacher: Does that mean the longer you know someone or something, the more knowledge you have about them (Q)? I've known my teeth ever since they grew in my mouth. Does that mean I know my teeth really well?

Tas: I guess so.

Teacher: But do you think I know my teeth better than my dentist knows them?

Tas: Of course not. Your dentist is an expert on teeth, including yours.

Teacher: But my dentist hasn't known my teeth as long as I have (Q). In fact, I changed dentists about two years ago. So do you think this new dentist still knows my teeth?

Anita: Yes, but that's different. She knows about teeth and so when she looks at your teeth, she understands more than you do.

Teacher: What do you mean?

Anita: Well, your dentist has studied teeth. She knows the names of all the teeth, what they're for and what they should look like.

Teacher: So she has knowledge about my teeth in the sense that she knows lots of facts about teeth? She knows the facts about teeth.

Kalim: Exactly.

Teacher: So if I know the names of all the planets in our solar system (B), does that mean I know those planets (A)?

Ellie: No, it means you have knowledge about them but it doesn't mean you know them.

Teacher: But how can that be? I thought we said at the beginning that knowledge (A) is about knowing things (B)?

Sam:	Well, it is about knowing things. It's about knowing the facts (B). For example, I know that the world is round.
Teacher:	That's a very interesting idea because people used to "know" that the world was flat. So what can we say about their knowledge?
Frances:	They were wrong. Their knowledge was wrong.
Teacher:	But I thought we said that knowledge is what we know to be right. So how can knowledge be wrong?
Paul:	Knowledge (A) is whatever you think is right at the time (B).
Mohammed:	But if I think I can fly, that doesn't mean that's right, does it?
Paul:	No, it means you're deluded.
Teacher:	Does that mean that when our ancestors knew the world was flat, they were deluded?
Paul:	Well, what is knowledge then?

Concept: Culture

Thirteen- to fourteen-year-olds

Teacher:	What is culture? (A)
Simon:	A group of people. (B)
Teacher:	We're a group of people (B). Does that mean we're a culture (A)?
Simon:	Sort of.
Teacher:	Do we all belong to the same culture then?
Mohammed:	No, not all of us. Some of us are a different color, and some of us believe different things.
Teacher:	Does that mean everyone who's black belongs to one culture (A) and everyone who's white belongs to another culture (A)?
Rachel:	No, that's to do with race, not culture.
Teacher:	What's the difference?
Shaheena:	Race is the color of your skin, whereas culture (A) is about what you believe and how you act (B).
Teacher:	So if culture (A) is to do with what you believe, then if we all believed a particular football player was the best in the world, would we all belong to the same culture (A)?
Tas:	No, that's just about football.
Teacher:	Is there no such thing as a football culture then? (not B)
Tas:	Yes, there is, but that's about liking football.

This is an extract from a transcript of an LC session about culture.

(Continued)

Anna:	And wearing jerseys and shoes and things.
Alison:	I wear sporty clothes but I hate football, so I'm not part of a football culture, am I?
Teacher:	So going back to the original question (what is culture?), are we saying that culture (A) is a group of people who like the same thing and perhaps wear the same things as well (B)?
Vijay:	Yeah, that's right.
Teacher:	But people who like the same thing and wear the same things aren't necessarily of the same culture, are they? For example, what about everyone who goes to see Taylor Swift live? Presumably, they all like the same thing (Taylor) and maybe all wear Taylor tour T-shirts.
Anita:	OK, that doesn't work but it does if you think about the Goths. They all wear black and like the same music.
Anna:	No, we don't.
Anita:	So are you saying you're not part of the Goth culture? (not A)
Anna:	No, I'm not saying that because I am part of the Goth culture, but I'm also part of the youth culture and maybe even this school culture, aren't I? But just because you're from the same culture doesn't mean you like the same thing, do the same thing or even wear the same thing.
Teacher:	So what does culture mean then?

This is an extract from a transcript of an LC session about fairness.

Concept: Fairness

Six- to seven-year-olds

Children:	That's not fair!
Teacher:	Why not?
Children:	Because we didn't all get cupcakes.
Teacher:	Why should I give sweets to everyone?
Children:	It's not fair if you don't.
Teacher:	But they're my cupcakes, so surely I can give them to whom I like?
Patrick:	But why did you pick those five?
Teacher:	They're my favorite students. What's wrong with that?
Catherine:	As a teacher you shouldn't have favorites.
Teacher:	So it's all right for you to have favorites but not me? Why not?
Children:	Teachers are supposed to make sure everything's fair.
Teacher:	Does that I mean I should treat all of you in exactly the same way?

Children:	Yes, of course.
Teacher:	So should I give everyone an A for effort, no matter how much effort they put into their studies?
Children:	No, but . . .
Teacher:	Or what about adults and children—should they all be treated in the same way?
Children:	Yes.
Teacher:	So children, even young ones, should be required to work, should they?
Children:	No.
Teacher:	But why not? It's only fair!
Children:	But children shouldn't have to work. That's what their parents are supposed to do.
Teacher:	Does that mean it would be unfair of me to ask you to help tidy the classroom? Should we expect someone else to tidy up after us?
Children:	No, but . . .

5.5 • CREATING COGNITIVE CONFLICT WITH COMPARISONS

A very good way to create cognitive conflict is to compare two or more concepts together. This technique is not so reliant on dialogue, so you might find particular groups of students prefer this approach. The technique might also be reassuring for you in early Learning Challenge episodes as you will be able to prepare some concept comparisons before you meet your students.

In the example dialogues shown earlier, one of the groups of students was thinking through the concept of culture. So to keep the same theme, here are some concept comparisons you might introduce:

- Culture and family
- Culture and group
- Culture and clique
- Culture and tribe
- Culture and team
- Culture and community
- Culture and civilization
- Culture and gang
- Culture and language
- Culture and religion
- Culture and race
- Culture and traditions

Comparing the similarities and differences between concepts is a good way to understand the nuances of a concept.

- Culture and nationality
- Culture and environment
- Culture and cuisine
- Culture and expectations
- Culture and being cultured
- Culture and fables

The list above brings together synonyms of culture, but we could equally look at antonyms, for example:

- Culture and individual
- Culture and unique
- Culture and random
- Culture and solitary
- Culture and nature
- Culture and accidental

Notice that the antonym list is much shorter. That is because I found it more difficult to think of words that represent the opposite to culture than I did to think of synonyms. This points to another useful technique for thinking: inviting your students to identify words that have the opposite meaning to the concept they are thinking about.

For example, you could ask your students to think of antonyms for the following concepts:

- Gang
- Dreams
- Perception
- Length
- People
- Bullying
- Pets
- Toys

The key to comparing two or more concepts together is to draw out connections and distinctions. As your students do this, you could suggest that they use a Venn diagram, such as the one in Figure 20, or other visual tool to help them order and record their thinking.

Venn diagrams are a very useful pit tool. More examples are shared in Section 6.3.9.

Once your students have created something similar to Figure 20, you could then ask other students to find exceptions to the characteristics assigned to the main concept (in this case, assigned to culture). For example: If you are saying people of the same culture (A) share the same values (B), then does that mean people who do not have the same values (not B) cannot be part of the same culture (not A)? For example, some members of indigenous cultures believe traditional stories should be passed on only orally, whereas others believe stories should be written down for posterity.

This wobbler will probably lead to a sense of cognitive conflict: on the one hand, culture is about shared values, but on the other hand, some people in the same culture do not share the same values.

▶ **Figure 20: Venn Diagram of Culture Versus Team**

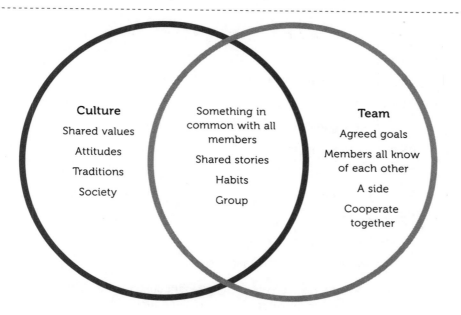

Following on from that, you can then ask whether "shared values" should be listed under "culture," to which your students will probably say no.

If you do the same for each of the characteristics given (in this case, values, attitudes, traditions and society), then that will leave your students with a blank circle (and probably blank faces!). This is one of the many ways you can encourage your students into the pit.

As your students grow in confidence and fluency with connecting and comparing concepts, encourage them to do the same thing in open dialogues. Remind them to use vocabulary such as *same, similar, different, identical, distinction* and *connection.*

5.6 • CREATING COGNITIVE CONFLICT IN CONTEXT

All of the techniques that follow are tried and tested ways to reveal different aspects of concepts that when put together can lead to cognitive conflict in the minds of your students. Past students of mine would call these *concept stretchers.*

5.6.1 • Variations of Meaning

This variation involves considering how the meaning of a concept might be different according to the context. For example:

Explain what *real* means in the following examples:

- She's the real deal.

- The cost of food in real terms has risen by 15%.

- Is that Rolex real?

- He sells real estate.

> Thinking about the different ways in which a concept might be used is a good way to understand the concept better.

- She's so in love, she thinks it's the real thing.

- Are you for real?

- Fractions are a type of real number.

- Is that your real name or just your nickname?

- Elton John's real name is Reginald Kenneth Dwight.

- We saw it happen in real time.

- There is nothing real about reality TV.

- It's all becoming very real.

- Get real!

- She is in real trouble.

- This is real life.

- It's the only real way to make sure.

- We should find out the real reason why.

These examples show how *real* can mean actual, not counterfeit, true, genuine, sincere, authentic and relating to things that are fixed (e.g., land, houses). You can use this wide variety of meanings to create cognitive conflict. For example, if your students say, "That apple is real," then you can ask what they mean by *real*. Once they respond, you can contrast their interpretation with a different use of *real*, for example, a real Rolex or real love.

5.6.2 • Variations of Circumstance

Another way to create cognitive wobble is to come up with contexts in which it is difficult to decide whether the examples fit the concept.

For example, in this exploration of fairness, ask your students say whether each statement represents fair, unfair or not sure (notice the three options emphasize the complexity of the concept).

1. Everyone in the school is given the same amount of homework.

2. Doctors are paid more than teachers.

3. Men are paid more than women for doing the same job.

4. Everyone is given a prize on Sports Day.

5. Children in some countries can't afford to go to school.

6. Some people live in very big houses.

7. A starving woman steals a loaf of bread to feed her family.

8. A student steals $5 from a wealthy banker.

9. Children are not allowed to drive cars.

10. Disabled people are allowed to park for free.

11. Someone breaks the law and so is sent to prison.

12. A grandmother can't pay her rent and so is sent to prison.

13. Adults do not have to go to school.

Looking at how the same concept can be used in different contexts helps to examine a concept further.

14. Some schools have longer holidays than others.

15. You have to be a particular height to go on some roller coasters.

5.6.3 • Variations of Type

Variations of type is concerned with deciding the quality or classification of examples given for a particular concept.

There are many ways to categorize according to type. A good way to start is to classify according to positive, negative and neutral examples. For example:

Positive examples

1. Standing up to a bully

2. Risking embarrassment to try out something you think is worthwhile

3. Battling a life-threatening disease

Negative examples

1. Putting the blame onto someone else when you have done something wrong because you are afraid to be blamed or punished

2. Not doing something you really want to do because you fear you might feel embarrassed

Neutral examples (neither positive nor negative)

1. Being extremely shy and not being able to get over it

2. Overcoming shyness and embarrassment by taking a pill

3. Stopping someone from bullying another person because you are a lot stronger than both of them

> Examining the classification of particular uses of a concept (for example, good/bad, human/physical, ethical/immoral) can help to identify different dimensions of a concept.

Giving examples, contrary examples and borderline cases for concepts is a useful way to get your students into the pit. Indeed, these are useful in dialogue generally. So when your students are used to analyzing concepts through examples, encourage them to recognize and reflect on concepts that arise spontaneously during interactions with each other. Help them grow used to questioning each other's assumptions about the meanings of concepts they are using and exploring the concepts through discussing examples.

5.6.4 • Variations of Opinion

Drawing out a range of opinions is another useful way to create cognitive conflict. This can be done in situ with your students, or you can prepare the range of opinions beforehand.

For example, here is a range of opinions about friendship:

• You should always trust your friends.

• It is OK to tell one of your friend's secrets to another friend.

• Pets can't be your friends.

• You can choose your friends, but you can't choose your family.

• Anyone who is nice to us can be our friend.

- The opposite of a friend is a stranger.
- Adults and children can't be friends.
- Teachers and their students can't be friends.
- People who can't understand each other can still be friends with each other.
- We should care more about our friends than about other people.
- Everyone should be a friend to everyone else.
- Opposing sports teams should always remain friends with each other.
- Being friendly is not the same as being friends.
- True friends are the ones who like you despite your flaws.
- True friends are hard to come by.
- Keeping friendships is harder than finding them.
- Enemies are made by what we say and friends are made by what we do.
- Friends have to have shared interests.

And here is a range of opinions about risk:

- Taking risks is exciting.
- Taking risks is dangerous.
- It is a risk to place a bet on something.
- Telling a joke in polite company is a risk.
- It is a risk to use social media.
- Taking a penalty shot is a risk.
- Saying nothing in class is a risk.
- Everything is a risk, so there is no point in trying to avoid risk.
- Without risk, life would be very boring.
- Traveling is a risk.
- Staying at home is a risk.
- It is a risk to write this book.
- It is a risk to read this book.
- To achieve anything, there has to be an element of risk.
- We are constantly taking risks.
- Risk provides us with opportunities.
- Risk allows you to conquer your fears.
- You should always take calculated risks rather than foolish ones.
- Don't risk everything unless you know you can handle it.
- Taking risks shows confidence and helps you stand out.

Each of the opinions above draws attention to the differing aspects of the concept being examined. These can then lead to cognitive conflict in the minds of your students. For example, if they agree that risk is both exciting and dangerous, this might lead to cognitive conflict if they are then asked to decide if risk is a good thing or a bad thing.

Here are some of the ways your students might think through these opinions:

1. Group the opinions into agree, disagree and not sure (notice the three options emphasize the complexity of concepts).

2. Use an Opinion Line to represent the degree of agreement. An Opinion Line would have "agree strongly" at one end and "disagree strongly" at the other. Your students should then place each opinion at an appropriate part of the line to illustrate how much they agree or disagree. More detailed instructions and lots of examples of Opinion Lines can be found in *Challenging Learning Through Dialogue* (Nottingham, Nottingham & Renton, 2017).

3. Opinion Corners offer four alternatives for agreement: agree, strongly agree, disagree and strongly disagree. Again, you can find out more about these in *Challenging Learning Through Dialogue* (Nottingham et al., 2017).

4. Your students could group the opinions into different categories. For example, common and unusual opinions; fact and opinion; what adults believe and what children believe; always true, sometimes true and never true. It is probably best not to give these categories to your students but instead ask them to come up with their own.

5. Give each group of students three opinions (or ask them to come up with three different opinions themselves). Then ask them to identify the reasons why each one might be the odd one out.

6. Use a 3x3 strategy in which your students select the three opinions they agree with the most, the three they disagree with the most and the three they are most ambivalent about. This can lead to discussion about why they have chosen those particular ones, which in turn can cause some of them to go into the pit.

7. Use any of the above strategies in a physical sense by asking your students to move to different parts of the room to identify their position on the matter. For example, Opinion Corners could be ascribed to the actual corners of the room rather than just drawn onto paper.

> There are many pit tools available to help LC participants think through concepts. As well as the ones listed here, there are others shown in Section 6.3.

5.6.5 • Variations of Condition

This technique involves "if" questions. For example:

Is a rule still a rule if . . .

- It's not written anywhere?
- No one enforces it?
- No one follows it?
- It's no longer possible to follow?
- It's not possible to break?
- Everyone always follows it?
- No one knows about it?
- No one remembers it anymore?
- It has many exceptions?
- There's no reason behind it?
- You can't help but break it?

> Asking "If this, then that" questions can help identify the effects of a concept.

- It doesn't help to keep the peace?

- It wasn't decided democratically?

- No one agrees with it?

Is a risk still a risk if . . .

- You know what will happen?

- No one takes it?

- No one knows about it?

- Everyone always does it?

- It does not hurt anybody?

- It is possible to be certain about the outcome?

- Someone takes it for you?

- Most people think it is safe?

- It is easy?

- Insurance companies do not class it is a risk?

- You have to do it?

- It is against the law not to do it?

- It is not dangerous?

- It is a pleasant experience?

When thinking about friendship, what if . . .

- There was no such thing as friendship?

- It was against the law to be friends with the opposite sex?

- You had too many friends?

- There was a limit to the number of friends you were allowed?

- You were allowed to be friends only with people you'd known for five or more years?

- Your parents got to choose whom you were friends with?

- The government paid you for every foreigner you were friends with?

- The government prevented you from making friends with foreigners?

- A limit was set on social media about the number of friends you were allowed online?

- There was a written test both parties had to pass before they could declare themselves to be friends with each other?

- You could spend time with your friends only online?

- Most of the time your friend wasn't very nice?

- There was no such thing as imaginary friends?

- You could only be friends with people?

- You could never really tell if someone was being friendly or not?

- You could build the perfect friend?

- You had to sign a legally binding agreement before you could be friends with someone?

5.7 • CREATING COGNITIVE CONFLICT WITH QUESTIONS

All of the techniques for creating cognitive conflict that have been covered so far have involved questioning. So it might seem strange to add a separate section all about questions. However, this section covers two additional approaches that seem to stand apart:

1. Prepared Questions
2. Socratic Questions

5.7.1 • Prepared Questions

It is always a good idea to have a set of prepared questions for Learning Challenge lessons, particularly if you are new to this approach. Indeed, if you look at all the lesson ideas in *Challenging Learning* (Nottingham, 2016) as well as in Chapter 10 of this book, you will notice all of them come with prepared questions to help extend and deepen the inquiry.

Here are some other examples:

> Coming up with prepared questions before an LC session can provide reassurance for facilitator and participants.

Bullying

- If I hit someone, am I a bully (even if I hit them during a game of football)?
- If someone makes me feel bad, are they bullying me (even if they tell me my cat has died)?
- Is it always wrong to bully someone? (What about bullying them into giving to charity?)
- Can someone bully you without being a bully?
- Is everybody a bully to somebody?
- Is it possible to get someone to do something that they don't want to do without bullying them?
- Is bullying the same as making fun of someone?
- Is it possible to bully someone by not doing anything?
- If three people confront another person—one hits them, another makes fun of them and the other one just watches—how many of them are bullies?
- What is the difference between a bully demanding money from someone and a tax collector demanding money from someone?
- Can someone bully you if you have never seen them?
- Is it still bullying if it doesn't bother you?
- Is it still bullying if you don't realize you are being bullied?

Dreams

- Is dreaming the same as thinking?
- Do you have to be asleep to dream?
- Is it good to dream?
- Do dreams have a beginning, middle and end?

- Do you think unborn babies dream?

- Can you make yourself dream?

- Are dreams a reflection of reality or are they entirely fictitious?

- Is there a difference between thinking while you're asleep and dreaming?

- People often use aspirations, dreams and wishes interchangeably. Are they the same? If not, what are the main differences?

- What do you think Lewis Carroll (the author of *Alice in Wonderland*) meant when he entitled a poem "Life Is but a Dream"?

- The philosopher Descartes (1596–1650) was convinced there are no definite signs to help us determine for certain whether we are dreaming or awake. Was he right?

- If dreams feel real, how do we actually know when we are awake and when we are dreaming?

- Is a dream still a dream if you don't remember it?

- Does our mind plan our dreams?

- Who has control over our dreams?

- How can we recognize we are dreaming before we wake up?

- How do blind people dream?

- Are dreams the same as aspirations?

Friends (Agreeing With Friends)

- Should we always agree with our friends?

- If we disagree with our friends, should we tell them we disagree?

- Are there times you have disagreed with a friend but not told them that you disagree?

- Are there times when we shouldn't tell our friends we disagree with them?

- Are there times when it is essential that we should tell our friends when we disagree with them?

- If you expressed your disagreement with a friend and he told you he would no longer be your friend, then was he a friend in the first place?

- How much would friends have to disagree with each other to stop them from being friends?

- Is it easier to agree to disagree with a friend or with a stranger?

- Do disagreements with your friends affect you more than disagreements with other people?

- Can you disagree fundamentally with a friend and still be friends with them?

Mind

- Is your mind inside, outside or the same as your brain?

- Do all your thoughts take place in your mind?

- When you talk to yourself, is that you talking or your mind talking?

- What does mind mean in "mind your own business," "I have a lot on my mind," and "don't mind me"?

- What is the difference between your mind and your brain?

- What is the difference between brainwashing and mind control?

- Are thoughts stored in your mind or created by your mind? Or both? Or neither?

- Does your mind feel as well as think?

- What is the difference between your mind and your wits?

- Is it really possible to mind read?

- Is your mind different from your body?

You

- What makes you you?

- If you looked different, would you still be you?

- If you forgot everything you know, would you still be you?

- Is there just one of you?

- Can you be sure that you are you?

- Do you know yourself better than other people know you?

- Which are you: the person you were, the person you are or the person you will be?

- Which part of you has remained constant throughout your life?

- If you read a so-called life-changing book, do you think you'd become a different you?

- If you had different beliefs or opinions, would you be a different you?

- When you say "I" do you mean your body? Or your mind? Or both?

- How you do you know that you are the same person as you were yesterday?

5.7.2 • Socratic Questions

Socratic questions come from the techniques reputedly used by the ancient Greek philosopher Socrates (469–399 BCE), who asked searching questions about such essential concepts as courage, beauty and a good life.

These questions are very useful for creating cognitive conflict as well as for helping your students climb out of the pit (see Chapter 6). I strongly recommend that you display these examples on your classroom walls or on cards that you and your students can readily refer to. This will make it much more likely that the questioning techniques will become part of everyday practice.

I have organized them into categories around a mnemonic, CRAVE Questions, to help you and your students refer to them more easily:

Clarification

Reasons

Assumptions

Viewpoints

Effects

Questions (about questions)

Socratic questioning techniques encourage people to clarify, give reasons, check assumptions, consider different viewpoints, think about effect and ask metacognitive questions.

C—Clarification

Questions that encourage clarity and depth

- Why are you saying that?
- What exactly does this mean?
- How does this relate to what we have been talking about?
- What do we already know about this?
- Can you give me an example?
- Are you saying . . . or . . . ?
- Can you rephrase that, please?

R—Reasons

Questions that check whether reasons support conclusions

- Can you give me an example of that?
- Are these reasons good enough?
- How might it be refuted?
- How can I be sure of what you are saying?
- Why is . . . happening?
- What evidence is there to support what you are saying?
- On what authority are you basing your argument?

A—Assumptions

Questions that check presuppositions and unquestioned beliefs

- What are you taking for granted?
- Are you assuming that . . . ?
- Please explain why/how . . . ?
- How can you verify or disprove that assumption?
- What would happen if . . . ?
- Do you agree or disagree with . . . ?
- Aren't you thinking that . . . ?

V—Viewpoints

Questions that seek interpretations of a situation

- What alternative ways of looking at this are there?
- Why is . . . necessary?
- Who benefits from this?
- Why is it better than . . . ?
- What are the strengths and weaknesses of . . . ?

- How are . . . and . . . similar?
- How could you look at this in another way?

E—Effects

Questions designed to reveal consequences and implications

- What would happen then?
- Doesn't it follow that . . . ?
- What are the consequences of that assumption?
- How does . . . affect . . . ?
- How does . . . fit with what we learned before?
- Are you suggesting that . . . ?
- What is the best . . . ? Why?

Questions

Questions about questions (metacognition)

- How effective was your question?
- Which of your questions turned out to be the most useful?
- What was the point of asking that question?
- Why do you think I asked this question?
- What does that mean?
- Can you improve any of your/my questions?
- What would you do to improve your questions in the future?

5.8 • REVIEW

In addition to the main points identified in the preview, this chapter has covered the following:

1. Wobblers are among the best ways to create cognitive conflict in dialogue.

2. The most useful wobblers are "If A = B" and "Not A."

3. Comparing two or more concepts together can often lead to cognitive conflict. The technique is not as reliant on dialogue as other approaches, so it might be more useful for beginners or more hesitant students.

4. Considering how concepts vary according to context is another productive way to create cognitive conflict. Variations include meaning, circumstance, type, opinion and condition.

5. Socratic questions are very useful for creating cognitive conflict as well as for helping your students climb out of the pit.

> "No one can teach, if by teaching we mean the transmission of knowledge in any mechanical fashion from one person to another. The most that can be done is that one person who is more knowledgeable than another can, by asking a series of questions, stimulate the other to think and so cause him to learn for himself."
>
> (Socrates, 469–399 BCE)

CONSTRUCT MEANING

6.0 • PREVIEW

This chapter focuses on how you can help your students construct meaning and climb out of the pit.

The most important points in the chapter include:

1. The purpose of Stage 3 of the Learning Challenge is for your students to emerge from the pit with a more sophisticated comprehension of the concept than they started with.

2. Dialogue is at the heart of the Learning Challenge and is particularly relevant to the Construct phase. This dialogue might be internal dialogue (also known as thinking), but it will be dialogue nonetheless.

3. The pit tools in Section 6.3 all provide an opportunity for your students to sort through and organize their ideas so that they can climb out of the pit.

4. The purpose of climbing out of the pit is not necessarily about reaching *the* answer because, depending on context, there might be many possible answers. Instead, it is about your students creating a more complex and thorough understanding of the concept.

6.1 • CONSTRUCTING MEANING

This stage of the Learning Challenge (LC) is about constructing meaning to climb out of the pit. Whereas being in the pit represents a state of cognitive conflict, climbing out of the pit is about connecting and explaining ideas so that a new sense of clarity is generated. Sometimes this happens in an impromptu manner, but often it needs to be constructed through the application of one or more of the pit tools described in this chapter.

Even if a question is patently open-ended and philosophical, with no agreed answer, your students might still feel frustrated if they do not arrive at an answer. In school, and often at home, many students are led to believe that learning is about finding the right answer to every question. Yet there are many questions that do not have one agreed right answer. For example: What is the best work-life balance? What can we do about climate change? What is the right thing to say to someone who is grieving? Why do seemingly good people commit atrocities?

> Constructing meaning helps LC participants climb out of the pit.

This chapter, then, is about helping your students create *an* answer for themselves even if *the* answer does not exist or can only ever be answered on a personal level maybe months or years later.

Before I share some of the best tools for building an answer, I do not want to overlook the impromptu light bulb moments. When these occur, they are a joy to behold. A lovely example occurred during the dialogue described in Section 5.4 in which some seven-year-olds and I were discussing the meaning of odd numbers. To a child, every single one of them thought an odd number could *not* be divided into two, and yet five cakes or $7 *could* be. Even at the age of seven, those children knew these two thoughts were contradictory. As the dialogue progressed and the children felt themselves getting more and more confused, some of them even started to appeal for clemency. Until one little fella, Darren, who according to his regular teacher wouldn't typically talk in math lessons other than to ask for help, shouted out, "I've got it. It's like odd socks, isn't it?"

I asked him to explain further, to which he replied, "My grandmother reckons that no matter how many socks she puts in the washing machine, she always gets an odd number out."

"What do you mean?" I asked.

"She takes them out, dries them and lays them out on the kitchen table. Then she takes one, puts it together with another and folds them. She does this until always at the end, there's one left over. Odd numbers are like that, aren't they?"

In response to this, Mary piped up, "Yeah, and you wouldn't want to cut your grandmother's socks, would you? You *could* but you wouldn't want to! So odd numbers are like socks— you *can* divide them but it becomes all very messy and nobody wants that!"

It was at this point that three children who had recently arrived from Poland had their *aha* moment. Up to that point, they had been a little lost with what was going on mainly because of the speed of conversation. But when they heard Darren describe his grandmother's odd socks and Mary add her definition, they immediately knew what was going on. They could relate to the analogy. This was made all the more meaningful because it had come from their peers. If the explanation had come from a teacher, it would have been another in a long line of adult-led descriptions. But in this instance, one of their peers had come up with the depiction, and it felt eminently more accessible to them.

This anecdote nicely describes some of the key features of Stage 3 of the Learning Challenge:

1. The Learning Challenge begins when your students have a basic idea about a concept. They then go into the pit as they identify contradictions and inconsistencies. Eventually they come out of the pit with a more sophisticated comprehension of the concept.

2. The sense of cognitive conflict your students feel in the pit creates a greater appetite for uncovering better answers and makes them more determined to persevere until they climb out of the pit.

3. The interaction between your students during the Learning Challenge is an important rehearsal of real-life social constructivism (a term used to describe how meaning and ideas are created by society).

4. As Joseph Joubert (1883) remarked, to teach is to learn twice. Throughout the Learning Challenge and particularly at Stage 3, your students will be explaining to and teaching each other and therefore learning more from the experience.

5. When a sense of clarity is reached spontaneously, your students will feel a sense of eureka. This in itself makes the whole endeavor feel so much more worthwhile (see Section 6.5).

> As some participants construct meaning, they should support others to climb out of the pit as well.

6.2 • USING DIALOGUE TO CONSTRUCT MEANING

Dialogue is at the heart of the Learning Challenge and is particularly relevant to the Construct phase. This dialogue might be internal dialogue (also known as thinking), but it will be dialogue nonetheless.

In the most basic sense, dialogue is the to and fro of talk between people who want to be understood. It is not mere conversation. Whereas a conversation might go nowhere (or indeed anywhere), a dialogue properly defined and conducted always goes somewhere (for example, answering a key question identified at the start of the Learning Challenge).

Furthermore, dialogue isn't just *between* people; it also takes place *within* people in that thinking is rather like an inner dialogue. At least some forms of thinking are. Perhaps not the subconscious, automatic type of thinking, but certainly the reflective, ponderous form of thinking can be said to be an internal dialogue. This makes dialogue all the more important. If the patterns of talk established in communication with others influence our patterns of internal dialogue, then dialogue leads to thinking itself.

> Exploratory dialogue is one of the best ways to construct meaning and so climb out of the pit together.

Dialogue is not the initiate-response-evaluate (IRE) model of questioning that is used in many classrooms. IRE is a teacher-led, three-part sequence that begins with the teacher asking a student a question or introducing a topic for the purpose of finding out whether the student knows an answer. Though this style of questioning does have some place in education, it tends not to be very productive in terms of the higher-order thinking that the Learning Challenge seeks to promote.

Dialogue is not debate either. Though many people use the term *debate* when talking about dialogue, they are not one and the same thing. The main purpose of debate is to win the battle and persuade others to agree with a particular view. This means that students may not listen properly to opposing points of view and instead just present their own perspective. There might also be less value placed on co-constructing new understanding or preparing counterargument, and more emphasis on preparing winning statements or assertions. In this sense, debate does not fit into the Learning Challenge culture.

What dialogue is—at least the dialogue that forms the basis for the Learning Challenge—is conversation *and* inquiry. Dialogue combines the sociability of conversation with the skills of framing questions and constructing answers.

Dialogue is about working collaboratively to understand what has not yet been understood and to form reasoned judgments and inferences. The IRE structure is compatible with dialogue, but it is not the same as dialogue. Dialogue can take participants further. It can help students become capable thinkers, willing and able to learn, reason and express themselves clearly and confidently. At its best, dialogue also fosters encouragement, engagement, understanding and exploration.

Dialogue is a supremely flexible and stimulating instrument of thought. As children get older, the issues they need to understand, the judgments they need to make and the relationships they need to maintain become more complex. The turn-taking structure of dialogue that leads a child to learn the rudiments of language also serves as a means of thinking about complex issues. Thus dialogue is holistic in its intentions and its outcomes.

> High-quality dialogue involves participants thinking together to form reasoned decisions.

Characteristics of Learning Challenge Dialogue

1. **Challenges ideas, reasons and assumptions**
2. **Makes participants "wobble"**
3. **Is based on exploratory talk that is characterized by longer exchanges, use of questions, reflection, explanation and speculation**
4. **Doesn't always result in the answer but maintains a focus on the principal question or concept**
5. **Follows the maxim "Not all of our questions answered, but all of our answers questioned."**

Dialogue strategies include the following:

Productive

Generating ideas, generating alternative ideas, listing

Collaborative

Listening, taking turns, suspending judgment, establishing and applying dialogue rules

Creating Meaning

Questioning, classifying, comparing, ranking, connecting, clarifying, exemplifying, offering analogies, interpreting, summarizing, defining, elaborating

Argumentative*

Agreeing, disagreeing, making an argument, questioning assumptions, assessing evidence

* Argument seen as the pursuit of truth rather than simply arguing as children might argue over a toy

Speculative

Hypothesizing, predicting, imagining, offering thought experiments

Reasoning

In addition to these five aspects of dialogue is the strategy of reasoning. If students are to think for themselves, then the language of reasoning should be developed deliberately and regularly in dialogue (as well as in writing).

Key terms of reasoning include the following:

Degree

The relative extent, intensity or amount of a quality, attribute or action

> All/some/none
>
> Always/sometimes/never
>
> More/less important
>
> Better/worse
>
> Impossible/possible/probable/likely/certain
>
> Only if

Discourse

The process of reasoning within a dialogue or writing

> Question/answer
>
> Statement/proposition/opinion
>
> Hypothesis/premise/argument
>
> Assumption/presupposition
>
> If . . . then
>
> Unless
>
> Agree/disagree
>
> Reason/grounds
>
> Principle/maxim
>
> Evidence
>
> Conclusion
>
> Consequence

Kind

A classification distinguished by common essential characteristics

> Quality/attribute
>
> Criterion
>
> All/some/none

The more that people are able to reason, the more reasonable they are likely to become. This list shows some of the best ways to reason.

Is/isn't

If . . . then

Group/class

Is/are

Part/whole

Example

Alternative

Addition

Relation

- -

The existence or effect of a connection or contrast between things

Cause/effect/consequence

Before/after/at the same time

Same/similar/different/opposite

Certain/possible/probable/impossible

Important/significant

Best/worst

If . . . then

Part/whole

Means/end/purpose

Connection/relation

All of these strategies should help your students build on the ideas of others rather than simply exchange ideas. And each of the moves shown under the subheadings can help your students understand, explore and make judgments within Learning Challenge dialogues. They will also be particularly effective at helping your students climb out of the pit and reach eureka moments together.

When used in conjunction with the pit tools shown in the next section, these strategies will be even more effective.

6.3 • TOP TEN PIT TOOLS

- -

Pit tools are so called because they help LC participants get into—and then out of—the learning pit.

This section presents the top ten tools for constructing meaning. Each of them provides an opportunity for your students to sort through and organize their ideas so that they can climb out of the pit. So long as you maintain a focus on active, meaningful, challenging, collaborative and reflective interactions, then your students should be able to use these tools to form reasoned judgments and inferences. Collectively, they are often referred to as pit tools or scaffolders.

Bear in mind that the purpose is not about reaching *the* right answer; rather, it is about your students creating a more complex and thorough understanding of the concept for themselves. Do not hesitate to guide and assist, but steer clear of giving them the solution.

6.3.1 • Concept Targets

- -

Your students can use a Concept Target to clarify the criteria and characteristics of a concept.

As your students identify contradictions and examine some of the nuances of a concept, they will find they have a lot of ideas buzzing around in the same space. To help them evaluate the quality of each idea, you could encourage them to use a Concept Target.

To use a Concept Target, your students should draw an inner circle and an outer circle, as shown in Figure 21. In the inner circle they should write the key concept they have been thinking about. In the outer circle, they should write all the ideas that have come out of the Learning Challenge dialogue so far.

▶ **Figure 21: Concept Targets: The Setup**

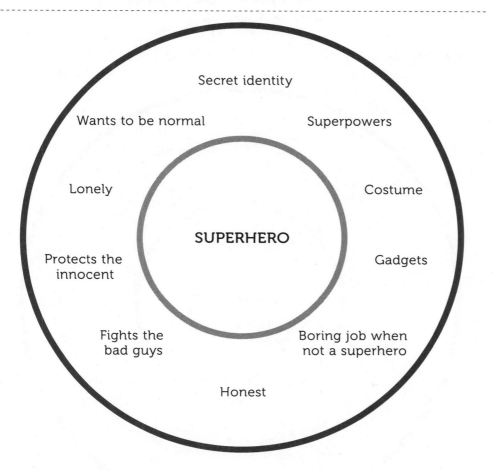

Then they should take each idea in turn and decide whether it is a necessary characteristic (in which case they should move it to the inner circle), a probable characteristic (in which case they should leave it in the outer circle) or a very rare characteristic (in which case they should move it outside of the outer circle).

Your students might like to use relative positions to describe the degree to which each particular idea is a characteristic of the concept. An example of this is shown in Figure 22.

Once your students are satisfied that they have accurately placed their ideas, they can then use the Concept Target to describe the concept. For example, if one group has placed their ideas as shown in Figure 22, then their description might read as follows.

> Concept Target tasks begin when your students place all the characteristics of a concept in the outer circle.

To use a Concept Target, LC participants should move the most important characteristics of a concept to the center and the less essential ones to the edges. The farther a characteristic is from the center, the less crucial it is thought to be.

A superhero possesses superpowers that ordinary human beings don't have. They use these to fight the bad guys and to protect the innocent. Very often they wear costumes and are lonely (because no one really understands what it is like to be them). A lot of them keep their real identity secret; some of them use gadgets and have boring jobs when not being a superhero. Very few of them (maybe even none of them) are honest because they keep secrets.

Another way to use a Concept Target is for one group to describe their answer to everyone else. Meanwhile, your other students could place the same descriptions onto a blank Concept Target. If the first group's portrayal is clear enough, then everyone else should be able to replicate relatively accurately the positioning of the ideas. If not, then their Concept Targets will look very different indeed. This can be a nice reminder to your students that accuracy of language is very important for understanding.

▶ **Figure 22: Concept Targets: The Next Step**

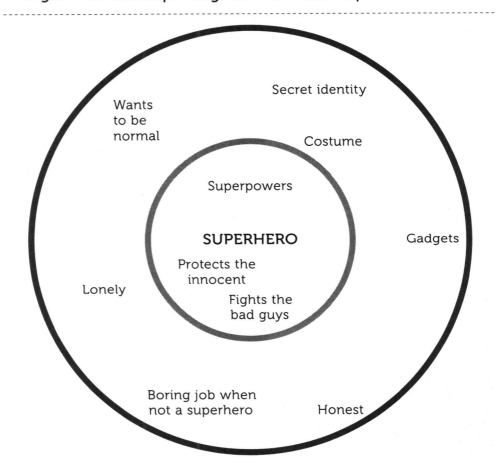

6.3.2 • Interchange

The Interchange strategy is a nice one for helping your students identify the interchangeable way in which many concepts can be used and decide which is the most applicable to their Learning Challenge experience.

Ask your students to think back over the Learning Challenge experience so far and to list the different ways in which they have used the central concept. For example, if the focus has been on the concept of growth, then they might have considered the following meanings:

1. Get bigger
2. Get older
3. Maturing
4. Develop
5. Cultivate
6. Expand
7. Lengthen
8. Deepen
9. Germinate
10. Progress

Once they have listed the many variations, ask your students to think of a sentence that each meaning could be used in. For example:

1. Fertilizer helps plants to grow. (get bigger)
2. We're all growing all the time. (getting older)
3. She was growing up too fast. (maturing)
4. He's grown as a football player. (developed)
5. If you cut rose heads off, it helps them grow. (cultivate)
6. When I eat too much chocolate, my waistline grows. (expands)
7. Pinocchio's nose grew when he told lies. (lengthened)
8. Their understanding of literature grew over the summer. (deepened)
9. Plants grow from seeds. (germinate)
10. I am growing as an artist. (progressing)

Now ask them to consider how many of the terms could be interchanged without changing the meaning. For example:

Original: Fertilizer helps plants to grow. (get bigger)

In this situation, *grow* could be interchanged with these terms:

Get bigger

Mature

Develop

Cultivate

Germinate

In this situation, *grow* could not be interchanged with these terms:

Get older

Expand

Lengthen (or maybe it could?)

Deepen

Progress

The Interchange pit tool encourages LC participants to consider which synonyms can replace the central concept and which ones can't.

Original: We're all growing all the time. (get older)

In this situation, *growing* could be interchanged with these terms:

Maturing

Developing

Progressing

In this situation, *growing* could not be interchanged with these terms:

Getting bigger (although this is true for children)

Cultivating

Expanding

Lengthening

Deepening

Germinating

By analyzing the ways in which the different meanings can and cannot be interchanged, your students should be able to create a clearer picture in their minds about the interpretation of the concept they are thinking about. This is turn should help them answer the principal question more lucidly and so climb out of the pit.

6.3.3 • Ranking

A commonly used and easily understood way for your students to sort through the many ideas they have come up with during the wobble phase is to rank those ideas. This can be done in a linear rank, diamond rank, pyramid rank or any such shape that will prompt your students to analyze the relative value of each answer.

Please note that some students will simply rank characteristics in alphabetical order, particularly when they find the idea of ranking too challenging. If your students do this, then gently remind them that the task is not to sort but to rank and that alphabetical order is not a rank. If alphabetical order was indeed a rank, then words beginning with *a* would be seen as more valuable than words beginning with *b, c* or *d*!

Diamond Ranking

The diamond ranking strategy encourages active participation. It will help your students prioritize information, clarify their thoughts and create reasons and reflections.

Ask your students to list the ideas they have generated so far in the Learning Challenge episode. These should be in relation to the key concept they have been thinking about thus far. Make sure they write each idea onto a separate piece of paper. Generally speaking, there would be nine slips of paper for a diamond rank, although for some groups it might be more appropriate to go for just four slips.

Now ask your students to place the idea they think is most important at the top. The next two most important should be placed underneath the first one but next to each other to show they are thought of as second equal. After that, there are three third equals, two fourth equals and then the single least important one at the bottom, as shown in Figure 23.

Ranking is a very useful pit tool for thinking about degrees of significance.

► **Figure 23: Diamond Ranking**

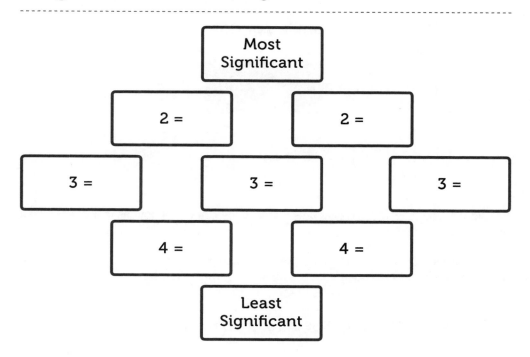

Below are the ideas that a group of students thinking about the concept of community came up with. The students initially worked in pairs to generate four characteristics each. They ranked these in a mini-diamond with one at the top, two in the middle and one at the bottom. After that, each pair teamed up with another pair, combined their eight characteristics together, came up with a ninth and then ranked them according to the scheme shown in Figure 22.

Here are some of the characteristics of community that they came up with:

Are fair

Develop friendships

Share beliefs

Celebrate diversity

Understand issues

Work hard to improve the whole community

Are reasonable

Are willing to compromise

Do not discriminate

Are clear about aims

Have shared thoughts

Cooperate with each other

Pyramid Ranking

Pyramid ranking is similar to diamond ranking except that it is in the shape of a pyramid or triangle. This allows different numbers of factors to be ranked compared to diamond ranking. Figures 24 and 25 show examples.

Which color makes you most calm, most cheerful, most agitated and so on?

▶ Figure 24: **Pyramid Ranking of Color Moods**

For older students, you could of course increase the number of options to six, ten, fifteen and so on.

In this example, the students listed the ideas that had come out of the Learning Challenge dialogue so far and then agreed on the ranking shown in Figure 25.

▶ Figure 25: **Pyramid Ranking of Happiness**

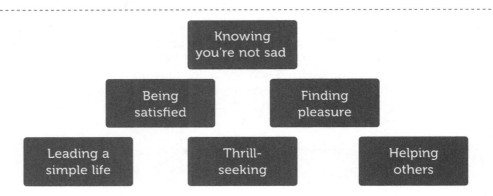

Having ranked their ideas, this particular group of students went on to describe happiness as follows:

> Happiness is valuing the opposite of what we know it feels like to be unhappy. We know it is normal to feel pain if we are hurt and feel sad when something bad happens, and it is only these experiences that make us value their absence when everything is OK. Happiness is also finding what gives us pleasure and knowing what to avoid so that we don't feel pain and suffering. As well as this, happiness comes from satisfying desires; this could be individual desires or life as a whole. Any other contributions to the idea of "What is happiness?" are too specific and are only meaningful when considering individuals.

Linear Ranking

A linear rank often leads to more deliberation than the other two styles of ranking because there are no equal spots. Instead, each characteristic should be given a position that is different from any other. As with all the other ranks, though, this position can be decided based on importance, relevance, significance or any other agreed quality.

▶ Figure 26: Linear Rank

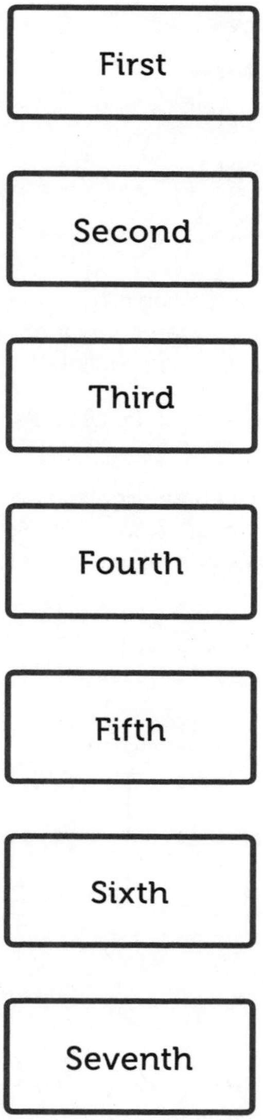

First

Second

Third

Fourth

Fifth

Sixth

Seventh

Example concept: Love

Words for your students to rank according to the structure shown in Figure 26:

Affection

Devotion

Admiration

Close

Considerate

Sympathetic

Drawn toward

Attraction

Passionate

Your students could create their own criteria to rank these qualities, or you could suggest one of the following:

Most important features of love

How to show you love your family

How to show you love your pets

How to show you love a hobby

6.3.4 • Opinion Lines

Opinion Lines are very useful for beginning to explore statements using examples, gauging degrees of agreement and disagreement or identifying degrees of preference. The best way to set up an Opinion Line is as follows:

1. Create a line long enough for all your students to stand along. It might help to mark this with a rope or some string.

2. Mark one end with a "Completely Agree" sign and the other with a "Completely Disagree" sign. Talk through the other descriptors shown in Figure 27 if you think it will help your students understand the degrees of agreement and disagreement:

▶ **Figure 27: Opinion Line Diagram**

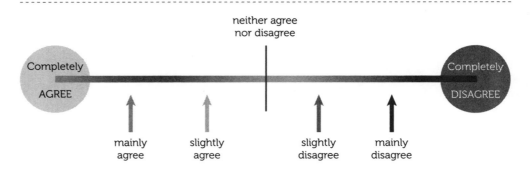

3. Formulate a statement that expresses a point of view relating to the central concept or key question in the Learning Challenge. Make it bold and contentious so that it increases the likelihood of everyone having an opinion. For example:

    •   Friends should never keep secrets from each other.

    •   There is no way of knowing for sure whether life is real or not.

    •   There is no difference between sports and war.

    •   People who do not listen are disrespectful.

    •   Fairness is impossible.

    •   There is no such thing as pure or original; everything is an adaptation of something else.

    •   Heroes do not exist.

    •   The world would be better without nations.

    •   The world would be better without religions.

    •   The world would be better without people.

    •   Truth and lies are simply matters of opinion.

    •   Telling lies is worse than stealing.

- Dreaming is just thinking with your eyes closed.

- Culture is the same as team.

- It is possible to get through a day without taking a single risk.

- Today you are a different you than the one you were yesterday.

- Our brain and our mind are the same thing.

- Everybody is growing all the time.

- If you choose not to eat meat for moral reasons, then you should become a vegan rather than a vegetarian.

- Some people are born talented.

- "Something" has always existed.

- Colors are in the mind not in the object.

- Ideas exist in our minds even before we are born.

- Pain can never be compared between people.

This list shows example opinions for students to respond to by standing at their chosen place on an opinion line.

4. Explain to your students that you are going to give them a contentious statement to think about. Say they will have time to think about it first and that then you will ask them to stand on the part of the line that corresponds with how much they agree or disagree with the statement. Give them the statement.

5. Once your students have taken a place on the line, get them to talk with the people around them to compare their reasons for standing where they are. The following prompts should help them to ensure their conversation is more exploratory than cumulative (for more information, see Sections 2.6.1 and 2.6.3 in *Challenging Learning Through Dialogue* [Nottingham, Nottingham & Renton, 2017]):

- What do you think?

- What are your reasons?

- I agree with you because . . .

- I disagree with you because . . .

- Is there another way of looking at this?

- What if . . . ?

- Have we considered all the factors?

- What have we agreed?

Incidentally, there are a number of others ways to use Opinion Lines in *Challenging Learning Through Dialogue* (Nottingham, Nottingham & Renton, 2017).

6.3.5 • Opinion Corners

Opinion Corners have a structure similar to Opinion Lines and so can be introduced in a similar way. The main difference is that using the corners will prevent your students from sitting on the fence because corners require them to choose from one of four descriptors: strongly agree, agree, disagree, strongly disagree. Set up Opinion Corners as shown in Figure 28.

Opinion Corners are better than opinion lines for polarizing views if the LC dialogue is in need of a bit more zest.

After you read a statement (examples follow), your students should stand in the corner that best represents their opinion on the matter. Tell them they have to choose one of the corners. They cannot stand somewhere in the middle. They must make a decision as to the one that is the best description of their opinion. They are allowed to move if they change their minds, but even then they should move from one corner to another rather than to the middle or off to a side somewhere.

▶ Figure 28: Opinion Corners

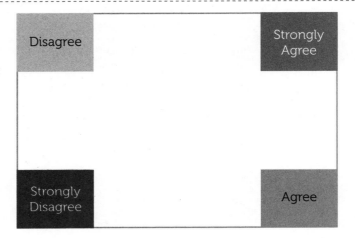

Once your students have chosen a corner, get them to talk about their choice with the people around them. After that, get a spokesperson from each corner to give a summary of the reasons why the people in their corner made the choice they did. This will give your students a chance to hear different perspectives on the issue.

Statements for Opinion Corners

Below are some statements to get you started with Opinion Corners. Of course, in practice the statements should come from the concept or question that lies at the heart of the Learning Challenge episode.

- It is wrong to steal.
- You should always support your friends.
- The truth is whatever society decides is the truth.
- Music is the same as sound.
- Bullying in school should be reported to the police.
- It is possible to do math without numbers.
- Stories and lies are the same thing.
- Everything has a shape.
- It is impossible to prove anything.
- There can never be a fair race.
- You can never truly trust your senses.
- It is right to censor things.
- People are naturally bad.
- War is never right.

6.3.6 • Concept Lines

Concept Lines also have a similar structure to Opinion Lines and so can be introduced in a similar way. The main difference is that the line now represents characteristics of a concept rather than degrees of agreement or disagreement.

Encourage your students to list all terms and ideas that they have used in connection with the central concept. Then get them to place the terms along the line, being careful to place them in order of meaning or significance. The examples in Figures 29 and 30 help to illustrate the technique.

A Concept Line invites participants to indicate the degree or extent to which each characteristic represents the concept.

▶ **Figure 29: Concept Line About Knowledge**

Concept: Knowledge

Proof   Fact   Evidence   Experience   Data   Thinking   Opinion   Belief   Guess   Ignorance

▶ **Figure 30: Concept Line About Friendliness**

Concept: Friendliness

Fanatical   Devoted   Forthcoming   Loyal   Dependable   Welcoming   Responsive   Approachable   Unsociable   Reserved   Disloyal   Distant   Hostile

6.3.7 • Concept Circles

Concept Circles usually have three circles: inner, outer and middle. The inner circle represents the concept that is central to the current Learning Challenge episode. The outer circle represents things that are not the concept. The middle circle represents the "not sure" position. Figure 31 shows this.

Concept Circles invite participants to place characteristics of the LC concept in the middle, characteristics that conflict with the concept in the outer circle and questionable characteristics in the middle circle.

Example concept: Anger

Words for your students to place in one of the three circles:

Furious	Happy	Heated	Calm	Mad	Indignant
Resentful	Loving	Satisfied	Impatient	Upset	Sorrowful
Vexed	Annoyed	Pleased	Joyful	Exasperated	Quiet
Energetic	Grumpy	Patient	Wrath	Irritated	Peaceful
Steady	Excited	Outraged	Ire	Satisfied	

Example concept: Like (as in "similar to")

Words for your students to place in one of the three circles:

Different	Other	Comparable	Identical	Same
Diverse	Various	Similar	Kindred	Unequal
Resembling	Uniform	Distinct	Equal	Akin
Parallel	Unlike	Related	Opposite	Dissimilar
Match	Peer	Alike	Strange	Opposed

Example concept: Before (in time)

Words for your students to place in one of the three circles:

Ahead of	After	Earlier	Later than	Prior to
Advance	Preceding	Same moment	Subsequent	Afterward
Finally	Then	Forward	Backward	Around
Beginning	Middle	End	Behind	In a while
Soon	Sooner	In preparation for	Finish	Result

▶ Figure 31: **Concept Circle Template**

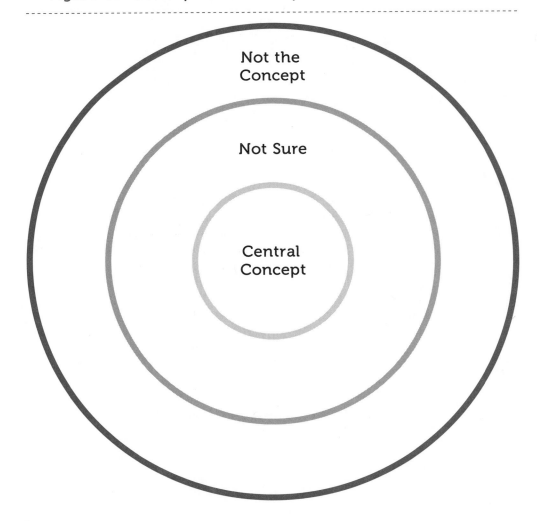

6.3.8 • Concept Tables

Concept Tables can help your students be more exact about the concept they are thinking about. Some Concept Tables can be created on the spot, whereas others will need some preparation. Either way, they can be really useful exercises to sit alongside a Learning Challenge episode. The possibilities are almost limitless, so Figures 32–39 are just a few examples:

▶ Figure 32: Concept Tables, Version A

Examples	Concept	Seems Like the Concept (but isn't)	Not the Concept	Not Sure

▶ Figure 33: Example of Version A Using the Concept *Real*

Examples	Real	Seems Real (but isn't)	Not Real	Not Sure
A rainbow				
The redness of blood				
A set of false teeth				
A plastic flower				
The smell of coffee				
A reflection in a mirror				
Your thoughts				
Cloud computing				
Praise from your teacher				
Praise from your friend				
Sunshine				
A book				
A fictional story				

▶ Figure 34: **Concept Tables, Version B**

Examples	Concept A	Concept B	Both	Neither

▶ Figure 35: **Example of Version B Using the Concepts *Exist* and *Visible***

Examples	Exist	Visible	Both	Neither
Blood cells				
Fire				
Happiness				
Thoughts				
Body smells				
Fear				
Music				
Words				
Jupiter				
Trust				
Darkness				
Salt in the sea				
Mosquitos				

Examples	Type A	Type B	Type C	Not Sure

► Figure 37: **Example of Version C Using the Concept** *Action*

Examples of *Action*	Making	Saying	Doing	Not Sure
Putting on your shoes				
Making a telephone call				
Painting				
Walking to school				
Inventing something				
Discovering something				
Opening a door				
Washing dishes				
Baking a cake				
Asking a question				
Sneezing				
Having a meal				
Talking while eating				

▶ **Figure 38: Concept Tables, Version D**

Examples	Meaning 1	Meaning 2	Meaning 3	Not Sure

▶ **Figure 39: Example of Version D Using the Concept *Just***

Examples of *Just*	Only	Fair	Exactly	Not Sure
According to the clock, it's only *just* 12 o'clock.				
I'm *just* going to make a telephone call.				
It wasn't *just* her idea; it was mine too.				
The decision was a *just* one.				
I didn't exactly fail, but I only *just* passed.				
It all went wrong, so he got his *just* deserts.				
I only *just* had enough money to buy that.				
Just give me five more minutes, please!				
I've *just* about had enough of your arguing.				
It's not *just* for me; it's also for my friend.				
Taking revenge is not a *just* thing to do.				

6.3.9 • Venn Diagrams

Venn diagrams are great visual tools for thinking. And they work with even the youngest students. In fact, one of the best lessons I've seen in a long time was in a nursery class in Thornaby-on-Tees, in the United Kingdom. The teacher asked her class of four-year-olds to sit in a circle, around which she placed fifty objects. She then showed the students a picture of a four-year-old boy and asked them each to pick one of the objects that they thought belonged to the boy and to place it in a hoop that she laid on the floor alongside the boy's picture. As they did this, she asked them to give reasons why they thought, for example, the toothbrush would belong to the boy.

Then she showed them a picture of a girl about the same age and asked them to do the same thing, only this time they were asked to place their chosen object into the hoop next to the girl's picture. The problem was, there were thirty children in the class, and they had begun with fifty objects, thirty of which were already in the boy's hoop. So she asked the ten children who didn't have an object to think of a solution to their problem. Of course, they suggested moving some of the objects from the boy's hoop into the girl's hoop, which they proceeded to do until the teacher asked the other children to challenge this if they so wished.

▶ Figure 40: Using Venn Diagrams With Young Children

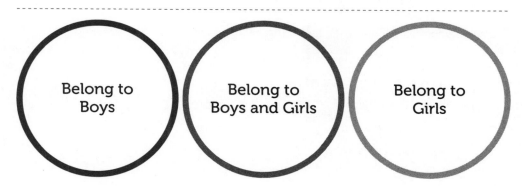

The children eventually decided that some objects could belong to boys and girls, at which point the teacher introduced a third hoop and laid it next to a picture showing a boy and a girl. The lesson finished with the children negotiating (by giving reasons, listening to each other and then making decisions) which objects should go in which hoop. Eventually, of course, all the objects ended up in the third hoop as the children realized they could all belong to boys *and* girls.

Of course, the normal way to draw a Venn diagram is as shown in Figure 41 with the overlapping circles.

▶ Figure 41: Using Venn Diagrams With Older Students

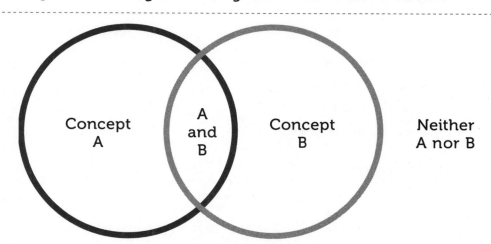

Example concepts: Mental Acts (concept A) and Verbal Acts (concept B)

Words for your students to place in the right location:

Shout	Command	Promise	Reason	Infer
Find	Say	Think	Warn	Notice
Name	Believe	Remember	Expect	Intend
Hate	Love	Suggest	Call	Deny

(Continued)

(Continued)

State	Agree	Inform	Rule	Swear
Pray	Beg	Greet	Thank	Welcome
Praise	Protest	Dare	Whisper	Sigh

Example concepts: False (concept A) and Metaphor (concept B)

Statements for your students to place in the right location:

1. My little sister is a pain in the neck.
2. Life is a box of chocolates.
3. The earth is a planet.
4. Dracula was a vampire.
5. This classroom is a zoo.
6. Life is a roller coaster.
7. Time is money.
8. The whole world is a stage.
9. My mother listened to me with a stony face.
10. Our teacher is such a dinosaur.
11. Yesterday was a complete nightmare.
12. Water flows downhill.
13. Blood was flowing like a river.
14. My best friend is a real clown.
15. He was a snake in the grass.
16. My head is spinning.
17. I'm a zombie by the end of the week.
18. His bedroom was a disaster area.
19. She cut him down with words.
20. I wandered lonely as a cloud.

Sometimes during a Learning Challenge dialogue, your students will find it useful to examine the relationship between two or more connected concepts. Venn diagrams can help with this. For example, you could ask them to decide which of the following variations best represent the relationship:

A good example of using Venn diagrams to identify the relationship between two concepts came out of a lesson with sixteen-year-olds recently. I began with a provocative statement: "Sports and war are the same thing." As predicted, the teenagers initially rejected this idea, so I suggested we use a Venn diagram to test the hypothesis. They came up with terms such as *attack, defend, bravery, rules of engagement* and *take no prisoners* and then started to place them into the diagram shown in Figure 42, option B.

As you might imagine, they struggled to think of reasons why all of these terms wouldn't go into both sports and war. Even the term *killing* went into both categories because of blood sports.

In the end, the students decided that they simply could not think of a characteristic that wouldn't fit into both categories. So I then asked them to use the diagrams shown in Figure 42, option C to decide whether all sport is war or all war is sport. Most leaned toward the first option, but some refused to agree to this, saying that simply can't be right!

▶ **Figure 42: Using Venn Diagrams to Identify the Relationship Between Two Concepts**

Venn diagrams can also be used to examine the relationship between two concepts as well as to identify the common characteristics between them, as shown by the different diagrams here.

Option A: Both concepts are distinct from each other

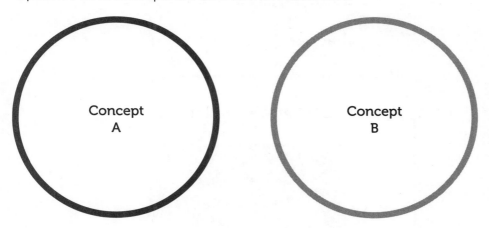

Option B: Both concepts are overlapping but not the same as each other

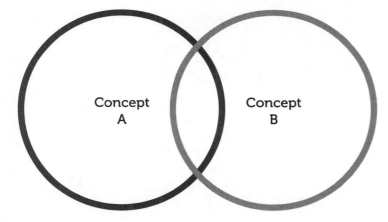

Option C: One concept is always a version of the other

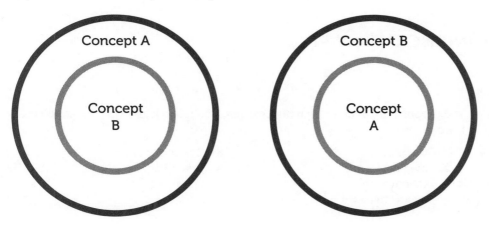

6.3.10 • Inference Squares

Inference Squares help to distinguish between what is known for certain, what can be inferred and what questions we could ask to find out more. They look like the diagram in Figure 43.

▶ Figure 43: **Inference Squares**

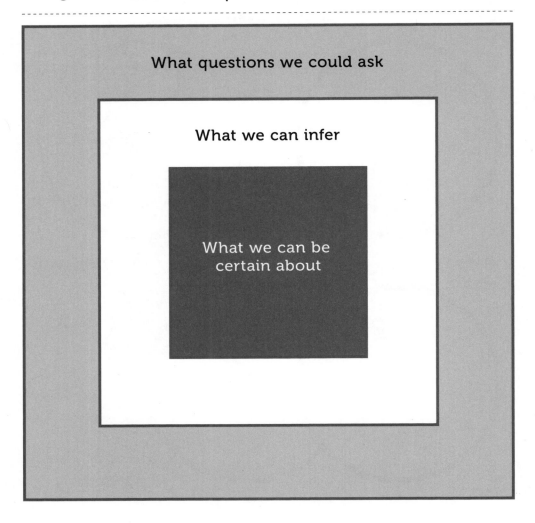

6.4 • TYPES OF THINKING IN THE PIT

The purpose of going through the Learning Challenge is to help your students become more

1. **Articulate**
2. **Imaginative**
3. **Adventurous**
4. **Critical thinkers**

5. **Communicative**
6. **Resilient**
7. **Wise**

For this to happen, your students will need to use many—maybe even all—of the thinking skills listed in Figure 44.

▶ Figure 44: **Thinking Skills to Use in the Learning Challenge**

Analyze	Anticipate	Apply	Causal link	Choose
Classify	Compare	Connect	Contrast	Decide
Define	Describe	Determine	Discuss	Elaborate
Estimate	Evaluate	Exemplify	Explain	Explore
Generalize	Give examples	Give reasons	Group	Hypothesize
Identify	Infer	Interpret	Mean	Organize
Paraphrase	Predict	Question	Rank	Represent
Respond	Sequence	Select	Simplify	Show how
Say why	Solve	Sort	Summarize	Support
Test	Verify	Visualize	What if	

The thinking skills here are the ones most commonly tested in national exams.

I created this list based on the skills of thinking that are frequently tested in national exams. Not because I am advocating that we should "teach to the test" but because some people I've met are worried that time spent on the Learning Challenge will distract from a focus on improving national test scores. My response is always the same: far from distracting from improving scores, it will actually help! The Learning Challenge teaches the very skills that will be tested. Of course, the first few questions in most exam papers require factual recall. But after that, the questions tend to look more like this (with the skills of thinking underlined in each case):

Interpret the diagram.

Estimate the effect of . . .

Give examples of . . .

Give reasons for . . .

Paraphrase what the author is saying.

Summarize the main points, giving examples.

Verify your answers by . . .

Examples of the types of thinking skills developed by the LC are underlined.

It is these questions, not the factual-recall ones, that tend to attract the greater number of points. So, far from distracting attention away from exams, the Learning Challenge can actually help your students achieve *better* results. And quite apart from that, it can help them become more thought*ful*, considered, adventurous and wise. Now, who doesn't want that?

When your students are in the pit, encourage them to use one or more of the skills listed in Figure 44 to help them connect ideas and explain their theories. For example, if your students are struggling to define a concept, then you can ask them to do one or more of the following (again, the skills of thinking are underlined).

Analyze the difference between your idea and someone else's idea.

Compare the central concept with another concept.

Decide if that is a causal link or simply a coincidence.

Group your ideas into definitely, maybe and not at all.

Elaborate on your earlier ideas.

Can someone summarize what has been said so far?

Can you sequence your ideas?

Why don't you rank your ideas according to how relevant they are?

In addition to the skills listed in Figure 44, is it worth noting that there are many other ways to think about thinking skills. To some experts, the teaching of good thinking should be concerned with developing dispositions so people become, for example, more curious, strategic, open-minded and evaluative. Other experts focus on skills such as locating relevant information, comparing, synthesizing and understanding. Benjamin Bloom (Bloom, Englehart, Furst, Hill & Krathwohl, 1956) emphasizes higher-order thinking, whereas Matthew Lipman (1988) promotes critical, creative and caring thinking.

Having studied many of these approaches, it seems to me that:

All good thinking is flexible, insightful and productive.

There is limited use for productive thinking if it is not flexible, nor for insights if they are unproductive. Thus, good thinking is a combination of all three of these characteristics.

As an aide mémoire for planning my lessons and to ensure that my students developed breadth as well as depth in their thinking, I developed a taxonomy using the acronym EDUCERE (from the Latin "to lead out"). It is, of course, the source of the English word *education*.

The EDUCERE acronym helps to identify the main categories of thinking developed during LC sessions.

Engage

Desire

Understand

Create

Explore

Reason

Evaluate

▶ **Figure 45: The EDUCERE Thinking Skills**

Engage

Paying attention, and thinking collaboratively with:

- Verbal acts such as saying, asserting, proposing, hinting, inferring, alleging and contending
- Mental acts such as focusing, committing energy and enthusiasm, and maintaining concentration
- Physical acts involving positive and interested body language

Desire

Having the inclination and desire to:

- Wonder and inquire
- Reflect upon and evaluate ideas and performances
- Take responsibility as well as calculated risks
- Work collaboratively as well as independently
- Imagine new possibilities and be open-minded
- Be resilient and tenacious
- Manage emotions and impulses
- Be thoughtful

Understand

Understanding information by:

- Locating relevant data
- Seeking clarity and precision
- Comparing and contrasting
- Sorting and classifying
- Sequencing
- Making connections
- Representing information
- Seeking deeper understandings
- Identifying misconceptions

Create

Creating new ideas by:

- Looking for alternatives and possibilities
- Generating hypotheses
- Innovating
- Assembling and formulating
- Suspending logic temporarily
- Searching for value
- Thinking flexibly
- Asking "What if?"

Explore

Exploring the current subject matter by:

- Asking relevant questions
- Defining problems
- Predicting outcomes
- Testing conclusions
- Seeking details to give depth
- Interpreting meaning

Reason

Developing reasoning by:

- Giving reasons
- Using precise language
- Inferring and deducing
- Applying logic
- Testing assumptions
- Presenting balanced arguments

Evaluate

Judging the value of something by:

- Developing criteria
- Checking accuracy
- Identifying improvements
- Testing relevance and significance
- Benchmarking
- Comparing with alternatives

6.5 • EUREKA!

Eureka is the sense of achievement LC participants feel when they climb out of the pit.

The best part about the Learning Challenge is when your students reach the eureka moment. This does not happen every single time, but when it does occur it is delightful.

Eureka moments occur when a person discovers a truth. It is when there is a sudden realization that they now understand something that they didn't understand before. It is that moment of blissful clarity. And that is what makes all the effort of going through the pit so worthwhile.

Back in June 2007, I was giving a keynote speech and mentioned the eureka moment. A woman in the audience jumped up and declared she'd just been married! Baffled, I inquired as to the relevance of such a statement. She then revealed (to the six hundred people in the auditorium) that her new husband was Greek so she'd been learning Greek and that *eureka* was Greek for "I found it."

Though bemused by the new Mrs. Papadopoulos's outburst, I was also very interested in this meaning of eureka. It does *not* mean "My teacher gave me the answer." It means, "I found it; I found my own answer to this problem and it feels great." Imagine when your students feel this sense of elation. What will they want to do with it? Share it, of course. They will talk and talk and talk about it at home and then when they return the next day. What will they want? More of the same! Compare this to the typical response students give when their parents ask them what they did at school: "nothing."

It is this sense of eureka that I think education ought to be about. We should be doing all we can to create the conditions for our students to reach an *aha* moment. Of course, this can't happen all the time—we'd be exhausted if it did! But it should happen *some* of the time and this is where the Learning Challenge comes in!

The key to eureka moments is that they come as a result of overcoming confusion. This feeling of aha will not be felt if your students reach an answer easily. If I had asked the youngsters mentioned in Section 5.4 what an odd number is and then accepted their first answer, they would not have felt any great sense of achievement. To reach their light bulb moment, they necessarily had to persevere, reflect, analyze and think. In other words, they had to go through the pit and come out the other side to have any chance of a eureka moment.

> **The eureka moment is one aspect of the Learning Challenge that makes the effort of going through the pit so worthwhile.**

6.5.1 • Eureka Teamwork

When some LC participants feel a sense of eureka, they can then be asked to support others to climb out of the pit.

Typically, it will be *some* of your students who reach the eureka moment at any given time. Very rarely will all of them have a light bulb moment at the same time. This can be turned to your advantage, though, as it allows you to pair your students up. You could say something along these lines:

> Those of you who have reached the eureka moment, please pair up with someone who is still in the pit. It is now your job to try to help your partner climb out of the pit. Show them how to construct an answer using one of the pit tools, or explain how you understand the concept now. Remember, though: your partner's task is to challenge and question you. They should try to pull you back down into the pit!

Easy answers won't last long enough. You need the most watertight answers you can construct so that you can keep using the ideas long into the future.

Having paired up students in the pit with students at the eureka point so many times, I can confidently say there is something quite captivating about the energy and purpose that come from such pairings.

> **The relationship between a student in the pit and a student at the eureka point is a balanced one: the eureka student aims to help their partner *construct*, whereas the pit student aims to help their partner *deliberate*. This is different from the usual instructor/instructed relationship that is so often a one-sided affair. It also means that the student in the pit does not feel stupid for asking so many questions; quite the opposite, in fact. That student now feels more discerning with each question asked and every challenge made.**

This in itself captures the essence of the Learning Challenge so very well. The whole endeavor is about challenge, inquiry, examining all options, connecting and explaining, collaboration, extending and relating. So it is a win-win for everyone concerned.

6.6 • REVIEW

In addition to the main points identified in the preview, this chapter has covered the following:

1. The top ten pit tools work best when supported by active, meaningful, challenging, collaborative and reflective interactions between your students.

2. Each of the pit tools can help your students form reasoned judgments and inferences.

3. Many types of thinking are developed by going through the Learning Challenge. These include interpreting, estimating, using supporting reasons, paraphrasing and summarizing, verifying and challenging.

4. The best part about the Learning Challenge is when your students reach the eureka moment. This does not happen every single time, but when it does occur it is delightful.

5. Pairing up students who have reached the eureka point with students who are still in the pit can generate a sense of focus, collaboration and inquiry.

> "Watch your thoughts, they become words;
> Watch your words, they become actions;
> Watch your actions, they become habits;
> Watch your habits, they become character;
> Watch your character, for it becomes your destiny."
>
> (Frank Outlaw, 1977)

CONSIDER YOUR LEARNING

7.0 • PREVIEW

This chapter focuses on how you can help your students review and transfer their learning journey.

The most important points in the chapter include:

1. Review: the learning journey is about using metacognition strategies.

2. Metacognition is when people think about their thinking. This can be usefully divided into cognitive awareness and cognitive regulation.

3. Cognitive awareness includes being mindful of how successful you have been in engaging, remembering, understanding and innovating.

4. Cognitive regulation includes the ability and willingness to select the appropriate strategy, monitor the effectiveness of the strategies you are using, search for the rationale for particular actions and evaluate the wisdom and accuracy of your own thinking.

7.1 • METACOGNITION

> Metacognition is when people think about their own thinking.

The final stage of each Learning Challenge episode is for your students to consider the learning journey they have been on and to look for ways to apply, adapt and transfer their learning.

In his book *Unified Theories of Cognition*, Allen Newell (1991) points out that there are two layers of problem solving: applying a strategy to the problem at hand and selecting and monitoring that strategy. Good problem solving, Newell observes, often depends as much on the selection and monitoring of a strategy as on its execution. The term *metacognition* (thinking about thinking) is commonly used to refer to selection and monitoring processes as well as to more general activities of reflecting on and directing one's own thinking.

> **Competent or successful learners can explain which strategies they used to solve a problem and why, while less competent students monitor their own thinking sporadically and ineffectively and offer incomplete explanations. (Newell, 1991, p. 312)**

The good news is that metacognitive strategies can be learned. They are not something that students either have or don't have. They can be acquired in a methodical way to begin with and then encouraged until eventually they become intellectual habits.

It is often useful to make a distinction between cognitive awareness and cognitive regulation. Figure 46 gives an overview of the differences.

Metacognition includes all of the considerations listed in Figure 46. Of course, it is unlikely that your students will have the time or energy to think about even half of these aspects every time they go through the pit. Nonetheless, they should aim to practice all types of metacognition over a series of Learning Challenge episodes.

▶ Figure 46: Types of Metacognition

Cognitive Awareness	Cognitive Regulation
An awareness of how well I am able to:	The ability and willingness to:
1. Engage Including: • Concentrating • Committing energy • Responding appropriately	1. Identify and select Including: • Locating relevant data • Hypothesizing • Benchmarking • Finding alternatives
2. Remember Including: • Factual recall • Situational recall • Procedural recall • Memory of and about people	2. Monitor Including: • Analyzing • Connecting • Predicting • Sequencing and classifying

3. Understand Including: • Its application • Its rationale • Making connections • Identifying relevance	3. Rationalize Including: • Finding reasons • Identifying motives • Challenging assumptions • Using precise language
4. Innovate Including: • Flexibility of thought • Finding alternatives • Asking "What if . . .?" • Establishing value	4. Evaluate Including aspects of: • Wisdom • Success • Application • Accuracy

7.2 • REVIEW QUESTIONS

Figure 47 neatly captures the key steps in reviewing a Learning Challenge episode. As such, it would be worth sharing with your students as they begin to review their learning.

There are, of course, many more questions that you could ask your students, as the following section shows. I am not advocating that you ask all of these! Instead, select two or three per section and then vary the questions from episode to episode.

Stage 1: Concept

Thinking about the *setting up* phase of the Learning Challenge:

1. Which concepts did you initially identify as interesting?

2. How did you choose the concept that became central to your Learning Challenge inquiry?

3. Why did you choose that one rather than one of the other concepts?

4. Now looking back, was that the best concept to go for?

5. What criteria would you use to decide what was best?

6. What questions did you create around your chosen concept?

7. On reflection, would there have been a better question to ask?

8. How did you choose the question you settled on?

9. What were some of your initial answers to your chosen question?

10. How accurate did these early answers turn out to be?

11. How confident were you with your early answers?

12. How did your thinking affect your first steps in the learning journey?

These are the sorts of metacognitive questions that could be asked to review an LC session.

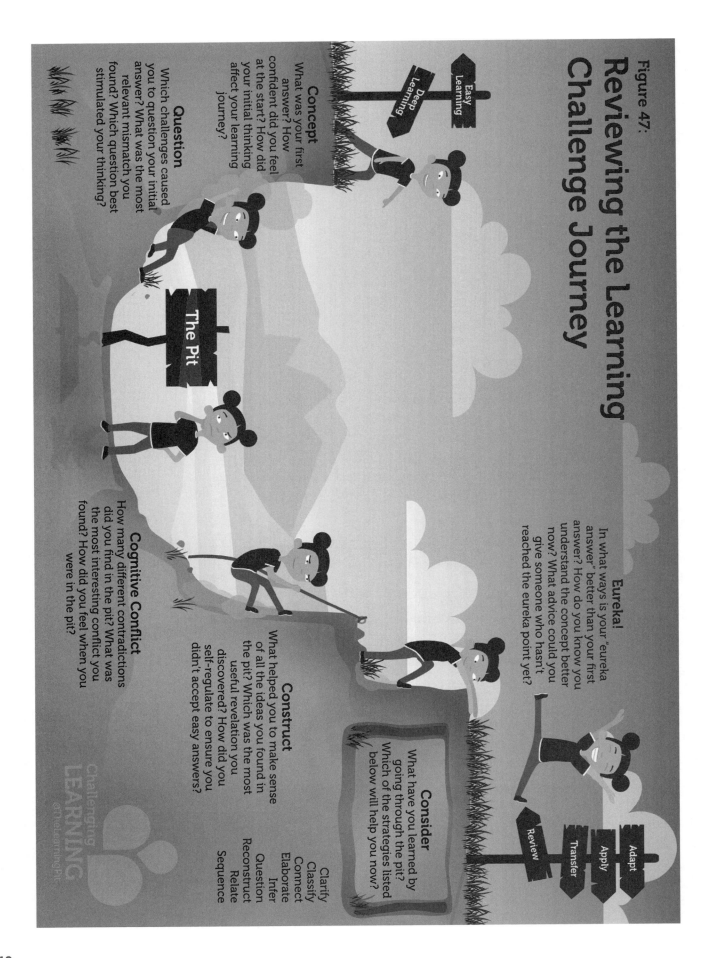

Figure 47:
Reviewing the Learning Challenge Journey

Concept
What was your first answer? How confident did you feel at the start? How did your initial thinking affect your learning journey?

Question
Which challenges caused you to question your initial answer? What was the most relevant mismatch you found? Which question best stimulated your thinking?

Cognitive Conflict
How many different contradictions did you find in the pit? What was the most interesting conflict you found? How did you feel when you were in the pit?

Construct
What helped you to make sense of all the ideas you found in the pit? Which was the most useful revelation you discovered? How did you self-regulate to ensure you didn't accept easy answers?

Consider
What have you learned by going through the pit? Which of the strategies listed below will help you now?

Clarify
Classify
Connect
Elaborate
Infer
Question
Reconstruct
Relate
Sequence

Eureka!
In what ways is your "eureka answer" better than your first answer? How do you know you understand the concept better now? What advice could you give someone who hasn't reached the eureka point yet?

The Pit

Easy Learning

Deep Learning

Review

Transfer

Apply

Adapt

Challenging LEARNING
@TheLearningPit

Stage 2: Conflict

Thinking about the *cognitive conflict* phase of the Learning Challenge:

1. What was it about the concept or the question that led to cognitive conflict?
2. Which two ideas formed the first cognitive conflict?
3. As you started to wobble, how did that make you feel?
4. How many examples of cognitive conflict did you create while you were in the pit? Can you list them?
5. Which two ideas conflicted the most and why?
6. Which ideas were dismissed easily and why?
7. Which skills of thinking did you use to analyze the conflict you felt in the pit?
8. Did you feel like giving up in the pit? If so, how did you resolve to keep going?
9. Which questions did you (or somebody else) ask that helped to wobble even more?
10. On which occasions were you most aware of the importance of precise language?
11. Which of the wobblers (see Section 5.4.1) did you use to create cognitive conflict?
12. Do you feel as if you examined *all* the options when you were in the pit?

Stage 3: Construct

Thinking about the *constructing meaning* phase of the Learning Challenge:

1. When did you start to make sense of all the conflicting ideas you had in the pit?
2. Which pit tool (see Section 6.3) did you use to help you connect and explain your ideas?
3. Which was the most useful revelation you discovered?
4. Which of the thinking skills (see Section 6.4) were most helpful in constructing your answer?
5. How sure can you be that you did not accept easy answers?
6. At any point, did you think you'd found clarity only to find another problem? If so, please explain.
7. What misunderstandings, misconceptions or assumptions did you uncover?
8. When you paired up with someone else who was already out of the pit, how did they help you?
9. Were you able to drag your pit partner back down into pit? If so, how? And how did they respond?
10. What did you do to check the accuracy of your answer?
11. If you had had time, what could you have done to improve your answer even further?
12. Do you feel satisfied with the learning journey you have been on?

Stage 4: Consider

Thinking about the *consider* phase of the Learning Challenge:

1. How did it feel to reach the eureka moment?
2. How do you know this was the eureka moment rather than merely a step on the way?
3. How did you self-regulate to help you on your learning journey?
4. In what ways do you understand the concept better now?
5. What would you do differently next time?
6. Which strategies did you use in this Learning Challenge episode that you could use in other contexts?
7. Is there a different sequence you could use next time to be more effective?
8. How could you adapt your new learning to another situation?
9. What analogy, metaphor or example could you create to explain your new learning?
10. What advice would you give others about going through a Learning Challenge?
11. What questions do you still have?
12. What is the next concept that you would like to explore?

As you will notice, the last set of questions are not just about looking back over the learning journey but also about looking forward to the next steps. That is one of the reasons I have been referring to Learning Challenge *episodes*. I do not see the Learning Challenge as a one-off event to run on special occasions. Instead, the Learning Challenge is a series of pits and peaks as your students develop and grow. Figure 48, designed by my longtime friend Mark Bollom, captures this nicely.

7.3 • THE ASK MODEL

The ASK model can be used throughout the Learning Challenge. It is particularly useful as a review and planning tool, though, which is why I have included it in this section.

ASK stands for attitudes, skills and knowledge:

- **Attitudes:** positive attitudes toward learning, including curiosity and persistence
- **Skills:** abilities to carry out those actions necessary for gaining understanding and achieving excellent performance in any given context
- **Knowledge:** familiarity with information, concepts, theories and practices in a given field

▲ Figure 48: The Learning Challenge as a Series of Pits and Peaks

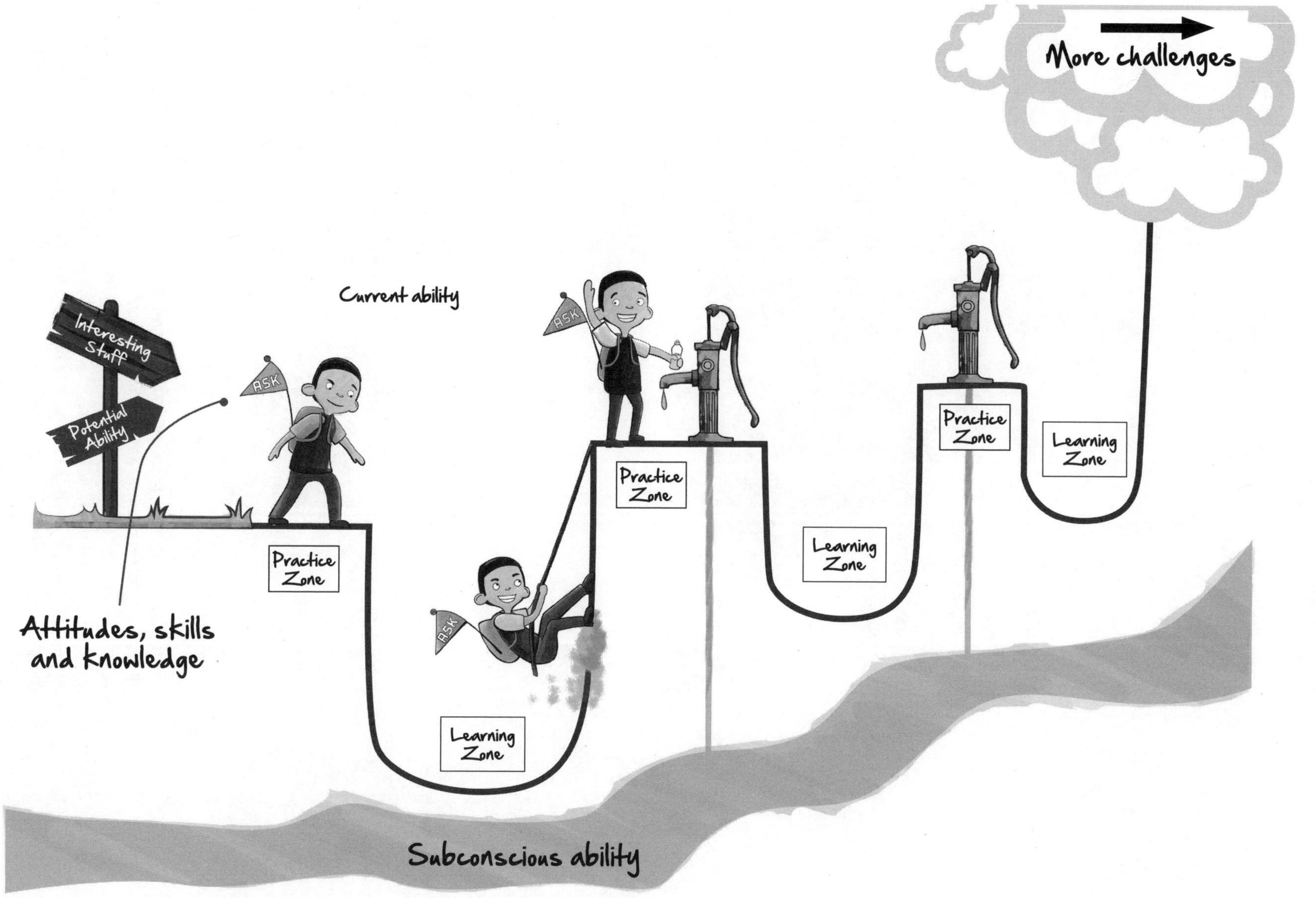

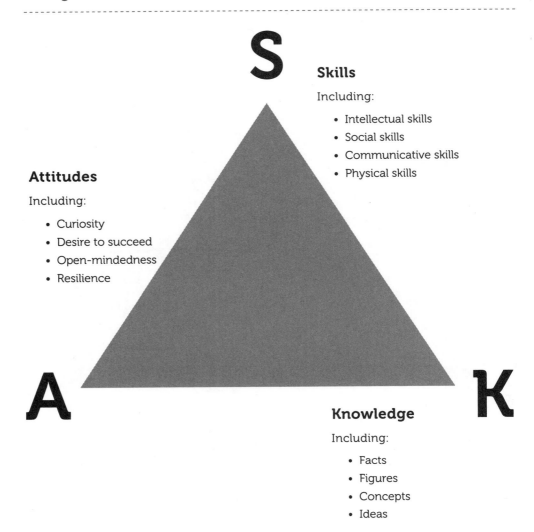

▶ Figure 49: The ASK Model

S Skills

Including:

- Intellectual skills
- Social skills
- Communicative skills
- Physical skills

Attitudes

Including:

- Curiosity
- Desire to succeed
- Open-mindedness
- Resilience

A

K

Knowledge

Including:

- Facts
- Figures
- Concepts
- Ideas

> The ASK model considers the role that attitudes, skills and knowledge play in learning *how* to learn.

When I use the ASK model with students, I tend to draw it as the triangle shown in Figure 49. That means we can plot a position along one of the lines to show the current emphasis for learning. So if we placed a cross in the middle of the line running bottom left to top right, then this would indicate a focus on attitudes and skills. For example, using curiosity (the attitude) to ask questions (the intellectual skill) about the Learning Challenge journey. Or if we placed a cross toward the left-hand side of the attitudes/knowledge line, then this would indicate an emphasis on attitudes with some need for knowledge. For example, the main focus has been on developing an attitude of thinking carefully when examining the difference between proven facts and presumed facts (knowledge).

A focus such as this will help your students reflect on their Learning Challenge journey. It will also remind them what learning *how* to learn (see Section 3.3) is all about. To become expert learners, your students will need to develop positive attitudes toward learning, be skillful in a number of aspects of learning and have good general knowledge and conceptual understanding so that they are able to find and assess information. In other words, they will need to grow in all three domains of the ASK model: attitudes, skills and knowledge. These are explained in the following sections.

7.3.1 • Attitudes

Think of the difference between teaching thirty students who value learning and fifteen students who don't. Or compare the likely progress of a student who is easily discouraged with one who persists and overcomes challenges. It seems attitudes play a major role in the outcomes of education.

Many believe that a combination of genetic dispositions and upbringing will determine the extent to which students value learning. They argue that we can work only with or against what is already given. And yet, the evidence is clear: it is possible to develop excellent attitudes toward learning by modeling, articulating and teaching the attitudes you want your students to learn.

That is easier said than done, of course, since finding agreement about which attitudes are the right ones to promote is a challenge in itself. Help is on hand, though, as there are many sources of inspiration, including Art Costa's (2000) *Habits of Mind* and Guy Claxton's (2002) *Building Learning Power.*

A very effective approach is to draw out some ideas from your students. To do this, ask your students to consider the following:

- Think of a goal or target that you have achieved—for example, learning to ride your bike, reciting your times tables, playing a musical instrument, writing a poem, making friends at a new school.

- Ask them what attitudes helped them achieve this.

- Record the answers that your students come up with and turn these into statements of intent (see below).

Sample Answers From Eleven-Year-Olds

- Always trying hard
- Being open to advice
- Thinking carefully
- Being willing to try new things
- "Never say die" attitude
- Learning from mistakes
- Staying focused
- Being open-minded

Corresponding Statements of Intent

- We always try hard.
- We are open to advice, offering support to each other.
- We think carefully about our studies.
- We are willing to try new things.
- We are tenacious (have a "never say die" attitude).
- We treat mistakes as opportunities to learn.
- We concentrate and remain focused during our learning.
- We are open to new ideas and different opinions.

Of course, it is not enough simply to decide the attitudes you wish to develop and then display them in the classroom. If that were all it took, then every school with pretty disposition posters (for example, TEAM: Together Everyone Achieves More) would have perfect students with perfect attitudes!

So to have a better chance of embedding the attitudes you want, you could try the following:

1. Identify the attitudes that you wish to focus on, using the approach shown.

2. Display these attitudes on the wall and talk with your students about their meanings. This includes developing from straightforward definitions to elaborations, including:

   • Students creating a poster to illustrate each of the attitudes

   • Identifying key role models for each attitude (e.g., Winston Churchill or J.K. Rowling for determination)

   • Exploring each attitude through storytelling, poetry, art or philosophical inquiry

3. Model each of the attitudes explicitly so it is obvious to your students how and when they are using each one to accomplish their learning goals.

4. Use every opportunity that presents itself to remind your students of the learning attitudes. For example, when they are stuck on a piece of work, remind them that this is an opportunity to practice perseverance.

5. Teach each of the attitudes as part of your Learning Intentions, using the ASK model.

7.3.2 • Skills

Skills are the abilities to carry out those processes necessary for gaining understanding, taking part in dialogue and achieving excellent performance in any given field. Children (and adults) develop their abilities through social interaction and from the social, cultural and educational context of their lives.

Intellectual Skills

These include the ability to identify, model and alter relationships or concepts; understanding relevance; drawing conclusions; comparing and contrasting; asking relevant questions and hypothesizing.

Social Skills

These include building rapport, respecting others' viewpoints, acting appropriately in particular contexts, self-regulation, working individually and as a team and encouraging others.

Communicative Skills

These include the ability to understand and be understood, listening and responding appropriately to others, talking persuasively and respectfully, requesting things politely, paying full attention to a speaker and reading body language.

Physical Skills

These include coordinated actions needed for such things as penmanship, manipulating objects to represent ideas, catching and throwing an object, dancing, drama, riding a bicycle, making art and playing a sport.

Specialized Skills

These include the abilities we need for specific types of action, such as using a map and compass, a ruler or tape measure, a paintbrush, sporting equipment, some weighing scales, a computer mouse, as well as driving a car.

Please note that I have included social skills because although many people will say that getting on with others has more to do with attitude than skill, I'm not sure this is the case. It seems that both attitudes and skills affect behavior. For example, one of your students may have a very friendly disposition but not, as yet, the ability to make friends. And of course the reverse might also be true: one of your students may know perfectly well how to make friends but does not have the inclination to do so. Therefore, a lesson focusing on how to build rapport with another person or how to begin a conversation with another person will develop very important life skills that many of your students might not have learned yet.

7.3.3 • Knowledge

I am assuming that each country or state has its own curriculum that identifies the knowledge that students are required to learn. So for that reason, I have not broken knowledge down into parts as I have with attitudes and skills.

7.4 • REVIEW

In addition to the main points identified in the preview, this chapter has covered the following:

1. There are questions that could be asked to review each stage of the Learning Challenge journey.

2. It is important to encourage your students to think about how their learning might transfer to other areas of their lives.

3. The Learning Challenge is a series of pits and peaks as your students develop and grow.

4. The ASK model (attitudes, skills and knowledge) can be a very useful frame of reference for helping your students review the gains they have made as a result of the Learning Challenge.

5. Figure 48 captures how the Teaching Target Model (see Section 1.1) fits together with the Learning Challenge and the ASK model.

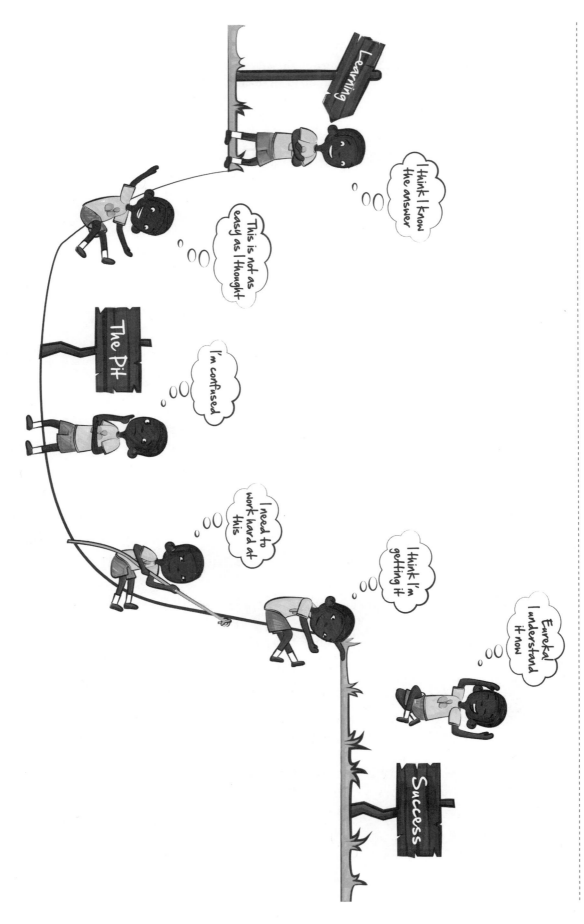

▶ Figure 50: Thoughts Through the Pit

MINDSET MATTERS

8.0 • PREVIEW

This chapter identifies the attitudes that are needed for success with the Learning Challenge.

The most important points include:

1. The purpose of the Learning Challenge is to take participants out of their comfort zone. This makes the sorts of responses shown in Figure 50 desirable as well as expected.

2. The Learning Challenge mindset includes an emphasis on effort, having a go, taking risks, trying new strategies, seeking advice, looking for challenges, questioning yourself and others, persevering and making progress.

3. A motto that neatly captures the essence of the Learning Challenge is "Proving is good; improving is better."

8.1 • THE LEARNING CHALLENGE MINDSET

Figure 50 captures some of the thoughts that often go through the mind of participants during the Learning Challenge. As you can see, it's not all sunshine and roses. That is not a particularly bad thing, though. As explained throughout the book (particularly in Sections 1.3, 3.4 and 9.3.1), the very purpose of the Learning Challenge is to take participants *out* of their comfort zone. So if we are not getting reactions such as "This is not as easy as I thought" and "I'm confused," then perhaps our students are not even in the pit!

Mindset is a term made popular by Carol Dweck, professor of psychology at Stanford University.

Earlier in the book, I shared the underpinning values of the Learning Challenge (see Section 1.3). These included the idea that learning can be made more interesting by making it more challenging, that process is as important as outcome and that your students are more likely to be in a *growth mindset* (Dweck, 2006) the more they go through the Learning Challenge.

As I noted in earlier chapters, the Learning Challenge focuses on effort, having a go, taking risks, trying new strategies, seeking advice, looking for challenges, questioning yourself and others, persevering and making progress. All of these are as essential to the Learning Challenge mindset as they are to Dweck's growth mindset. It is also something of a chicken-or-egg situation: the mindset of challenge, risk-taking and persistence is needed for the successful navigation of the Learning Challenge. At the same time, the Learning Challenge creates these exact same attitudes. This then leads to the Learning Challenge mindset that is captured in Figure 51.

▶ Figure 51: Qualities of the Learning Challenge Mindset

Personal abilities and attitudes, including:

- An inquiring outlook coupled with an ability to articulate problems
- A tendency to be intellectually proactive and persistent
- A capacity for imaginative and adventurous thinking
- A habit of exploring alternative possibilities
- An ability to critically examine issues
- A capacity for sound independent judgment

Social dispositions, including:

- Actively listening to others and trying to understand their viewpoints
- Giving reasons for what you say and expecting the same of others
- Exploring disagreements reasonably
- Being generally cooperative and constructive
- Being socially communicative and inclusive
- Taking other people's feelings and concerns into account

Put more succinctly, the Learning Challenge mindset is about a willingness to continually improve as a learner. Or as the motto for my company says:

Proving is good; improving is better.

8.2 • SELF-EFFICACY

As well as developing the mindset described in Section 8.1, the Learning Challenge is also focused on building participants' self-efficacy. It does this by showing participants time and again that they *can* change the outcome of their learning with the right effort, strategy and focus.

Self-efficacy is the belief a person has in their ability to effect, or bring about, a new outcome. Stanford psychologist Albert Bandura (1977) proposed the term as an alternative to the more widely used term *self-esteem*. Whereas the latter relates to how a person esteems or likes their self, the idea of self-efficacy relates more to a person's potency and influence. In my mind, this is what makes self-efficacy the more essential quality (though both would be even better!).

In her meta-analysis on teacher efficacy Rachel Jean Eells (2011) summarizes the work of Albert Bandura: "Efficacy involves more than positive thinking or optimism. It is tied to the construct of agency (the ability to make things happen) and to action" (p. 5).

Students who rate themselves very highly and yet are defeatist when faced with challenges could be said to have high self-esteem but low self-efficacy. Indeed, it is these students who tend to be quickest to shrug their shoulders and say something along the lines of "I don't care that I can't do it. I'm happy as I am." In some circumstances, that might sound reasonable, but what happens when it is actually coming from a fear of failure rather than a genuine disinterest? What if the shoulder shrug is a defense mechanism rather than a show of contentment? This is where self-efficacy comes in. If we help our students develop their self-efficacy, then they will be more likely to make decisions from a position of aptitude rather than aversion. Knowing they are in a position to effect or create a new outcome *if they wish to* is preferable to avoiding new experiences because of a sense of foreboding or fear.

Figure 52 summarizes the differences between low self-efficacy and high self-efficacy.

Incidentally, notice how similar the traits of low self-efficacy are to the behaviors associated with a fixed mindset (see Section 1.3.6): both are wary of change, both seem to prefer to prove rather than *im*prove themselves, and both are more likely to be frustrated by challenges.

> Self-efficacy is the belief someone has in their ability to influence outcomes.

▶ Figure 52: **Comparison of Low and High Self-Efficacy**

People with Low Self-Efficacy tend to be:	People with High Self-Efficacy tend to be:
1. Rigid in their thinking	1. Flexible in their thinking
2. Fearful of new and unfamiliar situations	2. Keen to experience new situations
3. Wary of change	3. Open to change
4. Cautious of other people	4. Cooperative with others
5. Keen to prove themselves	5. Keen to express themselves
6. Reassured by the familiar	6. Excited by challenge
7. Evasive in what they say	7. Honest in what they say
8. More likely to give up	8. More persistent
9. Easily frustrated	9. Tolerant
10. Less equipped to cope	10. Quicker to recover

Now compare the similarities in behavior between those with high self-efficacy and those in a growth mindset (also shown in Section 1.3.6). These include having better coping strategies, being open to new situations as well as to change and choosing growth and expression over playing it safe or showing off to others.

Furthermore, look at the behaviors associated with high self-efficacy, a growth mindset and the traits you expect your students to develop by going through the Learning Challenge: resilience, determination, curiosity, being more open to challenges and so on. Again, the links are clear: for our students to develop positive learning attitudes, we need them to go through the Learning Challenge.

As John Hattie (2009) remarked in his seminal work, *Visible Learning*, "The willingness to invest in learning, to gain a reputation as a learner and to show openness to experiences are the key dispositional factors that relate to achievement" (p. 47).

8.2.1 • Self-Efficacy and Learning Styles

Some years ago, I noticed a young man at the back of a math class flailing his arms around frenetically. All the other students were paying full attention to the teacher. This went on for the whole lesson. Afterward I asked the teacher whether this was normal, to which she replied, rather proudly, "Damian is a kinesthetic learner—he learns better when he moves."

> The misuse of learning styles can lead to a drop in self-efficacy.

What a load of rubbish! The boy doesn't have a medical condition; he's simply been told he's a kinesthetic learner, and gone along with it because it sounds fun. His teacher had asked her students to complete a learning styles questionnaire and then concluded that some were visual learners, others were auditory, and the rest were kinesthetic. She'd gone on to declare that visual learners had to see something written down to learn well, auditory learners had to hear something, and the kinesthetic lot—well, they had to bop and groove to learn!

Don't get me wrong: I agree we all have preferences. I seem to remember things better if I've seen them written down, but it's not impossible for me to learn through listening, despite what my wife would tell you.

However, as Frank Coffield and a team from my local university in Newcastle upon Tyne found when analyzing seventy-one different varieties of learning style assessments, "Some of the best known and widely used instruments (of learning styles) have such serious weaknesses (e.g., low reliability, poor validity and negligible impact on pedagogy) that we recommend that their use in research and in practice should be discontinued" (Coffield, Mosely, Hall & Ecclestone, 2004, pp. 138–139).

Furthermore, as Dylan Wiliam (2016) points out, "Learning-styles research is misguided because its basic assumption—that the purpose of instructional design is to make learning easy—may just be incorrect" (para. 9).

Learning styles can lead to people thinking they can only be good at some things and therefore avoiding the things they think they are not "naturally" good at. For example, the boy who asks his father for help with homework only to be rebuffed with "Don't ask me. I was never any good at spelling. Go and ask your mother!" What this implies to the boy is "Being bad at spelling is a family trait. It's no good fighting nature. Just accept you can't do it."

> One of the most damaging aspects of the "gift" mentality is that it makes us think we can know in advance who has the gift. This, I believe, is what makes us try to identify groups who have it and groups who don't—as in, "boys have it and girls don't," or those who show early promise have it and others don't. (Dweck, 2012, p. 7)

All of these examples point to *low* self-efficacy. They give the impression that the outcome is already set and that there is nothing a person can do to change it. That is not to say I am not arguing for or against the idea of fate. Instead, I want to draw attention to a crippling notion that there is nothing that can be done to affect how successful a person can be. This seems to me to be both discouraging and disabling. And quite frankly it is a belief that I sincerely hope no teacher holds, for if they did then surely that would make the process of teaching little more than one of sorting, classifying and controlling students. That kind of pessimism has no place in education.

Thankfully, though, these kinds of beliefs are rare. At least, they are in the schools I have worked in and with.

That said, it might still be worth reminding ourselves who sets the culture of our schools and our classrooms. In my mind, it is *not* the parents or politicians. It is the staff and students. Of course, society plays its role, but the biggest influence comes from the staff and students.

If you are skeptical about this, then cast your mind back to your own high school days. As a teenager, you moved from class to class to class, encountering different teachers for different subjects. I would be willing to bet you knew exactly which teachers had high expectations and which ones had low, which ones had a good sense of humor and which ones you suspected had not laughed since childhood. It is the same today: our students know which is which.

Now let me ask you: did you change your behavior and expectations depending on who was teaching you at the time? I bet you did! Most people I ask admit they did the same thing. And how about your peers? Again, did you change your behavior and expectations according to which classmates you were with for any given activity? Again, I'm assuming yes.

This then goes some way to emphasizing just how important beliefs are. And so it is with self-efficacy. If we believe we can significantly affect the future—in other words, if we have high self-efficacy—then we give ourselves much more chance of doing just that. But if we think that only students from the right side of town or with the right upbringing or without behavioral problems can learn, then we set a very different—and some might say disabling—tone in our classrooms. It is as the famous quote ascribed to Henry Ford goes: "Whether you believe you can do a thing or not, you are right."

To emphasize the point further, let's take a look at some of the recent research about the impact of efficacy in schools.

8.2.2 • Collective Teacher Efficacy

In 2015, John Hattie added the category *collective teacher efficacy* to his database of factors influencing student achievement. Based on a meta-analysis of twenty-six studies reporting a correlation between collective teacher efficacy and student achievement, Hattie calculated an effect size for collective teacher efficacy of 1.57. Bearing in mind the average effect of all factors in Hattie's database is an effect size of 0.4, this means that collective teacher efficacy can *quadruple* the typical effect on student achievement.

By collective teacher efficacy, the research means the perception that a group of teachers (and leaders) have about their ability to significantly and positively change the learning outcomes for their students. High collective efficacy means that the group of staff believe that together they can help not just some but *all* of their students make excellent progress in learning.

Looking at the original meta-analysis by Rachel Jean Eells (2011), a couple of quotes stand out. Citing Bandura and Tschannen-Moran, Woolfolk Hoy and Hoy, she writes:

Teachers set the culture of the classroom and as such have significant influence on students' self-efficacy.

Collective teacher efficacy (when the staff of a school believe they are capable of helping *all* students make excellent progress) is one of the most significant factors influencing student achievement.

As teachers in a school feel empowered to do great things, great things happen. If they feel powerless, and believe they cannot surmount the obstacles in front of them, they will be less likely to persist when challenged, and will not expend as much effort. (pp. 4–5)

Citing Bandura again, Eells affirms:

Highly efficacious teams or individuals will feel optimistic about success because they feel that they have the abilities needed to create that success. This engenders positive thinking, as limitations are seen as challenges rather than roadblocks, and the power of uncontrollable circumstances is weighed against that which can be controlled. (p. 5)

Years before Eells's report, Rosenthal and Jacobson (1968) showed that if teachers expected enhanced performance from selected students, then those students did indeed make greater-than-average gains. Describing this as the Pygmalion effect, the psychologists showed that raised expectations had a positive effect by creating self-fulfilling prophecies in classrooms. When teachers *believed* that they could help students overcome obstacles and make excellent progress, that is exactly what tended to happen. Unfortunately, the reverse was also true.

So it seems there really can be no mistaking the significance of efficacy. Which is why the Learning Challenge makes self-efficacy a principal aim.

> The very purpose of taking your students out of their comfort zone, challenging their assumptions and questioning their ideas is to build self-efficacy. The more your students go through the Learning Challenge, the more evidence they will have that they can positively influence the outcomes. With the right attitude and application, your students will come to realize they are in charge of their own learning success. And together they will generate a strong sense of collective efficacy.

8.3 • PRAISE AND THE PIT

As your students go through the Learning Challenge, resist the urge to praise them too much. Remember that praise is like currency: the more that's printed, the less valuable it becomes.

I am not saying that praise is a bad thing, but here is what I recommend:

Praise can inadvertently reduce self-efficacy, particularly if it is directed toward the child rather than their actions.

1. Be careful that praise does not become an extrinsic motivator replacing the intrinsic motivation of making it through the Learning Challenge. In other words, don't let the lure of praise become the reason your students go through the pit. Use the feeling of eureka as the goal.

2. When you do praise your students, focus it on something that will help to build their self-efficacy, for example, their effort, their choice of strategy, their perseverance and so on. Avoid praising the person (e.g., "good girl," "clever boy") as this can lead to frustrations later on if they feel that good people succeed and therefore bad people fail.

To be more specific about praise at each stage of the Learning Challenge, I recommend the following:

Stage 1: Concept

Avoid praise at the setup phase. Show interest in your students' first answers, of course. Also show that you are pleased they are willing to have a go, but don't praise them yet.

Do not confirm or challenge the ideas your students offer at Stage 1. You want them to explore possibilities, not spend energy guessing what's in the teacher's head! So leave your opinions at the door as much as possible. Remember: the Learning Challenge is about teaching your students *how* to think, not *what* to think.

Stage 2: Conflict

If you are inclined to praise your students, then this is the best point at which to praise. However, do not praise them for being right. Instead, praise their determination to persevere through the pit, for using a pit tool skillfully, for collaborating with others and for being willing to go beyond the obvious answers. In short, use praise to encourage them through the pit and out the other side.

Stage 3: Construct

As your students construct their answers, they may well need more of the praise used during the conflict stage. However, as they reach the eureka moment they shouldn't need any more praise; the elation of achieving newfound clarity should be reward enough. That said, if you are going to praise, then choose phrases that encourage internal reward. For example, use statements such as these:

- You should be proud of yourself for sticking at it. (rather than "I am proud of you")

- How good does it feel to have reached the eureka moment? (rather than "I'm impressed that you have reached the eureka point")

- As you look back over what you've achieved, what are you most pleased with? (rather than "I'm pleased with you")

By using statements such as the ones shown (rather than the ones in parentheses), you will emphasize the importance of intrinsic motivation as opposed to doing things for the sake of approval from others. This approach will encourage your students to engage in learning because it is a worthwhile endeavor, not because it will result in a pat on the head or another gold star.

Stage 4: Consider

Whenever I run a Learning Challenge session with a group of students, I invariably finish by inviting them to congratulate each other on a job well done. Phrases such as these give the right impression:

- Well done us for challenging each other's ideas.

- Well done us for persevering and seeking out better answers.

- Well done us for being willing to step out of our comfort zones.

- Well done us for finding new ways to think about things.

Avoid giving praise during the first two stages of the Learning Challenge.

During the third stage of the LC, give participants praise for persevering through the pit and not giving up.

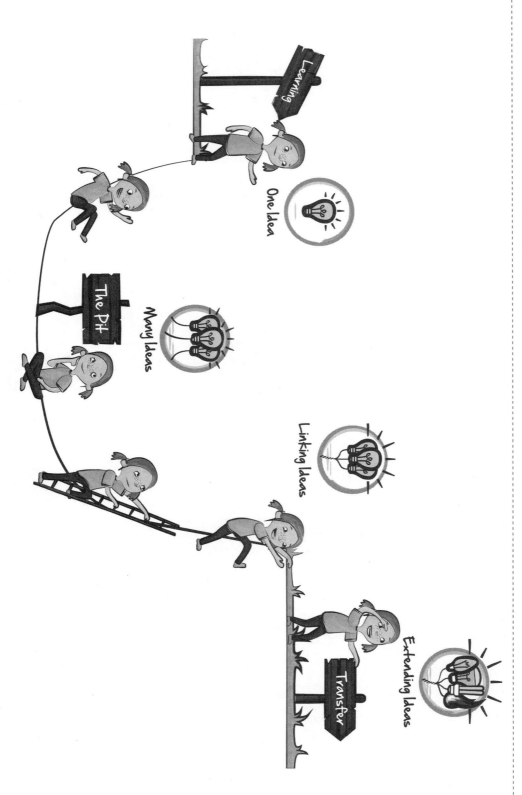

▼ Figure 53: A Blend of the Learning Challenge and the SOLO Taxonomy

8.4 • REVIEW

In addition to the main points identified in the preview, this chapter has covered the following:

1. The Learning Challenge focuses on building participants' self-efficacy. This is the belief a person has in their ability to effect or significantly influence the future.

2. A group of people together can also have a *collective* efficacy. In schools, this is often called collective teacher efficacy and has been shown to be one of the most powerful influences on student achievement.

3. Many things help to build self and collective efficacy. The Learning Challenge is one of them. Unfortunately, praise can have the opposite effect.

4. So long as we direct praise toward actions and do not overpraise, it can help build a sense of efficacy. Focus praise on the person or overdo it, though, and it is more likely to reduce self-efficacy.

LINKS AND PERSPECTIVES

9.0 • PREVIEW

This chapter shares some of the ways in which the Learning Challenge links with other approaches to learning.

The most important points include:

1. The SOLO taxonomy helps to explain the Learning Challenge and vice versa.

2. The similarities between Philosophy for Children and the Learning Challenge are considerable. In fact, the Learning Challenge was born out of the Philosophy for Children values and methodology.

3. The Learning Challenge can work with almost all students. For students with severe learning difficulties, considerable adaptations will be needed for it to be of any benefit. This chapter shares some examples.

4. The Learning Challenge can work across a whole school as well as in individual classrooms. There are some recommendations for leaders in Section 9.4.

There are many links between the LC and the SOLO taxonomy. These are explored over the next few pages.

SOLO stands for structure of observed learning outcomes. John Biggs and Kevin Collis (1982) first described it in *Evaluating the Quality of Learning: The SOLO Taxonomy*.

The SOLO taxonomy provides a useful reference point when describing learning progress from no knowledge through to deep understanding. There are also many commonalities between SOLO and the Learning Challenge (LC). Indeed, the SOLO taxonomy can help to explain each step of the Learning Challenge journey.

Figure 54 gives a summary of how the SOLO taxonomy and the Learning Challenge relate to each other. There is also a more detailed summary in Figure 59 at the end of this section. In between these two illustrations, you will find a more detailed description of the common features for each stage of the SOLO taxonomy and how they relate to the Learning Challenge.

To find out more about the SOLO taxonomy, you can read a full guide in *Challenging Learning Through Feedback* (Nottingham & Nottingham, 2017).

Prestructural Phase of SOLO: Before the Learning Challenge Begins

The prestructural phase of SOLO corresponds with a stage before the Learning Challenge begins. This is when your students have no knowledge of the concept you wish them to explore.

▶ **Figure 54: Prestructural Phase and Pre-Pit Stage**

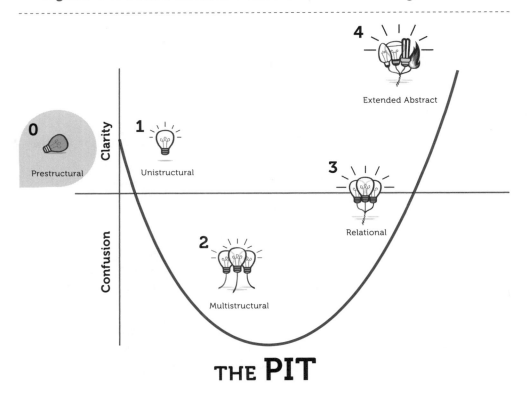

THE **PIT**

Here are some actions that your students might take in this phase:

• Saying they have no idea

• Attempting a task you've given them in an inappropriate manner

- Identifying irrelevant or incorrect information

- Missing the point

- Being unable (and perhaps unwilling) to make a start without a lot of support and encouragement

- Saying they need help

Unistructural Phase of SOLO and Stage 1 of the Learning Challenge

The unistructural phase of SOLO corresponds with the concept stage of the Learning Challenge. This is when your students have basic knowledge of the concept you wish them to explore.

▶ Figure 55: **Unistructural Phase and Concept Stage**

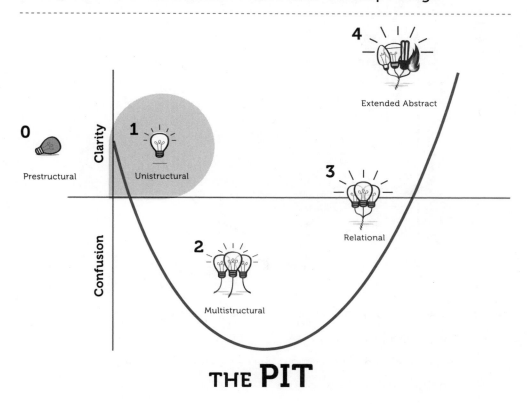

Here are the actions that your students might take in this phase:

- Saying they know something about the central concept

- Being able to identify, name, remember, match or list basic characteristics of the concept

- Having a go at defining the concept with simple answers

- Identifying relevant information

- Beginning to know the relevance of the concept

- Saying they are ready for the pit

Multistructural Phase of SOLO and Stage 2 of the Learning Challenge

The multistructural phase of SOLO corresponds with the conflict stage of the Learning Challenge. This is when your students have so many ideas about the concept that they are struggling to make sense of them all.

▶ **Figure 56: Multistructural Phase and Conflict Stage**

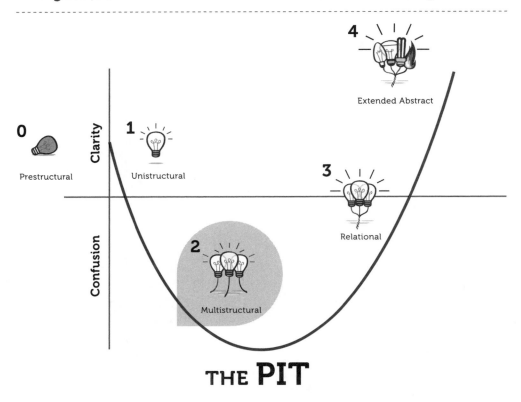

THE **PIT**

Here are the actions that your students might take in this phase:

- Finding many more ideas
- Being able to describe, compare, notice patterns and find exceptions
- Engaging animatedly in dialogue
- Perhaps being frustrated by not having reached a conclusion yet
- Developing their earlier ideas, adding complexity to their descriptions
- Having a good sense of the relevance and purpose of the task

Relational Phase of SOLO and Stage 3 of the Learning Challenge

The relational phase of SOLO corresponds with the construct stage of the Learning Challenge. This is when your students make sense of all the ideas they have been grappling with and construct an answer to climb out of the pit.

▶ Figure 57: Relational Phase and Construct Stage

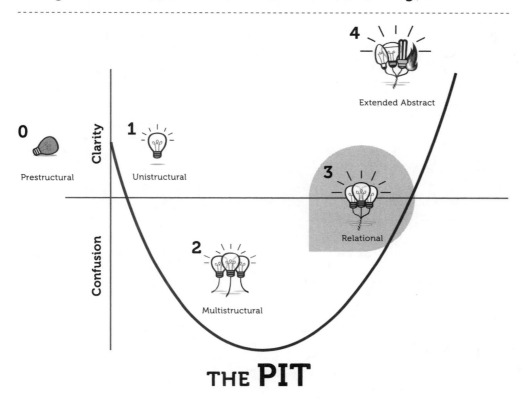

Here are the actions that your students might take in this phase:

- Connecting their ideas together

- Understanding patterns and how the ideas relate to each other

- Being able to explain cause, effect and significance

- Beginning to organize, distinguish, relate and analyze

- Explaining to others what steps to take to make progress

- Reaching a eureka moment

- Showing a sense of achievement

- Looking for ways to share or apply their newfound understanding

Extended Abstract Phase of SOLO and Stage 4 of the Learning Challenge

The extended abstract phase of SOLO corresponds with the consider stage of the Learning Challenge. This is when your students are considering their learning journey and looking for ways to apply their new understanding.

▶ **Figure 58: Extended Abstract Phase and Consider Stage**

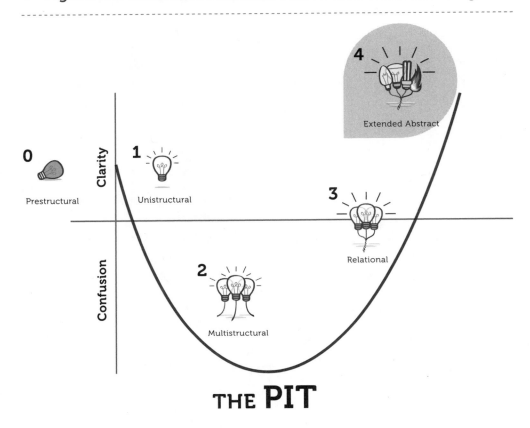

THE **PIT**

Here are the actions that your students might take in this phase:

- Reviewing, relating and understanding their learning journey

- Applying their understanding to new and different contexts

- Being able to generalize, hypothesize, prioritize, design, create, evaluate and perform

- Explaining how they developed their understanding and saying what they could have done differently

- Critiquing the process and strategies they used this time so as to identify how best to tackle other concepts

- Creating similar tasks or problems for others to try

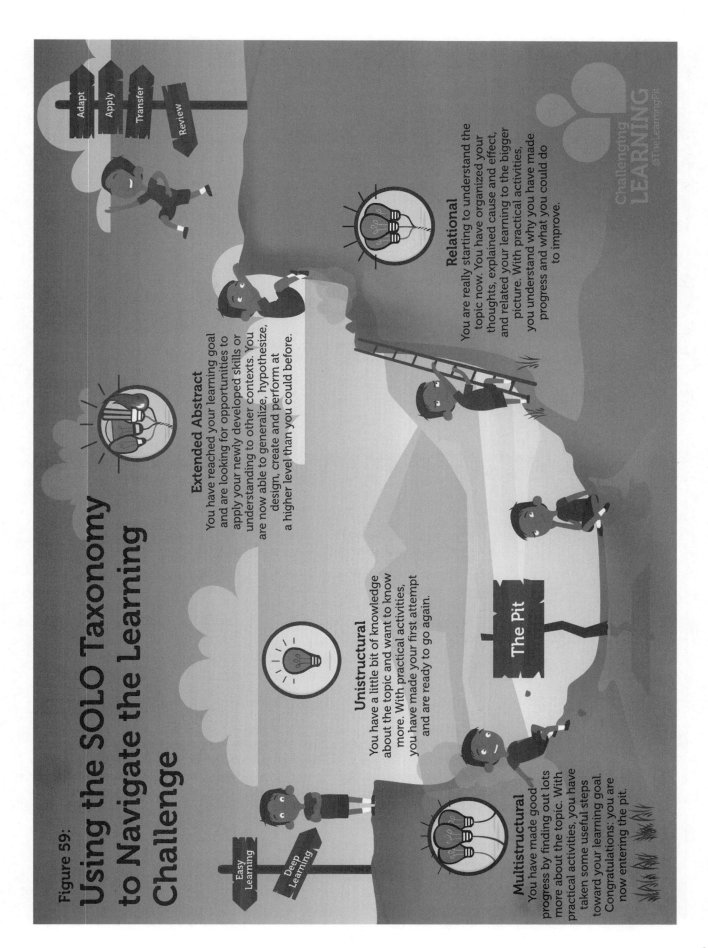

Figure 59:
Using the SOLO Taxonomy to Navigate the Learning Challenge

Extended Abstract
You have reached your learning goal and are looking for opportunities to apply your newly developed skills or understanding to other contexts. You are now able to generalize, hypothesize, design, create and perform at a higher level than you could before.

Relational
You are really starting to understand the topic now. You have organized your thoughts, explained cause and effect, and related your learning to the bigger picture. With practical activities, you understand why you have made progress and what you could do to improve.

Unistructural
You have a little bit of knowledge about the topic and want to know more. With practical activities, you have made your first attempt and are ready to go again.

Multistructural
You have made good progress by finding out lots more about the topic. With practical activities, you have taken some useful steps toward your learning goal. Congratulations: you are now entering the pit.

The Pit

Adapt
Apply
Transfer
Review

Easy Learning

Deep Learning

Challenging
LEARNING
@TheLearningPit

9.2 • PHILOSOPHY FOR CHILDREN AND THE LEARNING CHALLENGE

The LC comes from the Philosophy for Children tradition.

I first developed the Learning Challenge in the mid-1990s as a way to plan for, and facilitate, the Philosophy for Children (P4C) sessions I was running with students at the time. So to say that there is some commonality between P4C and the Learning Challenge would be an understatement. The Learning Challenge was born out of the Philosophy for Children values and methodology.

Philosophy for Children began as a way to teach wisdom, reflection, reasoning and reasonableness to students between the ages of six and sixteen. Since its inception in 1972, it has spread to more than sixty countries worldwide, has been well researched and has proved to have positive effects on student learning.

A central concept of P4C is that of the community of inquiry. This can be defined as a reflective approach to dialogue built up over time with a single group of students. The community embodies cooperation, care, respect and safety; the inquiry reaches for understanding, meaning, truth and values supported by reasons. Having read this book, you will see that the Learning Challenge shares exactly the same values.

Below are the ten steps that form the framework for a typical P4C session. I have grouped them according to the relevant Learning Challenge stage. Facilitators of a P4C session wouldn't necessarily follow all ten steps in one sitting, but they would certainly use Steps 1–3 and 6–9.

Stage 1: Concept

1. **Prepare:** Sit in a circle so everyone can see and hear one another. Give guidelines of conduct (see Section 3.4 for suggestions).

2. **Share a stimulus:** Present a stimulus to your students. The stimulus might be a narrative, a news item, a selection of contrasting arguments or explanations, a picture, a video, a work of art—anything that stimulates your students' thinking and prompts them to raise interesting ideas and questions (see Section 4.3 for suggestions).

3. **Identify issues and concepts:** Give time for individual reflection on the stimulus—maybe a minute of silent thinking or jotting down key words. Ask your students to share with a partner their thoughts about the issues raised. Write on the board their key words and some of their thoughts about what they thought was important or interesting about the stimulus.

4. **Create questions:** Split your students into small groups to generate open-ended, philosophical questions. When they have created a few, ask each group to choose their best one to present to the whole class (see Section 4.4 for suggestions).

5. **Air and choose questions:** Invite authors to explain or clarify their questions. Ask your other students to link, appreciate or evaluate any of the questions aired. Then get all your students to vote for what they consider to be the best question from the list you have collected from the groups. One way to encourage them to pick the best one rather than simply their favorite one is to say, "Pick the one you think will give us the best chance of an open-ended, philosophical discussion" (see Section 4.5 for suggestions).

6. **Dialogue: First thoughts:** Once the best question has been selected, ask the authors of that question to open the dialogue by sharing their initial thoughts—perhaps their expectations of where the question might lead or the answers they currently have in mind (see Section 4.6 for suggestions).

Stage 2: Conflict

7. **Dialogue: Build and challenge:** Bring other students into the dialogue by inviting comments, responses, examples, agreements, disagreements, reasons and so on. You might need to introduce other relevant perspectives or possible arguments if the dialogue is too limited in scope (see Chapter 5 for suggestions).

Stage 3: Construct

8. **Dialogue: Construct an answer:** Students are often frustrated if a dialogue does not finish with a conclusion or answer. That is not to say we should always answer a question; there are many times when it is impossible to do so or more beneficial not to do so. Nonetheless, you will find times when it is better to try to construct some sort of consensus (see Chapter 6 for suggestions).

9. **Dialogue: Final thoughts:** Even if you do come to consensus, it might also be worthwhile to give each student the opportunity to share their final thoughts with the community. Ask for volunteers or go around the circle, allowing students to say "pass" if they prefer not to speak.

Stage 4: Consider

10. **Review:** Invite reflective and evaluative comments about the inquiry. The guiding questions should always be along the lines of "What went well?" and "What could be improved?" (see Chapter 7 for suggestions).

9.3 • CONSIDERATIONS FOR STUDENTS WITH SPECIAL EDUCATIONAL NEEDS

Written by Mark Bollom

I taught for a number of years in special educational needs (SEN) schools across the United Kingdom. These schools catered for a mix of students with a wide range of needs. In one setting the students were defined as having moderate learning difficulties—one step away from their mainstream peers. These were very often young people who had started in a mainstream school but due to social, emotional and/or behavior difficulties, they had found themselves in a special school. These students tended to be just a little behind the curve and so the notion of the Learning Challenge made sense to them. I just had to modify the concepts a little so that they were more accessible, apply the principles of cognitive conflict and challenge in gentler way and everything worked well. Of course it wasn't quite as simple as that, but the route ahead was clear enough.

In some of the other settings in which I worked, it wasn't quite so straightforward. Sometimes I worked with students with severe learning difficulties and high levels of developmental delay, nonverbal students with autism spectrum disorder/autism spectrum condition (ASD/ASC), vulnerable students with profound learning difficulties and multisensory impairments. Therefore I offer some ideas as to how you might adopt and adapt the Learning Challenge principles to suit students with similar special educational needs.

This list is a comparison of the typical steps within a P4C session and how they relate to the LC.

The LC sometimes needs adaptation to suit students with special educational needs, as this section shows.

I'd like to start, though, by defining terms, or at least my terms of reference.

When I think about the definition of cognitive conflict and the examples of it in this book, and then I think of the difficult-to-reach, nonverbal students with severe and/or complex learning difficulties with whom I worked, then I confess, there is a tension there. I suppose it causes me to wobble! As I understand it, though, from the earliest stage of development people create schemas to explain the world around them. They then reformulate those schemas when they encounter another idea or piece of evidence that contradicts the original schema. For example, the youngest of children seem to have a schema that all creatures are friendly. Sadly, experience teaches them otherwise and so they reformulate their schema to be afraid of certain individuals or groups. Imagine the schemas that exist in the minds of students with complex learning difficulties. And then try to predict how they might respond to a schema as challenging as the Learning Challenge!

Trying to imagine the schemas that exist in the minds of students with complex learning difficulties or those with severe developmental delay is of course problematic. Nonetheless, those schemas exist. That means cognitive conflict exists because ideas and understandings are challenged through the daily experiences of these students. This creates the invitation to think about how to interpret and adapt the principles of the learning challenge and to think about how to make it meaningful and appropriate for students with special needs.

In the following sections, I describe how I would adapt, modify or reinterpret each stage to be more suitable for students with SEN. In some cases, I give examples of things I have done, and in others, things I would do had I known more about the Learning Challenge at the time. I offer this contribution acutely aware of the broad spectrum of needs incorporated under the umbrella of terms such as *special educational needs*, and in no way do I imagine that these thoughts and ideas are applicable to all SEN students or all settings.

Stage 1: Concept

When introducing or revisiting a concept you wish your students to gain a deeper understanding of, think about the following questions:

1. How can I make it relevant to the individual learning needs of my students?

In our attempts to make things age appropriate, as a result of curriculum guidance or the necessity to prepare our students for the world they inhabit, we sometimes lose sight of the developmental stage our students are at. Thinking about stage more than age is vital if we are to present a concept in a meaningful and useful way.

2. How can I make the concept real?

For many SEN students, it is vital that we make concepts real to them. In particular, those students with ASD may have difficulty dealing with abstract concepts. So it is important to provide concrete examples of the concept rather than simply hoping that students will somehow detect from us what it is we would like them to think about.

Some students' learning will be enhanced by providing them with a direct encounter with the concept you want them to identify with. If it's precipitation, then get outside in the rain, the snow or the fog. If it's self-care and personal hygiene, then students will need to see, smell and label clean and dirty things. If it's money, then dish out the notes and use them in real settings. If it's healthy eating, then you will probably have to engage in some healthy *and* unhealthy eating!

Make good use of educational visits and opportunities outside of the classroom. Focus these visits in terms of the introduction or identification of real concepts.

Multisensory experiences can also be valuable in terms of bringing concepts to life. It is no good exploring a concept like temperature if your students don't have a tangible reference point for terms such as *hot* and *cold*.

3. How can I communicate ideas and concepts effectively?

Supporting the communication of SEN learners is often of primary consideration. There are, of course, a number of ways to do this, and different learners will present different communication needs. So in addition to making the concept tangible and real, we may also need to use a range of augmentative communication strategies.

Props can be very effective links between the tangible experience and the abstract concept. For example:

a. **Objects of reference:** Something as simple as the minibus keys or seat belt clip from the transport used to and from the physical experience might be enough to make the link in the minds of your students. Picking up a feather during a visit to a bird sanctuary could help your students think back to the topic of animals that fly.

b. **Pictures and photographs:** In my experience, photographs work best. Take lots of photos—preferably with your students in them—and then use these as props when talking about the main concepts back at school.

c. **Alternative communication:** Students may already be using alternative communication strategies to support their communication. This might be through the use of picture and symbols cards, sign language or communication technology devices. In supporting these students, it is vital to ensure that the vocabulary they are capable of is available to them in relation to the particular concept they are focused on.

> Photographs of the concept in action can be very helpful in making the concept less abstract.

Stage 2: Conflict

> **When seeking to challenge students with SEN, we should be mindful of the fact that in so many ways their learning journey is already a challenge. Whether it's speech and language difficulties, sensory impairment, developmental delay, an autism spectrum condition or physical impairment, these characteristics can and do present learners with an array of obstacles on their learning journey.**

However, if we accept that the aim of the Learning Challenge is to actively listen to others and try to understand their viewpoints, give reasons for what you say and expect the same of others, explore disagreements reasonably, be generally cooperative and constructive and build a sense of self-efficacy, then plainly these are as relevant for students with SEN as they are for all other students. The main difference is in the nature of challenge and cognitive conflict.

SEN teachers are acutely aware that planning for learning requires a modification (slightly or fundamentally) of the curriculum and the breaking of tasks into small(er) steps. When thinking about cognitive conflict, though, we should all be mindful that the time outside the students' comfort zone, when they are wobbling, almost certainly needs to be shorter than for mainstream students. Or if we are to use the pit analogy, the challenge should be shallower. And that it is just shallow from our perspective!

Here is an example of what I mean:

Joe was a nonverbal seven-year-old boy with ASD and challenging physical behavior. His parents and his teachers wanted him to learn to swim for the obvious health and safety benefits. They also thought there would be some therapeutic benefit as well as enjoyment; after all, he already loved bubbles. However, Joe hated the very idea of swimming. He would refuse to enter the changing room and would scream and shout if he was asked to go near the pool. For Joe, the challenge was not getting him to swim unaided or even to get in the water. For him the learning challenge was to visit the swimming pool building, learn that it could be tolerable, leave the swimming pool with his behavior positively self-regulated and return to class where he could look at pictures of himself successfully sitting by the pool.

For Joe, this was the cognitive conflict:

1. I should cooperate with my teachers and parents.

2. They are asking me to do something I really don't want to do.

Things got worse before they got better. Joe would get very anxious on swimming day. He knew he was going to visit the swimming pool because his daily schedule told him so. And he knew that it would be a challenge because his task schedule told him it would be a challenge.

The skill of the staff supporting Joe was not just to ensure that he knew what was going to happen through carefully supported communication and the right amount of challenge. Their skill was also to see when the challenge of being near the pool was becoming too great, to attempt to extend the time Joe could deal with the challenge by looking for therapeutic actions that made the experience better and to celebrate with Joe his success and show him the progress he'd made. This included breaking things down into much, much smaller steps such as taking his swimming kit with him, hanging it up in the changing rooms, watching his friends in the pool and then collecting his kit again at the end of the session.

I've left that school now to work with the Challenging Learning team, but I heard recently that Joe is now a regular swimmer!

One of the many tools that can help students deal with challenge is language cards. Visual prompts such as the ones in Figure 60 can help.

► Figure 60: Language Cards to Support Learning

Think

Wobble

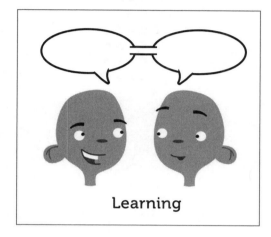

Learning

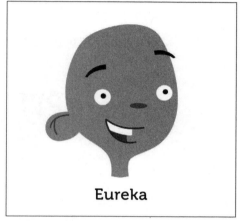

Eureka

Stage 3: Construct

When working with SEN students as they attempt to construct new understanding, it's worth bearing in mind that this stage will also need adapting to meet individual needs. Indeed, it is at this point that we should make every effort to help students feel most secure because if we can then they are likely to be more enthusiastic about future Learning Challenge experiences.

For students with SEN, the Learning Challenge journey is likely to look like Figure 61, with a longer Stage 1, a shallow Stage 2 and a long, gradually ramped Stage 3.

> The learning pit for SEN students would typically be shallower than normal.

The Learning Challenge for Students With Special Educational Needs

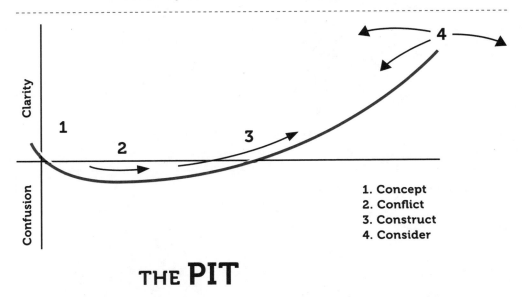

1. Concept
2. Conflict
3. Construct
4. Consider

THE **PIT**

Sophie's Coat

The shallow pit and long construct phase shown in Figure 61 can be illustrated by the story of a former student of mine, Sophie:

When I worked with Sophie, she was thirteen years old. She had Down syndrome, was visually impaired and had a range of other severe learning difficulties. She experienced her own form of cognitive conflict on a daily basis, in relation to a host of self-help and independent living skills. Her conflict was whether to try doing things for herself or to let other people do everything for her.

When people did do things for her, she would repeatedly say, "Naughty girl Sophie," while giggling to herself. She clearly loved the one-to-one attention the assistance afforded her, though. She faced enormous challenges, but her face was a picture of absolute delight when she really did achieve something and was told she had achieved something.

At the end of each day an adult from Sophie's class would hand her coat to her and suggest that she try to put in on. Invariably she would duly drop her coat, laugh and mutter (or worse). Although she would work at different times of the day and week on specific fine and gross motor skills, and clearly had adequate motor skills to put her coat on for herself, there was some barrier to her doing so.

With the advice and support of a highly skilled specialist visual impairment support worker, it was suggested that we should try *backward chaining*. Initially, Sophie would have her coat put on for her, she'd get the zip done up (with hand-over-hand support) and then she would be asked to just pat down the Velcro zip cover. After a few days she'd mastered this, so the next stage was to have everything done for her right up to the last 20 cm or so of her zip. Sophie would then finish this off and pat down the Velcro. By the end of the year Sophie had mastered the whole routine. She would still laugh and mutter (or worse) from time to time, so we needed to keep encouraging her, but she made real progress. By the end, she was much more frequently heard saying to herself, "You did it, Sophie."

Eureka Moments

A key point in the Learning Challenge is the eureka moment: that point at which your students realize they have found a new sense of clarity. This can be hugely motivating and typically acts as a powerful form of intrinsic motivation for further challenge.

However, for many students with SEN, they will need help in recognizing that eureka moment. They will benefit from hearing "*You* found it" or "You did it yourself." By highlighting their achievement to them, there is more chance that they will be motivated for future challenges.

> SEN students often need help in recognizing the eureka moment.

Stage 4: Consider

Meaningfully considering the learning journey and the thinking that has taken place (metacognition) could well be regarded as an all too ambitious step for some students with SEN. There are many students for whom everyday language is a challenge, never mind the language of reflection and review. That said, end-of-year and end-of-unit reviews are relatively commonplace in many SEN schools, so with the right adaptation, it may well be possible with some of your students.

The following are the sorts of activities that can help students with SEN review their Learning Challenge journey:

Photographs

Photographs are one of the best aide memoirs for students with SEN. Take lots of photographs of your students during their Learning Challenge experiences, print them out so that they can be handled, and then use them to talk about what students have been doing.

Hearing students with severe learning difficulties say, "That's me working," or name people they were collaborating with or identify where they were working can be a good starting point for exploring their reflections. Because they are discussing something as concrete as a photograph, it is possible to get a much more nuanced sense of their likes and dislikes, their understanding of the learning process and their enthusiasm for doing something similar again. If students can be given this tutorial time with an adult to discuss and reflect on their learning experiences, it can reveal a great deal. It can also enable students to think about their learning more deeply and provide them with a greater sense of ownership of the process.

> Photographs (particularly if they feature the students themselves), Sorting Circles and Learning Records can all help SEN students gain more from the LC.

Sorting Circles

An extension of the use of photographs can be achieved with Sorting Circles. Make sure you take photographs of your students working in different ways, in contrasting places and with a range of people. Then you can help your students sort the photographs into different binary categories such as easy/difficult learning, happy/unhappy feelings, fun/not fun, with an adult/by myself and so on.

Learning Records

Learning Records are so commonplace in SEN schools that they hardly seem worth a mention. However, with the right modifications, they can also be excellent supports for the consider stage of the Learning Challenge.

The best Learning Records have photographic records of student achievement together with short descriptions in student-friendly language of key learning moments. With a bit of adaptation, they could also make the following steps more explicit:

1. We were introduced to something new. (Identify the concept)

2. We worked through the challenges that this presented. (Cognitive conflict)

3. We learned this and so understood that more. (Construct understanding)

Conclusion

I offer these strategies as starting points. You may well already have tools in place that enable meaningful metacognition to take place. I also recognize that some of the ideas presented here may be too complex or too simplistic for some learners with SEN and that some of our students are extremely difficult to reach. But there's our challenge, and that perhaps is one of the reasons why we do what we do!

To conclude, I'd like to finish with a story about a group of older students with SEN that I worked with once upon a time. I share this being mindful of the previous chapter about teacher expectations and also as a caveat to some of the ideas I've shared in this section about keeping the challenge very shallow.

When I worked with sixteen- to nineteen-year-old students with severe learning difficulties, I organized a residential trip to an outdoor education center used by many of the local schools. Our school had never been to the center, and the staff there had little or no experience of working with students with these levels of learning difficulties. Needless to say, all these factors were comprehensively risk assessed before we headed off for a week of rock climbing, canoeing, caving and hiking.

The instructors at the center, while very much in charge of the safety aspects of all of the activities, had asked me to advise them at every stage on what I saw as an appropriate level of challenge. When I explained that many of these students struggled to step down from benches during PE in the hall at school or had issues with balance on ramps, they were surprised that I still thought a visit to a real rock face was viable.

On the first day, I accompanied a small group of students with Down syndrome to the rock face used by the outdoor center. What I knew about this location was that the rock face went from near vertical smooth rock, favored by elite climbers, around to easy routes that were typically used by the school groups who were brought here. There was also a rocky footpath, and this was the one that my students spent a whole morning navigating. They wore harnesses, roped up and climbed from the base of the cliff to a point on this path where they then rappelled down. Just as the smooth vertical rock face was beyond anything I'd contemplated climbing, so it was that this rocky path exceeded anything in terms of challenge that they'd ever encountered. But because this challenge was just right for them, the sense of accomplishment was enormous.

There were more high fives that day than I had ever witnessed before, with the students going through the full range of emotions one might expect from anyone rock climbing for the first time.

This set the tone for the whole week and reminded me just what people are capable of when encouraged and supported in the right way.

9.3.1 • Gifted and Talented Students

As an addendum to Mark's section about SEN students, I'd like to give a quick tip of the hat to students at the other end of the continuum: what many schools call "gifted education" or the "gifted and talented." Of course, this category is almost as varied and broad as the special educational needs category, but here are a few thoughts.

Having often worked with gifted students, I have found *some* of them to be wary of the Learning Challenge to begin with. For those students who have gained their gifted status by being remarkably capable of remembering information or for having a deep knowledge of specialized topics, they are thrown by the experience of going into the pit and not knowing the correct answer immediately. For other students who are used to being certain of their abilities, they often find the experience of cognitive conflict particularly confronting and unsettling. This is by no means the case for all gifted and talented students, but it is for a significant number of them.

> **Top students sometimes find the LC unsettling because they can't immediately spot the right answer. They soon get the hang of it, though, and begin to enjoy the extra opportunity to challenge, explore and engage with ideas.**

It is relatively straightforward to allay these misgivings by sharing the rationale for the Learning Challenge. What gifted and talent students—and indeed most students generally—need to know is what's in it for them. The Learning Challenge should not be sprung on them but introduced with reasons and an overview of the aims. You might like to use the following suggestions.

A rationale for the Learning Challenge

1. We learn more when we step out of our comfort zone.

2. One way to step out of our comfort zone is to find examples of cognitive conflict. This is when two or more ideas exist side by side and yet are in conflict with each other.

3. Examples of cognitive conflict include "stealing is wrong" but "Robin Hood was a good man," "equality is a good thing" but "not all people need the same thing" and "we should not lie" but "parents lie to their children about Santa, the tooth fairy and so on."

4. It can be confusing and sometimes frustrating to explore conflicting ideas, but ultimately that investigation can lead to a better understanding of important concepts such as existence, knowledge, right and wrong, thinking, art, community, science, politics and so on.

5. The Learning Challenge describes the journey we can take to explore these important concepts: Step 1, identify an interesting concept; Step 2, discover the contradictions and problems within people's understanding of that concept; Step 3, find connections and patterns between those ideas and then piece together a more complete definition; Step 4, reflect on the learning journey and think how this might be applied to other contexts.

6. Stepping out of your comfort zone is what one of the pioneers of educational psychology, Lev Vygotsky, called the zone of proximal development. In the Learning Challenge, this same zone is referred to as the pit. This term was chosen to evoke the feelings of discomfort and frustration many people feel when they are out of their comfort zone.

7. The pit is far less daunting when we are in it with others. That is why the Learning Challenge is a collaborative exercise. We are going to go into the pit together, and then we are going to help each other climb back out with much better ideas than we could have created by ourselves.

This rationale is as applicable to all students as it is to the gifted and talented ones.

9.4 • LEADING THE LEARNING CHALLENGE IN YOUR SCHOOL

Here are some suggestions for ways to get the Learning Challenge going across your school or college.

9.4.1 • Introduction

As the old cliché goes, first impressions count. So make sure the introduction to the Learning Challenge is a good one. There really is no substitute for seeing it working brilliantly in practice or hearing the model described by someone who knows it really well.

If that is not possible for you, then I recommend that you at least share the animated video of the Learning Challenge that is currently on Vimeo and YouTube. There are also some examples of the approach in practice on those sites. Resources are listed in Section 9.5.

9.4.2 • Background Reading

Encourage your colleagues to read as much of this book as they find interesting. As a minimum, I would recommend the following sections:

Chapter 1: introduction to the Learning Challenge

Sections 3.1, 3.2 and 3.4: the values and ground rules

Sections 5.1, 5.2 and 5.3: the role and rationale of cognitive conflict

Sections 6.1, 6.4 and 6.5: constructing answers and the eureka moment

Sections 8.2 and 8.3: self-efficacy, collective teacher efficacy and praise

A collaborative way to do some background reading would be through the use of Jigsaw Groups. This approach was designed by social psychologist Elliot Aronson (see www.jigsaw.org) to help weaken racial cliques in forcibly integrated schools. Here is one way to run Jigsaw Groups with your colleagues:

1. Divide your colleagues into groups of five. These are the home groups.

2. Assign one of the five segments of background reading shown above to each of the home groups.

3. Give each group time to read their section, question each other, discuss the main ideas and make notes.

4. Ask each person in a home group to number themselves 1 through 5.

5. Person 1 from each home group then moves to sit with all the other number 1s, Person 2 sits with all other number 2s on another table and so on. These new groups are now the away groups.

6. Each member of the away group takes it in turn to present their segment to the other members of their new group.

7. Once all of the information has been shared in the away group, everybody returns to their original groups to share what they have learned with each other.

9.4.3 • Ready-Fire-Aim

I find this a useful approach to professional learning. The routine is as follows:

Ready: preparing to have a go at something

Fire: having a few goes at the new ideas

Aim: returning to the source to ask more informed and nuanced questions

Ready

In the context of what I'm suggesting here, the *ready* section would begin with the introduction mentioned above plus the background reading. Following that, each of your colleagues should dip into the book to find some concepts or routines they think would be relevant for their particular students. Here are the best ways to begin this search:

Pick a concept (Sections 4.2, 4.2.1 and 4.3)

And/or create some questions (Sections 4.4 and 4.4.1)

Identify ways to create cognitive conflict (Sections 5.4, 5.5, 5.6 and 5.7)

Choose a construction strategy (Section 6.3)

> This list gives the main sections to read before having a go at a Learning Challenge.

> Jigsaw Groups are an effective way to engage in professional learning together.

> The Ready-Fire-Aim approach encourages a "try now, refine later" approach.

Fire

Now encourage (or expect?) your colleagues to have a go with at least one group of students. Remind them that it is very rare for the first few experiences to go according to plan. They might get deeply into the pit and stay there. Or they might find an answer all too quickly and easily and feel that they haven't really managed to get their students into the pit at all. Do not let this deter them. It takes time to build toward a complete and satisfying Learning Challenge. Meanwhile, the students will be learning *something*, be it how to think together, how to question more appropriately, what makes a good question and so on.

Aim

After your colleagues have attempted at least two or three Learning Challenge episodes, then bring them together for a reflection session. This is when the more focused and *nuanced* aiming is likely to take place. Ask them to split into groups to share what has worked and what hasn't. I recommend that you mix the groups in terms of different subjects or age groups taught. This will encourage them to explore a broader range of perspectives and (hopefully) stop certain faculties saying, "This just doesn't work for our curriculum subject."

One way to structure this review section is to use Edward de Bono's (2010) Plus Minus Interesting strategy. This means grouping reflections into the following categories:

Plus: the things that have worked well and why they have worked well

Minus: the things that have not worked well *yet* and why they haven't

Interesting: neither pluses nor minuses but things that would be interesting to find out, for example, "It would be interesting to see if that concept could be explored more successfully if we were to use physical props next time" or "It would be interesting to pause a session when students are in the pit to see if we can think of better challenges overnight"

Following this review, ask your colleagues in groups to list all the actions they think could be taken next. For example:

1. Try the same concept with a different group.

2. Run a full Learning Challenge session one afternoon without worrying about time or curriculum content.

3. Train older students to help facilitate Learning Challenge sessions with younger students.

4. Team teach, with one member of staff leading the session and the other one supporting with additional questions and challenges.

5. In teams, plan a full Learning Challenge for each member of the team to run with their students during the course of the week.

6. Arrange the students into mixed-age groups to see if that changes the quality of the Learning Challenge experience.

7. Divide a full Learning Challenge into four sections—concept, conflict, construct and consider—then run one section per day for four days.

8. Create a team of Learning Challenge champions who will plan the first three sessions for each year group in the school.

These are some of the actions a team might take to get the LC going in their organization.

9. Have a roll-out program in which a group of staff use the Learning Challenge much more regularly than others so that they are in a position to coach others later.

10. Meet once a month in faculty groups to review the successes and problems so far and to plan for the next set of Learning Challenges.

Once your colleagues have created the most complete list they can in the time they've got, ask each member of staff to commit to taking one of those actions over the coming weeks. It doesn't matter which they choose, so long as they choose one and do it to the best of their ability. It doesn't even need to be that every action on the list is claimed. So long as every person picks one action, even if it is the same as someone else's action, then there is likely to be forward momentum generated for everyone.

9.4.4 • Blending the Learning Challenge Into the Curriculum

On the one hand, the Learning Challenge often works best when it is not constrained by the requirements of the curriculum. So if you are able to run a session without worrying about the knowledge your students will gain at the conclusion, then you will be freer to focus on the other benefits such as developments in learning strategies and language.

On the other hand, curricula around the world are already bursting at the seams, so to try to find space in the timetable for yet another subject might seem unreasonable, at least to some. The following, then, are three approaches you might take in the hope of pleasing most of the people most of the time. They are guidelines only based on my own experience. Feel free to adapt the timing or the sequence of events—or dismiss them altogether!

9.4.4.1 • Phased Approach

A phased approach aims to strike a balance between the opportunity to develop the attitudes and skills of the Learning Challenge without worrying too much about curriculum aims and, at the same time, create the habit of taking students into the pit whenever and wherever it seems appropriate to do so. I have split the approach into four phases, but they could equally be blended into three phases if this suits your academic year better.

Phase 1   Approximately ten to twelve weeks

Create space in the timetable for every student to experience a full Learning Challenge episode three or four times in a ten- to twelve-week block.

A full session is likely to last between forty-five and seventy-five minutes depending on the concept chosen and the social/cognitive development of the students. One session might even be split into smaller sections if needs be.

The more staff you can involve in this phase, the more chance you will have of making the approach part of the learning culture of the school. So if you are able to encourage *all* staff—support staff and leaders as well as teachers—to take a group each, then the gains are likely to be more significant. It will also allow you to split students into smaller classes than normal, with the added benefit that this brings.

This phase is sometimes referred to as Learning to Learn in parent newsletters and within the school curriculum.

> A phased approach is probably the best way to embed the values and skills of the LC.

Phase 2   Approximately six to eight weeks

Create space in the timetable for every student to experience the Learning Challenge in a different group from normal and with a different teacher.

By organizing your students into mixed-age groups and getting them to work with a member of staff they are less familiar with, you are likely to enhance the sense of collaboration across the school. It also gives students the opportunity to learn from and communicate with a more diverse group than they might normally experience.

In some schools, this phase is called the Three Bears or Vertical Groups section. The former references the different ages and sizes of the bears in "Goldilocks and the Three Bears"; the latter refers to grouping students from the top, middle and lower levels in school.

Phase 3   Approximately ten to fourteen weeks

Do not timetable stand-alone Learning Challenge sessions. Instead, ask each member of staff to incorporate the Learning Challenge into the regular subjects studied at school. For example, one week students might encounter a Learning Challenge in history, the next time in science and so on. This might take a bit of overall planning for staff to ensure no groups are encountering too many Learning Challenges in the week while others are encountering none, but generally it tends to even out over the course of a month or two.

Phase 4   Approximately six to twelve weeks

Ask staff not to plan explicitly for Learning Challenge experiences. Instead, they should look for opportunities within normal lessons to take their students on a Learning Challenge journey when it seems appropriate to do so. So it might be that during a discussion about *Macbeth,* the opportunity arises to investigate what is meant by ambition or tragedy. Or when younger children are finding out about birds and mammals, a dialogue about pets might turn into a Learning Challenge.

9.4.4.2 • Curriculum Approach

The Learning Challenge provides ample opportunity to develop many learning attitudes and skills specified in academic standards. This gives you the opportunity to plan for Learning Challenge sessions at the same time as planning for curriculum development by matching the outcomes of your Learning Intentions and Success Criteria around these academic standards.

Many teachers use the LC to meet curriculum targets such as those shown.

Skills Developed	UK National Curriculum for England	USA Common Core State Standards—English Language Arts Anchor Standards	USA Common Core State Standards—Mathematical Practices	USA Texas Essential Knowledge and Skills (TEKS) and Texas College and Career Readiness Standards	Australian Curriculum Version 8.3
Communication	Speaking: including effectively for different audiences Listening: to understand and respond appropriately and participate effectively in group discussion	Present information, findings and supporting evidence such that listeners can follow the line of reasoning and the organization, development, and style are appropriate to task, purpose, and audience. (CCSS.ELA-LITERACY. CCRA.SL.4) Prepare for and participate effectively in a range of conversations and collaborations with diverse partners, building on others' ideas and expressing their own clearly and persuasively. (CCSS.ELA-LITERACY. CCRA.SL.1) Apply knowledge of language to understand how language functions in different contexts, to make effective choices for meaning or style, and to comprehend more fully when reading or listening. (CCSS.ELA-LITERACY. CCRA.L.3) Apply knowledge of language to understand how language functions in different contexts, to make effective choices for meaning or style, and to comprehend more fully when reading or listening. (CCSS.ELA-LITERACY. CCRA.L.3)	Attend to precision. (CCSS.MATH. PRACTICE.MP6) Construct viable arguments and critique the reasoning of others. (CCSS.MATH. PRACTICE.MP3)	Understand the elements of communication both in informal group discussions and formal presentations (e.g., accuracy, relevance, rhetorical features, organization of information). (Texas College and Career Readiness Standards, English Language Arts III.A) Apply listening skills as an individual and as a member of a group in a variety of settings (e.g., lectures, discussions, conversations, team projects, presentations, interviews). (Texas College and Career Readiness Standards, English Language Arts IV.A)	Speaking: learning how to speak expressively and clearly, always taking into account purpose and audience. Understand the use of persuasion and challenging others with a language that is respectful and thoughtful. Listening: to develop the skills of listening with empathy, listening to inform, listening to form opinion and listening critically.

(Continued)

Skills Developed	UK National Curriculum for England	USA Common Core State Standards—English Language Arts Anchor Standards	USA Common Core State Standards—Mathematical Practices	USA Texas Essential Knowledge and Skills (TEKS) and Texas College and Career Readiness Standards	Australian Curriculum Version 8.3
Application of Number	Developing the understanding and use of mathematical language related to numbers and calculations in order to process data, solve increasingly complex problems and explain the reasoning used Applying calculation skills and understanding of number to problems in other curriculum subjects and real-life situations		Model with mathematics. (CCSS.MATH.PRACTICE.MP4) Look for and make use of structure. (CCSS.MATH.PRACTICE.MP7)	Use mathematics as a language for reasoning, problem solving, making connections, and generalizing. (Texas College and Career Readiness Standards, Mathematics IX.A.3)	Mathematics aims to ensure that students are confident, creative users and communicators of mathematics, able to investigate, represent and interpret situations in their personal and work lives and as active citizens. Develop a common language in the use of number. Develop an increasingly sophisticated understanding of mathematical concepts and fluency with processes, and are able to create meaningful data, pose and solve problems and reason in number and algebra. Recognise connections between the areas of mathematics and other disciplines and appreciate mathematics as an accessible and enjoyable discipline to study.
Information Technology	Ability to make critical and informed judgements about when and how to use ICT for maximum benefit in accessing information, in solving problems or expressing work Ability to use ICT information sources includes enquiry and decision-making skills, as well as information processing and creative thinking skills and the ability to review, modify and evaluate work with ICT		Use appropriate tools strategically. (CCSS.MATH.PRACTICE.MP5)	Digital citizenship. The student practices safe, responsible, legal, and ethical behavior while using digital tools and resources. The student is expected to: (A) adhere to acceptable use policies reflecting appropriate behavior in a digital environment; (B) comply with acceptable digital safety rules, fair use guidelines, and copyright laws; and (C) practice the responsible use of digital information regarding intellectual property, including software, text, images, audio, and video. (TEKS §126.6.5)	Applying social and ethical protocols and practices When using ICT element Recognise intellectual property. Identify and describe ethical dilemmas and consciously apply practices that protect intellectual property. Use a range of strategies for securing and protecting information, assess the risks associated with online environments and establish appropriate security strategies and codes of conduct. Investigating with ICT element Select and use a range of ICT independently and collaboratively, analyse information to frame questions and plan search strategies or data generation. Use advanced search tools and techniques or simulations and digital models to locate or generate precise data and information that supports the development of new understandings.

			Communicating with ICT element

Select and use a range of ICT tools efficiently and safely to share and exchange information, and to collaboratively and purposefully construct knowledge.

Understand that computer mediated communications have advantages and disadvantages in supporting active participation in a community of practice and the management of collaboration on digital materials. |
| **Working With Others/ Collaboration** | Working with others including the ability to contribute to small-group and whole-class discussion, and to work with others to meet a challenge

Social awareness and understanding the needs of others | Prepare for and participate effectively in a range of conversations and collaborations with diverse partners, building on others' ideas and expressing their own clearly and persuasively. (CCSS.ELA-LITERACY. CCRA.SL.1) | Construct viable arguments and critique the reasoning of others. (CCSS.MATH. PRACTICE.MP3) | Learn to work in teams, small groups and in all collaborative learning situations.

Listen carefully to others, be supportive of others' learning ideas and effectively express own ideas with clarity and conviction. |
| **Improving Own Learning and Performance** | Pupils reflecting on and critically evaluating their work and what they have learnt and identifying ways to improve their learning and performance

Identifying purposes of learning, reflecting on the process of learning, assessing progress in learning, identifying obstacles or problems in learning and ways to improve learning | | | Students will be taught to improve their understanding of themselves as a learner and scrutinise their performance on given learning tasks.

Understanding the reason for learning and measuring their performance against specific and measurable success criteria will assist in developing reflective practices. |

(Continued)

Skills Developed	UK National Curriculum for England	USA Common Core State Standards—English Language Arts Anchor Standards	USA Common Core State Standards—Mathematical Practices	USA Texas Essential Knowledge and Skills (TEKS) and Texas College and Career Readiness Standards	Australian Curriculum Version 8.3
Problem Solving	Pupils developing the skills and strategies that will help them to solve the problems they face in learning and life Includes the skills of identifying and understanding a problem, planning ways to solve a problem, monitoring progress in tackling a problem and reviewing solutions to a problem		Make sense of problems and persevere in solving them. (CCSS.MATH. PRACTICE.MP1) Model with mathematics. (CCSS.MATH. PRACTICE.MP4)	Formulate a solution to a real world situation based on the solution to a mathematical problem. (Texas College and Career Readiness Standards, Mathematics VIII.C.1)	Students provided with ongoing opportunities to develop skills and strategies in problem solving, both in learning tasks and in their everyday lives. Students learn how to establish the root cause of a problem, the nature of a problem, what a solution needs to achieve and what features the solution would need to include. Students learn to review the processes they took in solving problems, analysing and evaluating worth and success.
Information Processing	These enable pupils to locate and collect relevant information, to sort, classify, sequence, compare and contrast and to analyse part/whole relationships	Analyze how and why individuals, events, or ideas develop and interact over the course of a text. (CCSS.ELA-LITERACY. CCRA.R.3) Determine central ideas or themes of a text and analyze their development; summarize the key supporting details and ideas. (CCSS.ELA-LITERACY. CCRA.R.2)	Make sense of problems and persevere in solving them. (CCSS.MATH. PRACTICE.MP1)	Interpret multiple representations of equations and relationships. (Texas College and Career Readiness Standards, Mathematics II.D.1)	Students experience learning key concepts, such as research, data collection and information, using some or all of the following processes to make sense of it: • Locating • Collecting • Classifying • Recognising • Organising • Sequencing • Identifying • Collating • Categorising • Comparing/Contrasting • Transposing • Analysing

Reasoning	Enable pupils to give reasons for opinions and actions, to draw inferences and make deductions, to use precise language to explain what they think, and to make judgements and decisions informed by reasons or evidence	Evaluate a speaker's point of view, reasoning, and use of evidence and rhetoric. (CCSS.ELA-LITERACY.CCRA.SL.3)	Reason abstractly and quantitatively. (CCSS.MATH.PRACTICE.MP2) Look for and express regularity in repeated reasoning. (CCSS.MATH.PRACTICE.MP8)	Analysing, synthesising and evaluating reasoning and results This element involves students analysing, synthesising and evaluating the reasoning and procedures used to find solutions, evaluate and justify results or inform courses of action. Students identify, consider and assess the logic and reasoning behind choices. They differentiate components of decisions made and actions taken and assess ideas, methods and outcomes against criteria. In developing and acting with critical and creative thinking, students: • Apply logic and reasoning • Draw conclusions and design a course of action • Evaluate procedures, outcomes and learning
Inquiry	Enable pupils to ask relevant questions, to pose and define problems, to plan what to do and how to research, to predict outcomes and anticipate consequences, and to test conclusions and improve ideas		Look for and make use of structure. (CCSS.MATH.PRACTICE.MP7) Look for and express regularity in repeated reasoning. (CCSS.MATH.PRACTICE.MP8)	Enquiring – identifying, exploring and organising information and ideas Students pose questions and identify and clarify information and ideas, and then organise and process information. They use questioning to investigate and analyse ideas and issues, make sense of and assess information and ideas, and collect, compare and evaluate information from a range of sources. In developing and acting with critical and creative thinking, students: • Pose questions • Identify and clarify information and ideas • Organise and process information
			Formulate topic and questions. (Texas College and Career Readiness Standards, English Language Arts V.A) Research/Research Plan. Students ask open-ended research questions and develop a plan for answering them. Students are expected to: (A) brainstorm, consult with others, decide upon a topic, and formulate open-ended questions to address the major research topic; and (B) generate a research plan for gathering relevant information about the major research question. (TEKS §110.18.22)	

(Continued)

(Continued)

Skills Developed	UK National Curriculum for England	USA Common Core State Standards—English Language Arts Anchor Standards	USA Common Core State Standards—Mathematical Practices	USA Texas Essential Knowledge and Skills (TEKS) and Texas College and Career Readiness Standards	Australian Curriculum Version 8.3
Creative Thinking	Enable pupils to generate and extend ideas, to suggest hypotheses, to apply imagination, and to look for alternative innovative outcomes	Present information, findings, and supporting evidence such that listeners can follow the line of reasoning and the organization, development, and style are appropriate to task, purpose, and audience. (CCSS.ELA-LITERACY. CCRA.SL.4)	Make sense of problems and persevere in solving them. (CCSS.MATH. PRACTICE.MP1)	Accept constructive criticism and revise personal views when valid evidence warrants. (Texas College and Career Readiness Standards, Cross-Disciplinary Standards I.A.2)	Creative thinking involves students learning to generate and apply new ideas in specific contexts, seeing existing situations in a new way, identifying alternative explanations, and seeing or making new links that generate a positive outcome. This includes combining parts to form something original, sifting and refining ideas to discover possibilities, constructing theories and objects, and acting on intuition. The products of creative endeavour can involve complex representations and images, investigations and performances, digital and computer-generated output, or occur as virtual reality.
Evaluation	Enable pupils to evaluate information, to judge the value of what they read, hear and do, to develop criteria for judging the value of their own and others work or ideas, and to have confidence in their own judgements	Evaluate a speaker's point of view, reasoning, and use of evidence and rhetoric. (CCSS.ELA-LITERACY. CCRA.SL.3) Delineate and evaluate the argument and specific claims in a text, including the validity of the reasoning as well as the relevance and sufficiency of the evidence. (CCSS.ELA-LITERACY. CCRA.R.8)	Construct viable arguments and critique the reasoning of others. (CCSS.MATH. PRACTICE.MP3)	Identify and analyze the main idea(s) and point(s)-of-view in sources. (Texas College and Career Readiness Standards, Social Studies IV.A.1) Evaluate sources for quality of content, validity, credibility, and relevance. (Texas College and Career Readiness Standards, Cross-Disciplinary Standards I.F.2)	Students are taught the concept of critical thinking, as a means of judging their learning and that of others, texts that they read and ideas or possibilities that they are asked to consider or formulate by themselves.

Planning a range of Learning Challenge lessons using these curriculum aims might look something like this:

Learning Challenge 1

Learning Intention

We are learning to work with others to meet a challenge and to contribute to whole-class discussion

Success Criteria

To reach our learning goal, we will be able to:

- Listen attentively to each other

- Encourage each other with supportive body language

- Allow thinking time and not rush people or interrupt them

- Respond appropriately using phrases such as "I agree with (name) because . . . " or "I disagree with (name) because . . . "

- Be able to identify or describe a cognitive conflict that took place during the dialogue

Learning Challenge 2

Learning Intention

We are learning to use precise language to explain what we think

Success Criteria

To reach our learning goal, we will be able to:

- Show that we have understood what someone else has said by paraphrasing their thoughts before building on what they said

- Show that we might have misunderstood what someone else said by asking clarification questions

- Identify examples of when the things that people said were understood correctly by others

- Identify examples of when the things that people said were misunderstood by others

- Compare the different examples and identify the top three reasons why

Learning Challenge 3

Learning Intention

We are learning to reflect on and critically evaluate a Learning Challenge experience

> Matching Learning Intentions and Success Criteria to curriculum targets can help to justify and embed LC sessions into school life.

Success Criteria

To reach our learning goal, we will be able to:

- Identify the contradictions we discovered in our own thinking

- Explain why the ideas we generated did or did not generate cognitive conflict

- Identify the strategies we have used to explain and connect our ideas

- Give suggestions for what we could have done to deepen the pit and/or improve our final answer

- Think of ways to apply and relate our learning to other contexts

9.4.4.3 Subject or Faculty Approach

Although it is possible to embed the Learning Challenge into all curriculum areas, there are some subjects that seem to be a more natural fit. These include personal, social, health education and citizenship; English; history; geography; religious education; and the sciences.

Although I would be reticent to recommend that the Learning Challenge be used exclusively in the subject areas listed, for pragmatic reasons this might be the way to go at least initially, after which I think it would be wise to look for opportunities to roll it across the whole school.

9.5 • LEARNING CHALLENGE RESOURCES

The following are examples, illustrations and additional teaching resources connected to the Learning Challenge:

Books

1. *Challenging Learning* by James Nottingham, 1st ed., 2010; 2nd ed., 2016

2. *Encouraging Learning* by James Nottingham, 2013

3. *Challenging Learning Through Dialogue* by James Nottingham, Jill Nottingham and Martin Renton, 2017

4. *Challenging Learning Through Feedback* by James Nottingham and Jill Nottingham, 2017

5. *Challenging Learning Through Questioning* by James Nottingham and Martin Renton, in press

6. *Creating a Challenging Learning Mindset* by James Nottingham and Bosse Larsson, in press

7. *Learning Challenge Lessons, Elementary* by James Nottingham, Jill Nottingham, Lucy Bennison and Mark Bollom, in press

8. *Learning Challenge Lessons, Secondary ELA* by James Nottingham, Jill Nottingham, Lucy Bennison and Mark Bollom, in press

9. *Learning Challenge Lessons, Secondary Mathematics* by James Nottingham, Jill Nottingham, Lucy Bennison and Mark Bollom, in press

10. *Learning Challenge Lessons, Secondary Science/STEM* by James Nottingham, Jill Nottingham, Lucy Bennison and Mark Bollom, in press

> The Learning Challenge is part of a series of books by the Challenging Learning team.

Online

The Learning Challenge Animation

Available on Vimeo (http://vimeo.com/128462566) and YouTube (www.youtube.com/watch?v=3IMUAOhuO78)

Example Illustrations From Around the World

---

www.jamesnottingham.co.uk/learning-pit

Downloadable Resources

---

http://www.challenginglearning.com/resources

9.6 • REVIEW

In addition to the main points identified in the preview, this chapter has covered the following:

1. When seeking to challenge students with special educational needs, we should be mindful of the fact that in so many ways their learning journey is already a challenge.

2. Some gifted and talented students can be wary of the Learning Challenge to begin with, especially if they don't know what the purpose of it is. So, as for all students, it helps to give them the rationale before beginning the first Learning Challenge.

3. Ready-Fire-Aim is a useful approach to professional learning. This means getting ready by doing some background reading, then firing by having a go with the ideas in practice and finally aiming by reflecting on the early experiences and asking more focused and nuanced questions.

4. Introducing the Learning Challenge across a whole school can be best achieved using a phased approach. This includes starting with stand-alone Learning Challenge lessons and then evolving into spontaneous experiences that are born out of normal curriculum experiences.

THE LEARNING CHALLENGE IN ACTION — 10

10.0 • PREVIEW

This chapter shares ideas for seven different Learning Challenge experiences.

The most important points include:

1. There are seven example concepts: color, drugs, killing, pets, social networking, proof and evidence, risk.

2. For each concept, there is an introduction plus some suggested questions to help create cognitive conflict and then some pit tools to help your students climb out of the pit.

3. The questions and activities are suggestions only. I do not imagine that you would use all the questions. Instead, I recommend that you select a few to use with your students and only if they are needed. It might be that other questions arise more spontaneously anyway.

> This final chapter shows worked examples for seven full LC sessions.

10.1 • COLOR

Age range: six to sixteen

Subjects: science, arts, media

Stage 1: Identify the Concept

Color is a particularly relevant concept for the Learning Challenge because of the ambiguities about what it is, where it comes from and whether it even exists in the physical world or whether it is purely a perception. In other words, would color exist if humans didn't perceive color?

Furthermore, color plays a central role in our lives. Visual experiences are deeply seated in color. People respond emotionally to color. And yet color might not even exist beyond the minds and perceptions of living creatures!

Are we seeing things that don't truly exist? For example, if we look at a banana, perhaps we see it as yellow; if we look away, is the yellow still there? Or is it our recognition of the fruit that triggers a sense of yellow in our mind?

You can have a lot of fun with your students by exploring the concept of color. Remember, though, that the point is not to reach the "right" answer but to guide your students through the Learning Challenge to create a more complex and thorough understanding of the concept.

Stage 2: Create Cognitive Conflict

Key Areas to Investigate Within and Around the Concept of Color

- The reality of color
- Our perception of color
- The illusion of color
- The social significance of color
- The psychological significance of color
- Our beliefs about colors
- Color in nature
- Identity
- Change
- Well-being
- Safety
- Color prejudice

Questions That Might Lead to Cognitive Conflict
WIth Students Age Six to Twelve

- What is color?
- Are colors real?
- If you were to write a book about colors, what would you write?
- How many colors can you see right now?
- Does everything have a color?
- What color are your dreams?
- Do you think in color?

- Do you feel in color?

- Do sounds have colors?

- Can you hear different colors?

- When you look at red, how do you know it is red?

- How is color created?

- Why do we see colors?

- Are rainbows real?

- If you were a color, what color would you be?

- What would the world be like without colors?

- Are some colors scarier than others?

- Does everything have a color?

- Are black and white colors?

- Are colors just names we use or do they tell us more?

- What things come in different colors? Do the following things come in different colors and, if they do, what colors do they come in: dogs, ice cream, the sky, flowers, grass, water, fire, people, footballs, winter, sadness, roller blades, a whisper, laughter, autumn?

- If an orange was not orange in color, would it be a different fruit? Why don't we call bananas "yellows" and plums "purples"?

Questions That Might Lead to Cognitive Conflict With Students Age Twelve to Sixteen

- Does every color have a name?

- If we look at this color, are we all seeing the same color?

- What color is the sound of a police siren?

- Do you think there will ever be new colors?

- What would it be like to change colors?

- Do colors change?

- Are there things that have no color (i.e., space, light)?

- Are there things that have many colors (i.e., space, light)?

- If something is red, can it also be blue? Can it be pink? Maroon?

- Is the color green made up of blue and yellow? If so, is all green just blue and yellow? Or is it something in itself?

- Do all green things look alike?

- What is the difference between a tint and a shade?

- Do all things that are blue feel the same way (i.e., the sky, a blue blanket)?

- Can colors make you feel a certain way?

- What color is a mirror?

- When is yellow yellower than yellow?

- Is there such a thing as the perfect color?

- Are there specific colors for specific people?

- Can you imagine a perfect color?

- Do we have the same color coding for danger as the color animals use to warn each other?

- Can the same color warn us and attract us?

- Is brown a good color for sweets? Is it a good color for chocolate?

- Why do we associate blue and not green with swimming baths?

- Does color affect our sense of smell and taste?

- Should we always believe our senses?

- Do certain colors make us have certain thoughts?

- Who told you that a specific color was a certain color?

- Can we really be sure we are all seeing the same colors?

- What do you think the effects of gender-specific color coding on young children are?

Stage 3: Construct Understanding

If your students are deeply in the pit and finding it difficult to climb back out, then you could invite them to use a Concept Corner such as the one in Figure 62. This is a derivation of the Concept Tables shown in Section 6.3.8.

Write the concept in the middle of the table. Then ask your students to think of examples for each of the categories shown in the corners. Example answers are shown in italics in Figure 62, but ordinarily you would give your students a version without the examples included.

▶ **Figure 62: Concept Table (With Examples Included)**

Phrases		Example
Phrases or sentences with *"color"* in them		Context in which "color" is important
Sample answers		Sample answers
• *The color of money*		• *Rainbows*
• *She hasn't got any color in her cheeks*		• *Fruit*
• *His rudeness colored her judgment*		• *Art*
		• *Warning signs*
	Color	
Synonyms and Antonyms		**Related Ideas**
Sample answers		Sample answers
• *Shade*		• *Art*
• *Tone*		• *Perception*
• *Hue*		• *Senses*
• *Tint*		

Another pit tool that would work particularly well with this concept is ranking. The tools of diamond ranking, pyramid ranking and linear ranking are all described in Section 6.3.3.

The criteria for ranking could be one of the following:

- Most/least exciting
- Most/least useful in everyday life
- Most/least meaningful
- Colors that make you feel calm, upset, confident, scared, thankful and so on
- Colors that act as warning signals

Stage 4: Consider

Sample Review Questions

- What is color?
- What effect does color have on our everyday lives?
- How does color affect our moods and personalities?
- What would the world be like without color?
- What colors do you think are gender stereotyped? Who do you think decided these?
- Is it possible that the gender color norms could possibly stem from the evolved differences between boys' and girls' favorite colors?
- Is color dictated by nature or nurture?
- Are we the only living creatures that see in color?
- What questions about colors are you left with?

10.2 • DRUGS

Age range: twelve to sixteen

Subjects: personal health, social and citizenship education

Stage 1: Identify the Concept

The concept of drugs dates back millennia. The coca plant has been considered a medicinal and sometimes magical drug going as far back as the Andean world more than four thousand years ago. There is also evidence of beer brewing from as early as seven thousand years ago, which again some people would consider to be a drug.

In many high schools, drugs education is an important aspect of the curriculum. It is also a hotly debated topic in political arenas around the world. All of this makes the concept an interesting one for a Learning Challenge experience.

Stage 2: Create Cognitive Conflict

Key Areas to Investigate Within and Around the Concept of Drugs

- Peer pressure
- Positive assertiveness
- Influence
- Risk
- Law
- Crime
- Legalization
- Legal and illegal drugs
- Prescription drugs
- Counterfeit drugs
- Drug dependence

Questions That Might Lead to Cognitive Conflict With Students Age Twelve to Sixteen

- What do we mean by the term *drugs*?
- Why do we have drugs?
- Are drugs bad for us?
- What do you think about drugs?
- Is it possible to go through life avoiding drugs completely?
- What is the difference between prescribed drugs and illegal drugs?
- Why is it justified for doctors to prescribe drugs that would otherwise be illegal?
- What are recreational drugs?
- How much drug use is too much?
- How much drinking of alcohol is too much?
- What is addiction?
- Have you ever done anything you didn't want to do?
- Why do we have laws?
- What do you know about laws regarding drugs?
- Do we have any rules to protect ourselves or just rules to protect other people?
- If you start using drugs, will you always continue to use them?
- If someone's aim in life is to be happy, and drugs make someone happy, is it then OK?

- What are the arguments for making all drugs legal?

- What effects do drugs have?

- What benefit to society is it to punish drug use?

- Can shame ruin your life?

- What motivates people to take drugs?

- Why might some people abuse drugs?

- Would legalizing more drugs cause more people to use them?

- Is it OK to have friends that you only party with?

- If something is legal, does that mean it is not harmful or addictive?

- Does the fact that we are told by the government that drugs are bad mean that they are?

- What are the risks involved in self-medicating when you feel unwell?

- Lots of substances are dangerous and damaging. Should the government ban unhealthy foods like donuts?

- If all drugs were legal, would emergency services have a duty to provide assistance if you overdosed?

- What if someone was hurt or unwell due to natural causes? Should emergency services assist that person first?

- Why do some people become addicted to drugs and others do not?

- Who influences you?

- Are we all addicted to something even if we don't realize it?

Stage 3: Construct Understanding

Your students could use a Concept Target to clarify the criteria and characteristics of the concept. This pit tool is described in Section 6.3.1.

Ask your students to draw an inner circle and an outer circle, as shown in Figure 63. In the inner circle they should write "drugs." In the outer circle, they should write all the ideas that have come out of the Learning Challenge dialogue so far.

For the examples given, I have assumed the starting question for the Learning Challenge was "Why would people use drugs?"

Then they should take each idea in turn to decide whether it is a necessary characteristic (in which case they should move it to the inner circle), a probable characteristic (in which case they should leave it in the outer circle) or a very rare characteristic (in which case they should move it outside of the outer circle).

► Figure 63: Concept Target (With Examples Included)

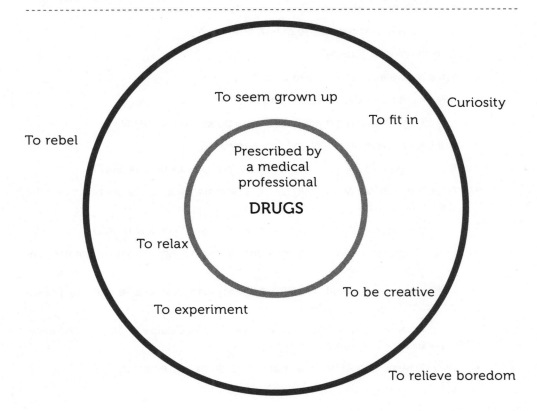

The diamond ranking activity described in Section 6.3.3 could be a useful pit tool for your students to use. The sorts of ideas that could be used with diamond ranking are shown in Figure 64. I have assumed the question is "What are important factors when making decisions about drug use?"

Stage 4: Consider

Sample Review Questions

- Why is age of first use of alcohol so critically important?
- Do you feel like you know where to go if you needed advice and help?
- Do you feel that you now know more about drugs and alcohol than you did at the start of the lesson?
- Do you think it is ever OK to use drugs? Under what circumstances?
- What questions about drugs are you left with?

▶ Figure 64: Examples to Place in a
　　　　　　Diamond Rank About Drugs

You are aware of how drug addiction develops and how drug use can seriously affect your body and the consequences it has.	When you are in trouble you have the confidence to seek help.	You hang out with people who share interests similar to yours.
You can cope well with pressures from others who try to involve you when you don't want to.	You think it feels right to do what you believe in.	You always think through your decisions carefully.
You thrive on being a role model and setting positive examples.	You have the ability to see when drug use is becoming a problem.	You like to keep up with trends and generally join in if "everyone is doing it."

10.3 • KILLING

Age range: ten to sixteen

Subjects: personal social health and citizenship, science

Stage 1: Identify the Concept

The concept of killing is an interesting one and has intrigued people for centuries. There are few moral beliefs that are more universal, unchanging and undisputed across different societies and throughout history than the belief that it is wrong to kill. However, it is clear this is contextual because so many people believe there are exceptions to the rule.

Stage 2: Create Cognitive Conflict

Key Areas to Investigate Within and Around the Concept of Killing

- Justifying
- Risk
- Law

- Murder
- Execution
- Choice

Questions That Might Lead to Cognitive Conflict
With Students Age Ten to Twelve

- What is killing?

- Is killing always wrong?

- Under what circumstances would killing be classed as a crime?

- Under what circumstances would killing not be classed as a crime?

- Is it always wrong to take another person's life?

- Is killing another person the worst possible thing anyone can do?

- Do some people extend the image of killing to the killing of all types of living beings and some concentrate only on humans?

- Are there exceptions that justify killing? Are there some situations in which it is morally acceptable?

- Is there ever a need to kill?

- What skills and knowledge should a person have in order to be in a position to judge what and when it is acceptable to kill?

- Murder is seen as unlawful because it deprives someone of life; however, life is common in all living things, like plants and animals. Is it therefore wrong to take away any living thing's life?

- Why is the killing of an animal normally less seriously wrong than the killing of a person?

Questions That Might Lead to Cognitive Conflict
With Students Age Twelve to Sixteen

- When we say or hear "it is wrong to kill," is the idea of wrongness a matter of degree?

- What do you think should be the punishment for murder (someone intentionally killing someone else)?

- If you were to create a set of rules for a person to fit into society, where would "not killing" rank?

- Do some of the reasons why killing a person is wrong not apply in the case of other living things?

- In a combat situation, is taking someone's life different? What about military on military and military on civilians?

- Do you think violence that is regularly shown on television, social media and video games and in films has made killing more acceptable? Has it made it more accessible?

- Is there a stronger moral belief that is more universal than "killing people is wrong"?

- Does partaking in activities such as smoking, drinking, engaging in dangerous sports and so on count as doing harm to one's own body, and would this be wrong if the result were death?

- Who owns one's life if not exclusively oneself? Can someone claim ownership over someone's life or a part of it?

- If we think about capital punishment, can anyone claim to be 100 percent sure that one criminal or another deserves to die?

- What expertise, skills and knowledge should somebody have to make life-or-death decisions?

- While many may believe it is wrong to kill people, is the killing of murderers an exception to the rule? Are there other exceptions to the rule?

- Is the death penalty a stronger deterrent than prison? Do crime statistics reflect this? Would the murder rate likely be higher without it?

Stage 3: Construct Understanding

As the dialogue progresses, your students could use an Opinion Line to register their (perhaps changing) opinions about the concept of killing. This pit tool is described in Section 6.3.4.

For this particular Opinion Line, you could do the following:

1. Create a line long enough for all your students to stand along. It might be helpful to mark this with a rope or some string.

2. Mark one end with a "Completely Justified" sign and the other with a "Completely Unjustified" sign. Talk through the other descriptors shown in Figure 65 if you think it will help your students understand the degrees of agreement and disagreement.

▶ **Figure 65: Opinion Line for the Concept *Killing***

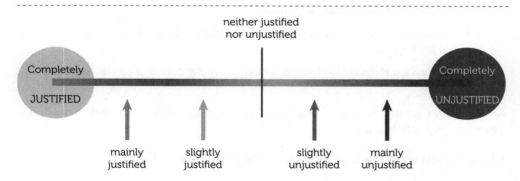

Suggested Topics for an Opinion Line About Killing
for Students Age Eight to Fourteen

- Killing a wolf before he kills the sheep

- Killing bacteria or viruses

- Killing for sport (e.g., fox hunting)

- Killing a nuisance like ants and mosquitos

- Killing accidentally and without noticing (e.g., a porcupine on a road)

- Killing animals to eat

- Killing plants to eat

- Killing slugs and snails that are eating your plants

- Two wrongs don't make a right

- Killing people is more wrong than killing animals. What if the person was guilty and the animal was innocent?

- Killing the guilty in defense of the innocent

Suggested Topics for an Opinion Line About Killing for Students Age Fourteen to Sixteen

- -

- Capital punishment for a serial murderer

- Capital punishment for a one-time murderer

- Capital punishment for a teenager who has murdered someone

- Killing yourself to save the life of another (e.g., a parent drowning while saving their child)

- War

- Euthanasia

- Suicide

- Assisted suicide

- An eye for an eye

- Someone gets pushed from a twelve-story building, killing the person they land on. The person who did the pushing and the person who was pushed are both punished.

- Killing someone by refusing an organ transplant for them because someone else was more deserving of the transplant

- There is only enough air in the tank to save one of two scuba divers, so one person is left to perish.

- Conjoined twins will both die in a matter of months, or one can be separated and saved.

An alternative pit tool to use in this Learning Challenge is a linear rank. This tool is described in Section 6.3.3.

Example question: When is killing most justified?

- War

- Stepping on a snail

- Pest control exterminators

- Capital punishment

- Animal euthanasia

- Human euthanasia

- Defense

- Revenge

- Carelessness

Stage 4: Consider

Sample Review Questions

- Do we have a degree of acceptability when it comes to killing different living things?

- Can someone ever value all life equally?

- Is killing ever right?

- Can murder ever be justified?

- What questions are you left with about killing?

10.4 • PETS

Age range: six to sixteen

Subjects: math—comparing animals; biology—life processes and living things

Stage 1: Identify the Concept

The concept of pets offers an opportunity to inquire into concepts such as nature, companionship and habitual practices.

The relationship between humans and other animals may have played an important role in human evolution. How is it that some animals transitioned from food to friends, and what is the significance of this relationship? With 46 percent of households in the United Kingdom owning a pet (Pet Food Manufacturers Association, 2015), making an animal part of the family is something plenty of us do. But why?

Stage 2: Create Cognitive Conflict

Key Areas to Investigate Within and Around the Concept of Pets

- Responsibility

- Wants and needs

- Choice

- Decision making

- Animal welfare

- Care

- Human nature

- Companionship

- Habitual practices

The ideas for the questions below are arranged into different wobblers. You can read about these in Section 5.4.1. The text below uses the same annotations that are used in Section 5.4.2:

(A) represents the main concept

(B) represents the students' main answer

(not A) is when the opposite of concept (A) is being tested

(not B) is when the opposite of answer (B) is being tested

(G) is a generalization

Questions That Might Lead to Cognitive Conflict With Students Age Six to Twelve

----

Wobbler 1

Question: What is a pet? (A)

Answer: Something that lives in our homes. (B)

Question: So is everything that lives in my home (B) a pet (A)? For example: the mice in my attic, the plant in my kitchen, the mold in the fridge?

Wobbler 2

Question: What is a pet? (A)

Answer: Something that lives in our homes. (B)

Question: So does that mean something that does not live in our homes (not B) cannot be a pet (not A)? For example: a rabbit that lives in the hutch outside, a horse that lives in the field, a fish that lives in a pond, a dog that lives in the kennels while you are away?

Wobbler 3

Question: What is a pet? (A)

Answer: An animal kept for company. (B)

Question: Do pets always (G) have to provide company? For example: what if your pet wasn't with you during the day (S)? Would that mean they were no longer your pet (G)?

Wobbler 4

Question: Can any animal be kept as a pet? (A)

Answer: No, not if they are too big. (B)

Question: How big? (A)

Answer: Bigger than your front door. (B)

Question: So if an animal is bigger than my front door (B), does that mean I definitely can't have them as a pet? (not A)

Answer: No.

Question: And what about if I have a really big door, like a barn door (B)—does that mean I still can't have them as pets (not A)?

Answer: No. But the smaller the animal the more likely you are to choose them as a pet.

Question: Really?

Questions That Might Lead to Cognitive Conflict With Students Age Six to Twelve

- Is keeping a pet right or wrong? Is it always right or wrong?
- Can we ever know our pets?
- What makes one animal a pet and another not?
- Why are some animals companions and others food?
- Plants are living things. Can you keep plants as pets?
- Does a pet have to be an animal?

Questions That Might Lead to Cognitive Conflict With Students Age Twelve to Sixteen

- What separates one animal from being domesticated and another from living in the wild?
- Pets in one part of the world are food in another. Is that OK?
- Does what people want out of a pet always match the pet's needs?
- Do human beings serve the needs of animals, or do animals serve the needs of human beings?
- Is it OK to keep practical animals, that are useful, to relieve some of our workload, like a living tool?
- Is it reasonable to keep a pet and disagree with animals being kept in captivity?
- Are humans the only animals that keep pets?
- Can a human be the pet of their animal?
- If your pet is seen as a member of your family, is it no longer a pet?

Stage 3: Construct Understanding

Depending on the progress of the dialogue, Opinion Corners could well provide a useful way for your students to begin explaining and connecting their ideas. Opinion Corners are described in Section 6.3.5.

▶ **Figure 66: Opinion Corners for the Concept *Pets***

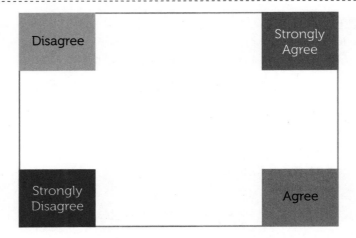

Statements to Use for Opinion Corners on Pets
With Students Age Six to Twelve

- Keeping a pet is acceptable.

- An animal's strongest desire is to be free.

- Owning pets makes us feel human.

- A pet is a person with fur.

- People should always keep two of the same pet so that they have company when their human companions aren't home.

- It's OK to keep animals as a type of decoration, such as a goldfish.

- Animals are responsible for their actions.

- You should rehome a pet if you can provide it with a better-quality life.

- If pets don't run away that means they want to stay.

- Pets couldn't survive or be happy if they lived in the wild.

- Pets are different from other animals in that we see them as friends rather than food.

- Animals have something to offer everyone.

- Pet stores are just pet prisons.

- Only certain people should be allowed to own a pet.

Statements to Use for Opinion Corners on Pets
With Students Age Fourteen to Sixteen

- It is a selfish desire to own a pet.

- It is human instinct to want to keep a pet.

- It would be in the animal's best interest if the institution of pet keeping never existed.

- Fundamentally, pets are stuffed toys that can move without batteries.

- We deprive animals if we keep them as pets.

- Humans should have the power over all other living creatures.

- Only sad, inadequate human individuals would wish to keep members of other species as captives.

- Pedigrees are not natural; they exist only because we made them, so we now have a responsibility for caring for them.

- If somebody didn't understand the concept of pets, they would assume pets were in charge.

- Choosing a pet is no different from choosing a lifelong partner.

- Human beings provide a safe and nourishing life for pets and protect them from the dangers they would otherwise face.

- It is unfair to the pet to treat it as an equal member of the family.

- Pets need to know who their master is.

- It is cruel to treat pets as if they were humans.

An alternative pit tool that would be appropriate for this topic is a Concept Line. These are described in Section 6.3.6.

▶ Figure 67: Concept Line for the Concept *Pets*

Trained	Restricted	Wild

Example words to place along the line:

- Disciplined

- Domesticated

- Tame

- Controlled

- Confined

- Undomesticated

- Natural

- Feral

Stage 4: Consider

Sample Review Questions

- How does your idea of pets differ from the one you had at the beginning of the lesson?
- In what ways does keeping an animal as a pet differ from keeping an animal captive?
- What are pet owners responsible for?
- What do pets depend on their owners for?
- What characteristics make some animals good household companions?
- What questions about pets are you left with?

10.5 • SOCIAL NETWORKING

Age range: six to sixteen

Subjects: information and communication technology; personal, social and health education

Stage 1: Identify the Concept

Social networking seems to be a twenty-first century phenomenon, and yet in some ways the practice has existed throughout human history. This is partly what makes the concept an interesting one to explore, particularly within a Learning Challenge context. The popularity of social networking among students provides an added curiosity and its inherent dangers another.

Stage 2: Create Cognitive Conflict

Key Areas to Investigate Within and Around the Concept of Social Networking

- Innovation
- Computing
- Safety online
- Friendships
- Perceptions of reality
- Advertising
- Community
- Communication
- Social skills

Questions That Might Lead to Cognitive Conflict
With Students Age Six to Twelve

- What does *online* mean?

- How safe are you online?

- How can you communicate with people who are not in front of you?

- Is it important to remember that they're not in front of you?

- Why do people use social networks? Which social networks do you use?

- How should people decide whom they add to their friends list?

- What is friendship? Is it possible to have friends that are only online?

- Do you ever check into places? Do you share your location with your friends online?

- If you do, how private is your profile? Does it help to set your profile to private? Is privacy a good thing? Can it be a bad thing?

- Do your parents or guardians know what you're doing online?

- Would it ever be helpful for your parents or guardians to know what you are doing online?

- Do you think posting personal information and pictures can affect your future?

- Does social media have a positive impact on a person's character?

- Can two people meet online?

- What is the difference between posting something to someone online and saying it to them in person?

- Is it possible to keep in touch with friends and social events without being online?

Questions That Might Lead to Cognitive Conflict
With Students Age Twelve to Sixteen

- If the Internet went down, would that mean that it would be impossible to social network?

- Does social networking increase our popularity?

- If social media makes us popular, does that mean that to be popular we have to use social media?

- If you do not engage in social networking, does that mean that you are not popular?

- How many online friends or contacts do you need to have to be considered popular?

- Can using social networks be dangerous? If so, what are the possible dangers?

- Are there some old-fashioned values that aren't fitting with our digital age? Is this sad or is this inevitable?

- Does technology affect us or do we affect it?

- Do social media sites compensate for face-to-face contact?

- Have social media sites changed the way you view yourself?

- Are social media sites changing the way people view each other?

- How are social media sites changing the way that you think?

- What is community? Can community be something different from being in physical proximity? Can people sitting at computers or on electronic devices ever truly be described as a community?

- Does social media have more positive or negative effects on society?

- What is friendship (may have been defined above)? What different levels of friendship are there? Can we be socially and mentally healthy when we have friendships with people we've never seen? Compared to the people we have around us?

- Can you care for another person on social media?

- Can you mistreat someone on social media?

- Would someone behave differently on social media than they would face to face or on the telephone? Why or why not?

- Would someone be responsible if an idea they created on social networking turns into a crime in the real world?

Stage 3: Construct Understanding

By sorting and classifying characteristics that best describe social networking and those that describe face-to-face communication, your students could gain a clearer insight into the defining characteristics of the concept. Venn diagrams can be of use in this regard. They are of course well known, but there is also a guide in Section 6.3.9.

▶ **Figure 68: Venn Diagram of Social Networking**

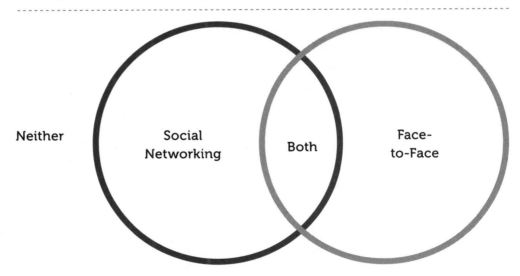

It can be dangerous.	You may not know the person you are talking to.
It is easy to recognize how someone is feeling.	You have to be careful what you say.
You can pretend to be older or younger than you are.	You can estimate how old someone might be.
You can be sure of the identity of someone if you have met them before.	You can tell if someone is joking or being serious.
It is easy to know what the person means because you can hear the tone in their voice.	Facial expressions help you understand the person.
It's easier to chat privately.	It's a good way to share thoughts and ideas.
Some people find it easier to communicate this way.	Bullies may use this way to tease someone.
It's a great way to stay connected with friends and family.	You can meet and interact with others who share similar interests.

Stage 4: Consider

Sample Review Questions

- What advice would you give someone choosing a username?
- When choosing a password, what should you do?
- Who could you tell if someone asks for personal information?
- What should you do if online friends want to meet you in person?
- What are the best and worst parts of social networking sites?
- What can you do to prevent criminals from using a social networking site to target you?
- What should you do if someone sends you a message that discusses private matters that make you feel uncomfortable?
- What skills have you had to use in this lesson?

- How could what you've thought about today or the way you've thought about it be useful in the future?

- What questions about social networking are you left with?

10.6 • PROOF AND EVIDENCE

Age range: nine to sixteen

Subjects: sciences and math

Stage 1: Identify the Concept

It is notoriously difficult to prove anything beyond all doubt. For example, a student might say they can prove who they are by showing their passport, but this might be a forgery. Or they might say they can prove that the sun will rise every morning, but there is a minute possibility that the world will end before tomorrow and with it all sunrises! This may seem facetious, but it is actually a rich vein of thought to explore with students. You can have a lot of fun, and students will gain a greater insight into the problems of proof and evidence.

Stage 2: Create Cognitive Conflict

Key Areas to Investigate Within and Around
the Concepts of Proof and Evidence

- Confirmation

- Certification

- Verification

- Data

- Test

- Guarantee

- Warranty

- Declaration

The following is an extract from a real-life dialogue that took place between a teacher and her students:

Teacher: I bet you cannot prove anything to me!

Adam: I can! I can prove that I'm sitting here.

Teacher: How?

Adam: Well, look, here I am! (waving)

Teacher: But how do I know that I'm not just imagining you?

Rachel: You could walk over and touch Adam.

Teacher: But when I touch things in dreams, it doesn't mean I've actually touched them, so perhaps I'm dreaming this whole conversation.

Rachel: But you need to be asleep to dream and you're not asleep.

Tas:	No, you don't. You can daydream without being asleep.
Teacher:	Good point, Tas. So can anyone prove that this isn't all a dream?
Annie:	You don't smell things in your dreams, but I can smell things here.
Teacher:	But how do you know people can't smell in their dreams?
Annie:	Well, I never have.
Teacher:	Is that enough evidence to prove that people can't smell in their dreams?
Laurie:	I guess not.
Teacher:	OK, let's take an example. Could we ever prove that ghosts do or do not exist?
Anita:	Yes. If someone were to see a ghost, that would prove ghosts exist.
Teacher:	But what if no one else could see this ghost?
Anita:	OK, if everyone could see the ghost that would prove the existence of ghosts.
Teacher:	Does that mean that if just one person cannot see the ghost, then there are no ghosts?
Kalim:	No. If the majority of people can see the ghost, then that would be enough.
Teacher:	So is proof to do with what the majority believe?
Ellie:	Yes.
Teacher:	But there was a period of history, in the tenth century, when the majority of people thought the world was flat. So had they proved the world was flat?

Questions That Might Lead to Cognitive Conflict
With Students Age Nine to Twelve

- If we can touch, taste, smell, hear and see something, is that enough evidence to prove it exists?

- If our gut instinct tells us something is real, does this prove its existence?

- If my pet is a bird, is that enough to prove that my pet can fly?

- If I have a pet dog, does that prove my pet can bark?

- Do you have enough evidence to prove beyond all doubt who you are?

- If no counterevidence can be found, does that mean something has been proved?

- It's the beginning of December and Tom the Turkey is reflecting on his life. Every day for the past three hundred days, Tom has been cared for by Farmer Jones. He's been well fed, watered, sheltered and given medicines whenever he needed them. Is this enough evidence to prove that Farmer Jones loves Tom?

- The sun has risen every day since the earth was formed. Is this enough evidence to prove that the sun will rise tomorrow?

- If your fingerprints were found at the scene of a crime, does that prove you were there?

- You see smoke. Is that evidence or proof (or neither) that there is a fire?

- There has never been an occurrence of someone living forever. Does that prove that one day I too will die?

- Does evidence need to be incontrovertible to prove something?

- If one has absolute proof for the repeated occurrence of an event, is that enough to predict with absolute certainty that it will happen in the future?

- How could you prove to a blind person that there are colors?

- The philosopher David Hume wrote, "A wise man proportions his belief to the evidence." What did he mean by this?

- Has anything ever been proved for all time?

- How much evidence is required to prove something?

- Can you prove that you are not simply a figment of someone's imagination?

- If you are able to prove something that is later found to be false, was it ever proved?

- Do we really need proof?

Stage 3: Construct Understanding

What are the similarities and differences between the following?

- Proof and evidence

- Evidence and data

- Proof and facts

- Proof and truth

- Proof and knowledge

- Proof and faith

- Proof and observation

- Evidence and facts

Examples	Proof	Evidence	Both	Neither
Martha tells everyone that her name is "Martha."				
Martha shows everyone her passport that states her full name is "Jane Martha Smith."				
John explains fractions to his younger brother by cutting one cake into four pieces.				
Emma says she has two pet guinea pigs.				
Emma shows photographs of her guinea pigs.				
Mia says she can count to 100 in Portuguese. Her mother confirms this.				
Michael says his pet parrot can fly. Then he shows a video of the parrot flying.				
The museum guide shows some dinosaur bones and says dinosaurs lived about 200 million years ago.				

Stage 4: Consider

Sample Review Questions

- Is proof the same as evidence?

- How much evidence do we need to prove something?

- Is it possible to prove anything without hindsight?

- Why is it important to search for evidence and proof?

- What are the problems with evidence and proof?

- How do your ideas of proof and evidence differ from the ones you had at the beginning of the lesson?

- What questions about proof and evidence are you left with?

10.7 • RISK

Age range: seven to eighteen

Subjects: science, PE, media, citizenship

Stage 1: Identify the Concept

The concept of risk impinges on many aspects of people's lives, with children and teenagers not immune from this. There is often a mismatch between our perceptions of risk and the likelihood of an event or outcome occurring, and that can be explored in this lesson.

When considering this concept, the following topics could provide a useful departure point for a concept diagram or mind map.

Stage 2: Create Cognitive Conflict

Some of the Key Areas to Investigate Within and Around the Concept of "Risk" Include:

- Risk assessment
- Consequence
- Personal risk
- Unavoidable risk
- Unknown risk
- Age-related risks
- Danger
- Psychological risk

Questions to Ask Your Students About Risk

- What is risk?
- Who has taken a risk today?
- Am I taking any risks standing here now? If so, what are those risks?
- If I teach a bad lesson and you don't learn anything, is that a risk? Is it a risk to me? Is it a risk to you?
- Should we consider all potential risks before we do something?
- Would I have been safer to stay in bed this morning? Would there have been any risks if I had done that?
- Would those risks have been realized immediately?
- If there are risks to being here now and risks to not being here now, how do I decide what to do?
- Is there a limit to how much risk a person should take? Is that the same for all people?
- Who should decide how much risk to take? For a soldier? For a school student? For a surgeon?

- Have you made decisions about all the risks you've faced today?

- Should we take risks only if they are unavoidable or worth it in terms of reward?

- Is it silly to take risks for pleasure?

- Can risk taking give us pleasure? Is that logical?

- Why do people do extreme sports? Do people who do extreme sports think about the risks?

- Who has better control of the risk: a rock climber, a rugby player or a show jumper? Are any of these considered extreme sports?

- Is it weird to like risk?

- Do we need people in the world who can cope with risk? Why?

- Do we need people in the world who identify and measure risk? Why?

- People who look at the consequence of risk realize that if very young children use a Bunsen burner they could badly burn themselves and that if people have an accident in a swimming pool they could drown. So why do we take young children swimming but not let them use Bunsen burners until they reach secondary school?

Questions That Might Lead to Cognitive Conflict With Students Age Seven to Eleven

----

- Do all living things take risks?

- Do animals think about the risks they are taking?

- Are there any risks we can't see?

- Are risks always things we can touch, taste, smell, hear or see?

- Can risks make us scared?

- Is fear always a bad thing?

- What is it right to be scared of?

- What is it unnecessary to be scared of?

- If you are not scared of something, does it mean it's not a risk?

- Are other people a risk?

- Should we avoid risky people?

- How do we know if someone is risky?

- Is risky the same as dangerous?

- If we think someone is a risk to us, should we be scared of them?

- If we've decided not to be scared of someone who is a risk to us, how should we behave toward them?

Questions That Might Lead to Cognitive Conflict With Students Age Twelve to Fourteen

----

- Is it ever sensible to take a risk that has potentially serious consequences?

- Is there a limit to how much risk I should take to keep my family safe?

- Is physical risk always scarier than psychological risk? Can psychological risk be dangerous?

- Is having money a risk? Is having a lot of money a bigger risk?

- Should I take a risk with my money if it might mean my family will be better off?

- Should I take a risk with my money if doing so makes me happy?

- Is it riskier for a poor man or a rich man to gamble?

- Are groups or individuals more likely to take risks?

- Do groups help us be brave or stupid in the face of risk?

Questions That Might Lead to Cognitive Conflict With Students Age Fourteen to Eighteen

- Is it true that young men take more risk than old men?

- Do women have a different attitude toward risk than men? Is this nature or nurture?

- Could repeated risk taking be seen as an addiction? Is the addiction itself dangerous or damaging or just the risk?

- What risks would a person with a young family take that a person without a family wouldn't take and vice versa?

- Is a professional soldier risking it all solely for their country?

- The ability of human beings to perceive and deal with risk has allowed humankind to prosper. In the modern world risk can now be measured. Are we better off being aware of statistical risk, or should people continue to react to their instinct and gut feelings?

- Is all risk equally presented to us?

- In adult life should managing risk be the individual's responsibility?

- Why do people ignore or not listen to safety advice?

Stage 3: Construct Understanding

What are the similarities and differences between the following?

- Risk and danger

- Risk and fear

- Risk and consequence

- Risk and likelihood

- Risk and probability

- Risk and thrill seeking/gratification

- Risk and risk aversion

- Risk and health and safety

- Risk and necessity

- Risk and foolhardiness

- Risk and courage

- Risk and bravery

- Risk and reward

- Risk and personality

- Risk and attitude

- Risk and vulnerability

- Risk and rationality

Ask your students to consider the list of risks below and decide which quadrant in Figure 71 each one would fit into. Some of the risks listed are deliberately vague (e.g., theft) to promote further dialogue.

- A road accident

- A stomach upset

- Falling off a bike

- Falling off a skyscraper

- A fight

- Bankruptcy

- Unemployment

- A burn

- A plane crash

- A building fire

- Theft

- Violence

- A terrorist attack

- A cut finger

- Losing a bet

- Hunger

- Homelessness

- Failure

- Loving someone and losing them

- A dangerous person

- An accident in water

- War

▶ **Figure 71: Severity Versus Likelihood Graph**

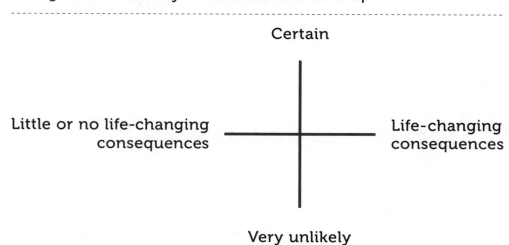

Extension for Older Students

Random Pairs

Use the list of people and the list of risks below to draw out random pairs.

Person

> Elderly widower
>
> Mother of young children
>
> Eighteen-year-old man
>
> Ten-year-old child
>
> Thirty-year-old city banker/dealer
>
> Middle-aged academic
>
> Homeless twenty-five-year-old

Risk

> Long-term debt
>
> Dangerous but life-saving operation
>
> Stress
>
> Physical hardship
>
> Physical combat/violence
>
> Exposure to extreme weather
>
> Excess alcohol

Using the Think-Pair-Share technique, ask students to consider each of the individuals' possible attitudes to the risk they're matched with. Invite a range of perspectives.

Possible facilitative questions:

- Why would they have that attitude to that risk?
- Would that attitude be different from another person's?
- What could cause them to have that attitude?
- If their life changes, could this affect their attitude toward risk?

Stage 4: Consider

Sample Review Questions

- What is risk?
- Has your understanding of the concept of risk changed over the course of this lesson?
- When you encounter risk or witness how other people respond to risk, will your reaction be revised in any way by the understanding you've now developed?

- Will your behavior in response to risk be changed by the process of this lesson?

- Will you be more aware of your behavior in response to risk as a result of the consideration you have made during this lesson?

- Are there any questions about the concept of risk that you are left with?

- Is a deeper understanding of risk useful?

- Is being able to objectively measure risk useful?

APPENDIX

Here is a list of books that provide a good stimulus for drawing out concepts (see Section 4.3 for more information).

Book Details	Concepts	Ages	Overview and Potential Questions
Aaaarrgghh, Spider Lydia Monks Houghton Mifflin Company	• Appearance • Belonging • Fears • Learned behavior • Pet • Prejudice • Scary	5–13	A story about a spider who wants to be a family pet. Can her remarkable skills persuade the family to let her stay? What happens when the spider invites all her friends around? • What makes one pet better than another? • What makes us afraid of something? • Are we only afraid of frightening things? • Do we all need to belong? • Is it possible to avoid prejudging?
The Bear Under the Stairs Helen Cooper Picture Corgi	• Dreaming • Imagination • (Ir)rational • Power of belief • Real/not real • Scared .	6–11	A little boy believes there is a bear living under his stairs. He feeds the bear but doesn't talk to the bear. He dreams about the bear and imagines what the bear is like. Eventually he ventures in. • If we believe in something enough, can that make it real? • Just because we can't see it, does that mean it doesn't exist? • Are we all scared of something? • Does it give us comfort to have something to be scared of? • Do we need to confront our fears in order to overcome them?
The Big Orange Splot Daniel Manus Pinkwater Scholastic Paperbacks	• Conformity • Independence • Our obligations to our community • Creativity • Promises	3–12	When Mr. Plumbeans's house is splashed with bright orange paint, he decides a multicolored house would be a nice change. A story about creativity and individuality. • What causes conformity? • How do you break free without breaking apart? • What do I mean by "going with the flow"? • Are there ever any good reasons to follow the crowd?

(Continued)

Book Details	Concepts	Ages	Overview and Potential Questions
Bottomley the Brave Peter Harris Red Fox Picture	• Bravery • Greed • Imagination • Lies • Truth	5–11	The story of a plump, lazy but highly imaginative ginger cat whose hair-raising account of his confrontation with a gang of ruthless burglars is curiously at odds with the reality of the illustrations. • What's the difference between telling lies and telling stories? • Is it sometimes OK to tell lies? • When is it not good to tell stories? • Can scaredy cats sometimes be brave?
Changes Anthony Browne Walker Books	• Appearance • Arrival of a new sibling • Changes • Normality	5–11	A day in the life of Joseph, in which everything seems to change in the most peculiar of ways. The book explores the boy's state of mind as he prepares for the return of his parents with his new baby sister. • Is change inevitable? • If one thing in your life changes, can it cause everything else to change? • Can one thing change and everything else stay the same? • Is wondering worse than knowing? • If normal means everything staying the same, does that mean nothing is normal?
Chalk Bill Thomson Marshall Cavendish	• Imagination • Magic • Intrigue • Discovery	3–7	This wordless picture book is about three children who discover a bag of chalk while strolling in the park one rainy day. The children begin to draw and then . . . magic! • Have you used your imagination? • How do you read a story with no words? • What does imagination mean? • What is real and what is not real?
Crispin, the Pig Who Had It All Ted Dewan Corgi Children's Books	• Appreciation • Being spoilt • Making friends • Using imagination • Values	6–11	A tale about a pig who is spoiled and lonely. He has lots of toys that he gets bored with easily and ends up breaking, until he receives the most modest gift of them all, which teaches him to use his imagination and thus how to engage with other pigs. • Are our friends worth more than our possessions? • Can our imagination make anything into a toy? • Can you have too much of a good thing? • Why was the empty box the best toy? • Are money and value the same thing?

Book Details	Concepts	Ages	Overview and Potential Questions
The Conquerors David McKee Andersen Press	• Culture • Domination • Fascism • Imperialism • Influence • Integration • Megalomania • Power	8–16	A tale about a very large country that's ruled by a general with a very strong army. Through conquering a small country the general finds that his own country had changed and had adopted many of the ways of the small country he had "conquered," but why? • Can you have power without influence? • Do ignorance and arrogance always come together? • Is every society a multicultural one? • What is the difference between influencing and conquering? • Is friendship a greater force than intimidation? • Does anyone have the right to tell others how to live their lives?
Egg Drop Mini Grey Red Fox	• Ambition • Dreams • Knowledge • Patience • Personal fulfillment • Youth	6–11	This is the dramatic story of a local egg who had dreamed of being high up there, flying with them all. So the egg went to a very high place . . . and jumped . . . • Is it good to be ambitious? • Does youth make us ignorant? • Does age make us wise? • If we believe we've achieved our goals, does that mean we have? • Should we limit our dreams? • Should we only have aspirations that others think we can achieve?
Fish Is Fish Leo Lionni Demco Media	• Contentment • Envy • Friendship • Habitats • Imagination • Self-acceptance • Self-awareness	7–12	The fish and the tadpole are inseparable friends until the day that tadpole discovers he has legs. Soon a frog, the tadpole decides to discover more of the world, leaving the fish behind. However, he returns with stories full of wonderful pictures. So the fish jumps on to the land to discover this world for himself, only to have to be rescued by the frog. He now realizes that the frog was right when he said, "Frogs are frogs and fish is fish," and you can't be something you are not. • What makes you you? • How do you know what your limitations are? • Is aspiring to be something else a bad thing? • Why do other people's lives often look more interesting than our own? • Do you have to know yourself before you can accept yourself?

(Continued)

Book Details	Concepts	Ages	Overview and Potential Questions
The Fish Who Could Wish John Bush and Korky Paul Oxford University	• Aspirations • Contentment • Greed • Revenge • Wisdom • Wishing	6–11	A story about a fish with a special gift. The story teaches us how to be humble, through the fish making one final wish. • Is it wrong to wish a selfish wish? • Is it foolish to wish to be like everyone else? • Can you teach someone a lesson by taking revenge? • Is wisdom something you have to work at? • Should we be happy with whom we are?
Frederick Leo Lionni L'École des Loisirs	• Communities • Collectivism • Human interdependence	6–12	Always the daydreamer, Frederick is preparing a surprise that will warm the hearts and feed the spirits of his fellow mice when they need it most. • Do you think Frederick is working? • What makes a community? • What constitutes work? • Is it fair that Frederick gets to eat the food? • Did Frederick violate the social contract by not also helping to gather food? • If Frederick were a famous poet, would his poetry be more valuable?
Frog Is Frog Max Velthuijs Andersen Press	• Acceptance • Envy • Loving oneself • Talents • Trying to be someone else	8–13	Frog is very happy with himself. Lots of animals have impressive skills and he is not one of them! Eventually, Hare helps him realize that he has many talents, including jumping and swimming. Frog is Frog! • Are we all talented? • Should we accept who we are? • Is envy a bad thing? • Is it natural to want what someone else has got? • Are we our own worst judge?
The Girl Who Never Made Mistakes Mark Pett and Gary Rubinstein Sourcebooks Jabberwocky	• Mistakes • Personal best • Responsibility • Flexibility	3–12	Beatrice Bottomwell is a young girl who never makes mistakes. Life for Beatrice is sailing along pretty smoothly until she does the unthinkable: she makes her first mistake. And in a very public way! • Are mistakes good or bad? • How do you feel when you make a mistake? • How can you learn from your mistakes? • Which do you think is better, trying something new or always being perfect?

Book Details	Concepts	Ages	Overview and Potential Questions
Gorilla Anthony Browne Walker Books	• Busy parents • Hopes and dreams • Imagination • Private adventure • Time • Zoos/captivity	7–12	Hannah is obsessed with gorillas. She watches them on TV, she reads about them and draws pictures of them, but she's never seen one in real life. The night before her birthday, a toy gorilla that she finds at the bottom of her bed comes to life and takes her on an adventure. • Can our imagination make our dreams come true? • Should we keep animals in zoos? • Is it all right to have private adventures? • Is some people's time more important than others?
The Gruffalo Julia Donaldson and Axel Scheffler Macmillan Children's Books	• Being scared • Believing • Bravery • Eating animals • Predictions • Reality • Telling lies	5–11	An absolute classic. More often than not, the Gruffalo is the first story we use with a primary group for their first philosophy session. It is a rhyming story of a mouse and a monster. The little mouse goes for a walk in a dangerous forest. To scare off his enemies, he invents tales of a fearsome creature called the Gruffalo. Imagine his surprise when he meets the real Gruffalo! • Is the Gruffalo real? • How can you tell when someone is telling lies? • How did the mouse know what the Gruffalo was like? • Why were the animals scared of the little mouse? • Is it OK for animals to be eaten?
The Hole Øyvind Torseter Enchanted Lion Books	• Investigating • Existentialism • Ignorance • Acceptance	11–16	The protagonist of *The Hole* has discovered a hole in his apartment and tries to find an explanation for it. He seeks expert advice. But not everything can be explained. • Do things still exist if they can't be explained? • Do we marvel at existence simply because we can? • Why is there always something rather than nothing?

(Continued)

Book Details	Concepts	Ages	Overview and Potential Questions
I'll Always Love You Hans Wilhelm Hodder Children's Books	• Aging • Death • Friendship • Life cycle • Love • Playing	5–10	A story about a boy and his dog. They're inseparable friends, always playing and getting up to mischief. But over the years, Elfie the dog grows old and slow. The story tells the tale of the young boy's loss. • What does it feel like to lose something we love? • What does *always* mean? • Is something more special if it belongs to you? • Is it important to do things together with those we love? • Can a pet be your best friend?
The Important Book Margaret Wise Brown and Leonard Weisgard HarperCollins	• Change • Identity • Important	4–9	The pattern of the book is that the author suggests various things like rain, a spoon or a daisy. For each item, the author lists some qualities or purposes and gives an opinion as to the most important. The book ends on the subject of "you." • What makes something important? • What makes you you? • If you had a different name, would you still be you? • Does everything about you change over time? • Will you still be the same you when you are old?
The Kiss That Missed David Melling Hodder Children's Books	• Being in a hurry • Bravery • Fairy tales • Love • Magic • Monsters/dragons	5–9	The little prince's goodnight kiss has gone missing. It escaped into the forest where it had no place to be. So the brave and fearless knight is sent on a mission to bring it back. But is the knight brave and fearless enough? • Does love have magical powers? • Do dragons exist? • What makes someone brave and fearless? • Does love always make things better? • Does hurrying make things go faster or slower?

Book Details	Concepts	Ages	Overview and Potential Questions
A Lion in the Meadow Margaret Mahy Puffin Books	• Assumptions • Believing other people • Having no name • Imagination • Reality	5–11	This story is based on the dilemma of believing there is a lion in the meadow even though your mother does not believe you. What might happen if the boy discovers it is really there? • How do you know when to believe other people? • How does it feel when people don't believe you? • What would life be like if we were all referred to as "boy" or "girl" rather than by our own names? • In what way were the lion and the dragon real? • Was the mother wrong to assume there was no dragon in the matchbox?
Little Hotchpotch Brian Patten and Mike Terry Bloomsbury	• Appearances • Commonality • Identity • Names • Wisdom	6–11	A story about a little creature who doesn't know who or what he is and his quest to discover his real identity. Eventually a wise owl tells him he's a "hotchpotch." • What makes you you? • Do we have something in common with everyone? • Does it matter what we look like? • If you don't have a name, do you not have an identity? • Is a false identity still an identity?
Little Mole Werner Holzwarth Chrysalis Children's Books	• Evidence • Expertise • Investigating • Knowledge • Revenge	7–13	A little mole pops his head out of the ground only to find a poo dropping on his head. So he sets off on a journey to find out who was responsible. At the end, the mole is seen taking his revenge on Basil the butcher's dog. • Is it wrong to take revenge? • Should we always trust an expert? • How do we know what evidence to believe? • Can revenge ever be fair? • Do two wrongs make a right?

(Continued)

Book Details	Concepts	Ages	Overview and Potential Questions
Night Monkey, Day Monkey Julia Donaldson and Lucy Richards Egmont Books	• Compromise • Differences • Friendship • Give and take • Sharing	5–11	A story about two friends, a night monkey and a day monkey. They are best friends but live in very different worlds. In the end they come to understand that they can have different interests and beliefs yet still be best friends. • Do you have to compromise to be friends? • Can we see the world as others see it? • Is friendship built upon shared experiences? • Do friends always have something in common with each other? • Can you be friends with someone who's the complete opposite of you?
Nothing Mick Inkpen Hodder Children's Books	• Identity • Personality • Nature • Memory • Experiences • Physical attributes	6–12	A little creature lies in the attic, alone and forgotten. It cannot even remember its own name. One day the attic door is flung open, and so begins Nothing's search to discover who he really is. • How did Nothing get found? • What did the mouse feel about new people? Why? • Why do you think Nothing was upset when he met the cat? • Which bit of Nothing is Nothing? • As you grow, does any part of you stay the same? • Can you change your identity?
Oscar Got the Blame Tony Ross Andersen Press	• Blame • Imaginary friends • Pretend • Reasons	4–9	Oscar and Billy were the best of friends, but when Billy dressed the dog in Dad's clothes Oscar got the blame, and when Billy put frogs in Granny's slippers Oscar got the blame. It's just not fair when your invisible friend is such a naughty boy. • In what ways do imaginary friends exist? • Can imaginary friends make you do things? • Was it fair that Oscar got the blame for everything? • Is someone always to blame? • Can some things happen without any reason?

Book Details	Concepts	Ages	Overview and Potential Questions
"Quack!" Said the Billy-Goat Charles Causley and Barbara Firth Candlewick Press	• Animals talking • Communication • Language • Subverting expectations	3–7	"Quack!" said the billy-goat. "Oink!" said the hen. "Miaow!" said the little chick running in the pen. So begins the story of animals evidently making the wrong noises. • Can animals talk? • Why does it sound wrong for a billy-goat to say "quack"? • Is it impossible for a goat to sound like a duck? • If so, does that mean goats can't talk to ducks? • Can dogs talk to cats, or cows talk to sheep?
The Rainbow Fish Marcus Pfister North South Books	• Arrogance • Beauty • Humility • Popularity • Self-satisfaction • Vanity	4–9	The Rainbow Fish is the most beautiful fish in the sea, but he has no friends because he is just too beautiful to play with any of the others. The Rainbow Fish gives away his shiny scales one by one, but gains a sense of satisfaction from pleasing others as well as gaining a group of new friends. • Should we change ourselves in order to be popular? • Is it important to please other people? • What makes something beautiful? • Is vanity a weakness? • Is popularity the same as being liked?
The Red Tree Shaun Tan Simply Read Books	• Darkness • Despair • Fate • Hope • Nothingness • Patience • Passing of time • Understanding	9–14	This story covers the topics of good events passing you by and the inevitability of bad things happening. This book helps to remove the rose-tinted glasses of early childhood without being morose or depressing. • How can you tell if something is worth waiting for? • Is there such a thing as fate? • Why do troubles seem to come all at once? • Is it possible for "nothing to happen"? • Would you get rid of the bad times if it meant you also lost the good times?

(Continued)

Book Details	Concepts	Ages	Overview and Potential Questions
Room on the Broom Julia Donaldson and Axel Scheffler Campbell Books	• Fantasy • Friendship • Helping others • Magic/reality • Scariness • Stereotyping	6–11	This is the story of a good-natured witch and her cat that collect other friends as they fly through the sky on their broomstick. • Is it always a good thing to help others? • What makes this witch a good witch? • Is magic real? • If you do something nice, should you expect something nice in return?
Slow Loris Alexis Deacon Red Fox	• Being bored • Being different • Captivity • Nicknames • Reasons • Secrets • Zoos	6–11	Slow Loris is a sloth. All the other animals in the zoo think he's boring because he never seems to do anything. They call him names and make fun of him behind his back. But Slow Loris has got a secret! He gets up to all sorts of fun during the night. When the other animals discover this, will they join in? • Do we all have secrets? • Is it good to share (or have) a secret? • Can something that is boring also be interesting? • Should we use nicknames? • Are animals kept in zoos for people's entertainment?
The Smartest Giant in Town Julia Donaldson and Axel Scheffler Macmillan Children's Books	• Altruism • Appearances • Generosity • Gratitude • Kindness • Familiarity • Personal pride • Self-satisfaction	6–10	This story tells the tale of George, who sees others who are more needy than himself. The animals send him a crown and a thank-you card declaring him the kindest giant in town. • Is there such a thing as a totally selfless act? • Are we most comfortable with the things we know the best? • Is what other people think of you important? • Does it matter what we look like?
Something Else Kathryn Cave and Chris Riddell Puffin Books	• Belonging • Friendship • Identity • Self-esteem • Strange	6–11	Something Else just doesn't fit in. Then, one day an even odder "Something" turns up. Something Else thinks Something is very strange and asks him to leave. But when Something looks sad, Something Else realizes how similar they are and they become best of friends. • Is everyone different? • When should we try to fit in with everyone else? • Why do we all have a need to belong? • Do two people need something in common to become friends? • When we look in the mirror, do we see what everyone else sees?

Book Details	Concepts	Ages	Overview and Potential Questions
A Squash and a Squeeze Julia Donaldson and Axel Scheffler Macmillan Children's Books	• Advice • Contentment/discontentment • Personal fulfillment • Trust • Wisdom	6–11	A little old lady living alone was grumbling because she felt her house was too small. The wise old man advised her to bring her animals into the house one at a time. By the time the old lady had five animals in her house, it really was a squash and a squeeze! • Do we only realize the real value of what we have once it is gone? • Does wisdom come with age? • What does it mean to be wise? • How can we tell which advice we should trust? • Do we need to experience discontentment in order to achieve contentment?
Supposing . . . Alastair Reid New York Review Children's Collection	• Presume • Imagine • Assume • Consider • Pretend	6–12	What if all the things you did when you were little you didn't really do? What if you just imagined them? Then it wouldn't matter if your supposings were silly, impossible or even a little naughty—because they're all just in your head. • Questions can be formed around each supposing in the book. After looking at each individual supposing, provide further questions starting with "What if" and "How so."
The Teddy Robber Ian Beck Corgi Children's Books	• Forgiveness • Possessions • Reasons • Stealing	5–9	Someone is stealing teddies. But who could it be? Who is the Teddy Robber? When Tom's own teddy is snatched in the dead of night, he is determined to get to the bottom of the mystery. • If someone returns what they have stolen, does that make it OK? • Is there a reason for every action? • Would it be possible to steal anything if we didn't have possessions? • Is stealing ever right? • Is it OK to take back something that has been stolen, or is that still stealing?
Three Monsters David McKee Andersen Press	• Discrimination • Exploitation • Ignorance • Intelligence • Laziness • Prejudice • Racism • Wisdom	7–12	When the yellow monster discovers the other monsters' intentions, he proceeds to use their ignorance to his advantage. • Is racism ever acceptable? • Do we all prejudge? • Is ignorance a form of laziness? • Is the unknown threatening? • What is the difference between intelligence and wisdom? • Why are some people exploited and not others?

(Continued)

Book Details	Concepts	Ages	Overview and Potential Questions
Tuesday David Wiesner Houghton Mifflin	• Beneath the surface • Events • Other worlds • Strangeness • Time	8–12	On Tuesday, just as the full moon is rising, the lily pads take off flying—each topped by a serene, personable frog. • Can we ever really know how other creatures live? • Is it possible that some creatures exist in another world than our own? • Is time important only to people? • Do strange things really happen during a full moon? • Is there an explanation for everything?
The Tunnel Anthony Browne Walker Books	• Differences • Fears • Risk • Selflessness • Sibling rivalry/ bond • Support	8–12	A story about a brother and a sister who are very different characters. At first they resent having to spend time together, but when the brother disappears inside a tunnel, his sister puts her own fears of the dark and witches and wolves behind her to go inside and rescue him. • Is love stronger than fear? • Do siblings have a special bond? • Does love make you selfless? • Would you risk your own safety to save another? • Do you need to experience loss before you really appreciate what you have?
Tusk Tusk David McKee Red Fox	• Color/race • Difference • Hate • Peace • War	7–14	A story that explores the concept of race through the idea that once elephants came in two colors: black and white. They loved all creatures but hated each other. So they went to war. When eventually this is resolved, it is discovered that recently the big-eared elephants have started giving the small-eared elephants strange looks. • Does color matter? • Why do we fight? • Is it wrong to hate others? • If we were all the same, would there still be conflict? • Is war inevitable?

Book Details	Concepts	Ages	Overview and Potential Questions
Two Monsters David McKee Red Fox	• Agreement and disagreement • Destruction • Fallibility • Name calling • Perspective • Shared views	6–12	Two monsters live on either side of the mountain and talk to each other through a hole. Because of their different positions, they see things in very different ways and are constantly arguing. When there's no mountain left, they finally see each other's point of view and agree that they were both right. • Can we ever see things from exactly the same perspective as someone else? • Can destruction ever be constructive? • Do we need to have shared views to be friends? • Do we all make mistakes? • Would it be good if we all agreed with each other all the time?
Voices in the Park Anthony Browne Corgi Children's Books	• Different perspectives • Narrow-mindedness • Open-mindedness • Outlooks • Perceptions • Personalities	7–12	Four different voices tell the story of the shared experience of a walk in the park. Each person shares a different perspective on the same event and illustrates how different personalities and outlooks can perceive the same thing in many different ways. • Is it possible to experience exactly the same thing as someone else? • Do we only ever see what our mind allows us to see? • Does our personality dictate the experiences we have? • Is it good to see things differently than other people?
War and Peas Michael Foreman Andersen Press	• Anti-war • Inequality • Difference • Imbalance • Metaphors • War and peace • Poverty and greed • Drought and hunger • Food/water • The growth cycle • Climate and weather	6–12	King Lion is sad because it has not rained in his country for too long. He needs help and decides to ask his rich neighbor. Will it all turn out to his advantage? • Why is inequality a problem? • Should inequality worry us? • What is poverty? • What should be done about poverty?

(Continued)

Book Details	Concepts	Ages	Overview and Potential Questions
Where the Forest Meets the Sea Jeannie Baker Walker Books	• Development • Progress • Past/future • Environment • Extinction • Care • Wondering	5–11	A tale of a young Australian boy and his father. His father takes him by boat to a tropical rainforest. The boy explores, musing about the nature of the forest, its history and future until it's time to go eat the fish his father has caught and cooked. • Can human development ever be good for nature? • Do humans have the right to change the landscape? • What makes a good environment? • Should people be allowed to live in the countryside? • Would the planet be a better place without humans?
Where the Wild Things Are Maurice Sendak Red Fox	• Adoration • Dreams • Fears • Imagination • Monsters • Reality • Time • Wild/tame	6–11	After making mischief at home, Max is called a "wild thing" by his mother and is sent to bed without any supper. While he is in his bedroom, a forest and a sea begin to grow in front of him. This is just the start of Max's wild thing adventures. • What does it mean to be wild? • Do we all have a wild side? • Why does time pass quickly sometimes and slowly at other times? • What would life be like without imagination? • What is a monster?
Who Are You, Stripy Horse? Jim Helmore and Karen Wall Egmont Books	• Being unique • Helping each other • Friends • Identity • Knowledge • Talents • Wisdom	5–9	The story of a forgotten toy who can't remember his name and embarks on an adventure to meet Ming, a wise and ancient Chinese vase cat, who is the only person in the shop who might be able to tell him who he is. • Are you who others think you are? • What's the difference between being wise and being clever? • Does everybody have talents? • What are friends for? • Does everyone and everything have a name?

Book Details	Concepts	Ages	Overview and Potential Questions
Why? Nikolai Popov North-South Books	• Aggression • Retaliation • Violence • War	9–16	A frog sits peacefully in a meadow. Suddenly, for no apparent reason, he is attacked by a mouse. The frog retaliates. This provokes further retaliation until there is a full-scale war between the mice and the frogs. • Does every action have a reason or motive? • Is it wrong to retaliate? • Can war ever be justified? • Does everyone lose in a war? • What's the difference between a war and a fight?
Willy and Hugh Anthony Browne Red Fox	• Appearance • Bravery • Differences • Friendship • Strengths	6–11	No one wants to be friends with Willy because they all think he's a wimp. But one day he meets Hugh, who's much bigger than Willy and looks very menacing. Despite their differences, Willy and Hugh become good friends and help each other out in tricky situations. • Do you have to be big to be strong? • What does it mean to be brave? • Do differences matter? • Can any two creatures be friends? • Is appearance always misleading?
Willy the Dreamer Anthony Browne Walker Books	• Aspirations • Awake/asleep • Dreaming • Empathy • Fears • Imagination • (Sub-)conscious	6–11	Willy loves to dream. He dreams about good and bad things, things that have already happened and things that may never happen. • Can you dream only when you're asleep? • Are dreaming and imagining the same thing? • Is it good to dream? • Does dreaming help us be empathetic? • Does dreaming mean we want to be something we're not?

(Continued)

Book Details	Concepts	Ages	Overview and Potential Questions
Zoom Istvan Banyai Picture Puffin Books	• Culture • Leisure • Perspective • Significance • Size	8–16	This book features vivid images that effortlessly pull the reader into a thoughtful progression, as each image turns out to be only a fragment of a larger picture. • Can we ever see the whole picture? • Can two people share the same perspective? • Do we all share the same world or different worlds? • What does "taking a closer look" mean?

INDEX OF CONCEPTS

Action: a key concept for Concept Tables in Section 6.3.8

Anger: a key concept for Concept Circles in Section 6.3.7

Before: a key concept for Concept Circles in Section 6.3.7

Bully: used as an example in Figure 19, an example for Wobbler 1 in Section 5.4.1 and an example of Prepared Questions in Section 5.7.1

Bravery: the main focus for one of the dialogues in Section 5.4

Color: an example for a Pyramid Ranking exercise in Section 6.3.3 and the focus for the lesson plan in Section 10.1

Community: an example for a Diamond Ranking exercise in Section 6.3.3

Courage: a key concept for Variations of Type in Section 5.6.3

Culture: the main focus for one of the dialogues in Section 5.4.2 and the concept for comparisons in Section 5.5 and Figure 20

Democracy: an example for Wobbler 2 in Section 5.4.1

Dream: an example for Wobbler 2 in Section 5.4.1 and an example of Prepared Questions in Section 5.7.1

Drugs: the focus for the lesson plan in Section 10.2

Evidence: the focus for the lesson plan in Section 10.6

Exist: a key concept for Concept Tables in Section 6.3.8

Fairness: an example for Wobblers 1 and 2 in Section 5.4.1 and the main focus for one of the dialogues in Section 5.4.2

False: a key concept for a Venn diagram in Section 6.3.9

Food: an example for Wobbler 1 in Section 5.4.1

Friend: a main concept in Figure 17, an example in Figure 19, an example for Wobblers 2, 3 and 4 in Section 5.4.1, a key concept for Variations of Opinion in Section 5.6.4 and Variations of Condition in Section 5.6.5 and an example of Prepared Questions in Section 5.7.1

Greed: a main concept in Figure 13 with associated questions in Sections 4.3 and 4.4

Growth: the central concept for the Interchange strategy in Section 6.3.2

Happiness: an example for a Pyramid Ranking exercise in Section 6.3.3

Home: as an example for Wobbler 1 in Section 5.4.1

Just: a key concept for Concept Tables in Section 6.3.8

Killing: the focus for the lesson plan in Section 10.3

Knowledge: the main focus for one of the dialogues in Section 5.4.2 and a Concept Line in Section 6.3.6

Lies: as an example in Figure 19 and an example for Wobbler 2 in Section 5.4.1

Like: a key concept for Concept Circles in Section 6.3.7

Living things: as an example for Wobbler 3 in Section 5.4.1

Love: an example for a Linear Ranking exercise in Section 6.3.3

Mental acts: a key concept for a Venn diagram in Section 6.3.9

Metaphor: a key concept for a Venn diagram in Section 6.3.9

Mind: an example of Prepared Questions in Section 5.7.1

Odd numbers: the focus for one of the dialogues in Section 5.4

Pets: the focus for the lesson plan in Section 10.4

Poem: an example for Wobbler 1 in Section 5.4.1

Proof: the focus for the lesson plan in Section 10.6

Real: the main concept throughout Chapter 2 plus a key concept for Variations of Meaning in Section 5.6.1 and in Concept Tables in Section 6.3.8

Risk: a key concept for Variations of Opinion in Section 5.6.4 and Variations of Condition in Section 5.6.5 and the focus for Section 10.7

Rule: a key concept for Variations of Condition in Section 5.6.5

Social Networking: the focus for the lesson plan in Section 10.5

Stealing: an example in Figure 19

Superhero: the central concept in Figures 21 and 22

Thinking: an example in Figure 19

You: an example of Prepared Questions in Section 5.7.1

Verbal acts: a key concept for a Venn diagram in Section 6.3.9

REFERENCES

Alexander, R. (Ed.). (2010). *Children, their world, their education: Final report and recommendations of the Cambridge Primary Review*. Abingdon, UK: Routledge.

Bandura, A. (1977). Self-efficacy: Toward a unifying theory of behavioral change. *Psychological Review, 84*(2), 191–215.

Biggs, J. B., & Collis. K. (1982). *Evaluating the quality of learning: The SOLO taxonomy*. New York, NY: Academic Press.

Bjork, R. (1994). Memory and metamemory considerations in the training of human beings. In J. Metcalfe & A. P. Shimamura (Eds.), *Metacognition: Knowing about knowing* (pp. 188–205). Cambridge, MA: MIT Press.

Bloom, B., Englehart, M., Furst, E., Hill, W., & Krathwohl, D. (1956). *Taxonomy of educational objectives: The classification of educational goals. Handbook I: Cognitive domain*. White Plains, NY: Longman.

Bruner, J. S. (1957). On perceptual readiness. *Psychological Review, 64*(2), 123–152.

Bryk, A., & Schneider, B. (2002). *Trust in schools: A core resource for improvement*. New York, NY: Russell Sage Foundation.

Claxton, G. (2002). *Building learning power*. Bristol, UK: TLO.

Coffield, F., Moseley, D., Hall, E., & Ecclestone, K. (2004). *Learning styles and pedagogy in post 16 learning: A systematic and critical review*. London, UK: Learning and Skills Research Centre. Retrieved from http://sxills.nl/lerenlerennu/bronnen/Learning%20 styles%20by%20Coffield%20e.a..pdf

Conoley, J. C., & Kramer, J. K. (Eds.). (1989). Myers-Briggs Type Indicator. In *The tenth mental measurements yearbook*. Lincoln, NE: Buros Institute.

Costa, A. (2000). *Habits of mind*. Alexandria, VA: Association for Supervision and Curriculum Development.

De Bono, E. (2010). *Teach yourself to think*. London, UK: Penguin.

Dewey, J. (1916). *Democracy and education*. Simon & Brown. (Original work published 1916)

Dweck, C. S. (2006). *Mindset: The new psychology of success*. New York, NY: Ballantine Books.

Dweck, C. S. (2012). *Mindset: How you can fulfil your potential*. London, UK: Robinson.

Dweck, C. S. (2014). The power of yet. Retrieved from http://www.youtube.com/watch?v=J-swZaKN2Ic

Edwards, J., & Martin, B. (2016). *Schools that deliver*. Thousand Oaks, CA: Corwin.

Eells, R. J. (2011). *Meta-analysis of the relationship between collective teacher efficacy and student achievement* (Doctoral dissertation, Loyola University Chicago). Retrieved from http://ecommons.luc.edu/luc_diss/133

Erickson, H. L., & Lanning, L. A. (2013). *Transitioning to concept-based curriculum and instruction: How to bring content and process together*. Thousand Oaks, CA: Corwin.

Freire, P. (1970). *Pedagogy of the oppressed*. New York, NY: Bloomsbury.

Green, M. (2016, July 3). Develop mental agility with a plunge into the learning pit. *Financial Times*. Retrieved from http://www.ft.com

Hattie, J. (2009). *Visible learning: A synthesis of over 800 meta-analyses relating to achievement*. Abingdon, UK: Routledge.

Hattie, J. (2011). *Visible learning for teachers*. Abingdon, UK: Routledge.

Hattie, J. (2015). The applicability of visible learning to higher education. *Scholarship of Teaching and Learning in Psychology, 1*(1), 79–91.

Joubert, J. (1983). *The notebooks of Joseph Joubert*. New York, NY: New York Review of Books. (Original work published 1883)

Lankshear, C., & McLaren, P. (1993). Introduction. In C. Lankshear & P. McLaren (Eds.), *Critical literacy: Politics, praxis, and the postmodern* (pp. 1–56). Albany: State University of New York Press.

Lennon, J. (1971). Imagine. On *Imagine* [record]. London, UK: Apple Records.

Lipman, M. (1988). Critical thinking: What can it be? *Educational Leadership, 46*(1), 38–43.

Lipman, M. (2003). *Thinking in education* (2nd ed.). Cambridge, England: Cambridge University Press.

Newell, A. (1991). *Unified theories of cognition*. Cambridge, MA: Harvard University Press.

Nottingham, J. A. (2010). *Challenging learning*. Berwick Upon Tweed, UK: JN.

Nottingham, J. A. (2013). *Encouraging learning*. Abingdon, UK: Routledge.

Nottingham, J. A. (2015). James Nottingham's learning challenge (learning pit) animation. Retrieved from https://www.youtube.com/watch?v=3IMUAOhuO78

Nottingham. J. A. (2016). *Challenging learning* (2nd ed.). Abingdon, UK: Routledge.

Nottingham, J. A., & Nottingham, J. (2017). *Challenging learning through feedback*. Thousand Oaks, CA: Corwin.

Nottingham, J. A., & Larsson B. (in press). *Creating a challenging learning mindset*. Thousand Oaks, CA: Corwin.

Nottingham, J. A., Nottingham, J., & Renton, T. M. (2017). *Challenging learning through dialogue*. Thousand Oaks, CA: Corwin.

Nottingham, J. A., & Renton, M. (in press). *Challenging learning through questioning*. Thousand Oaks, CA: Corwin.

Nottingham, J., Nottingham, J., Bennison, L., & Bollom, M. (in press). *Learning challenge lessons, elementary*. Thousand Oaks, CA: Corwin.

Nottingham, J., Nottingham, J., Bennison, L., & Bollom, M. (in press). *Learning challenge lessons, secondary ELA*. Thousand Oaks, CA: Corwin.

Nottingham, J., Nottingham, J., Bennison, L., & Bollom, M. (in press). *Learning challenge lessons, secondary mathematics*. Thousand Oaks, CA: Corwin.

Nottingham, J., Nottingham, J., Bennison, L., & Bollom, M. (in press). *Learning challenge lessons, secondary science/STEM*. Thousand Oaks, CA: Corwin.

Outlaw, F. (1977). What they're saying. *San Antonio Light,* 7-B.

Pet Food Manufacturers Association. (2015). Pet population 2015. Retrieved from http://www.pfma.org.uk/pet-population-2015

Postman, N. (1969). *Teaching as a subversive activity.* New York, NY: Dell.

Rosenthal, R., & Jacobson, L. (1968). *Pygmalion in the classroom: Teacher expectation and pupils' intellectual development.* New York, NY: Holt, Rinehart & Winston.

Rowe, M. B. (1972). *Wait-time and rewards as instructional variables: Their influence on language, logic and fate control.* Paper presented at the annual meeting of the National Association for Research on Science Teaching, Chicago, IL.

Stahl, R. (1990). Using "think time" and "wait time" skillfully in the classroom. *ERIC Digest.* Retrieved from http://www.ericdigests.org/1995-1/think.htm

Vygotsky, L. (1978). *Mind and society.* Cambridge, MA: Harvard University Press.

Wegerif, R. (2002, Autumn). The importance of intelligent conversations. *Teaching Thinking, 9,* 46–49.

Wiliam, D. (2016, April 28). Learning styles: What does the research say? [Blog post]. Retrieved from http://deansforimpact.org/post_Learning_styles_what_does_the_research_say.html

Willingham, D. (2008–2009, Winter). Ask the cognitive scientist: What will improve a student's memory? *American Educator,* p. 22.

Yeats, W. B. (1979). The second coming. In K. Raine, *From Blake to "a vision."* Dublin, Ireland: Dolmen Press.

INDEX

A SAGE Publishing Company

Helping educators make the greatest impact

CORWIN HAS ONE MISSION: to enhance education through intentional professional learning.

We build long-term relationships with our authors, educators, clients, and associations who partner with us to develop and continuously improve the best evidence-based practices that establish and support lifelong learning.

Solutions you want. Experts you trust. Results you need.

AUTHOR CONSULTING

Author Consulting

On-site professional learning with sustainable results! Let us help you design a professional learning plan to meet the unique needs of your school or district. www.corwin.com/pd

INSTITUTES

Institutes

Corwin Institutes provide collaborative learning experiences that equip your team with tools and action plans ready for immediate implementation. www.corwin.com/institutes

ECOURSES

eCourses

Practical, flexible online professional learning designed to let you go at your own pace. www.corwin.com/ecourses

READ2EARN

Read2Earn

Did you know you can earn graduate credit for reading this book? Find out how: www.corwin.com/read2earn

Contact an account manager at (800) 831-6640 or visit
www.corwin.com for more information.